The Endless Kingdom

The Endless Kingdom

Milton's Scriptural Society

David Gay

DELAWARE

Newark: University of Delaware Press
London: Associated University Presses

Associated University Presses
440 Forsgate Drive
Cranbury, NJ 08512

Associated University Presses
16 Barter Street
London WC1A 2AH, England

Associated University Presses
P.O. Box 338, Port Credit
Mississauga, Ontario
Canada L5G 4L8

Library of Congress Cataloging-in-Publication Data

Gay, David, 1955–
    The endless kingdom : Milton's scriptual society / David Gay.
        p. cm.
    Includes bibliographical references and index.
    ISBN 0–87413–777–2 (alk. paper)
    1. Milton, John, 1608–1674—Political and social views. 2. Politics and literature—Great Britain—History—17th century. 3. Christianity and literature—England—History—17th century. 4. Literature and society—England—History—17th century. 5. Milton, John, 1608–1674—Religion. 6. Kings and rulers in literature. 7. Social values in literature. 8. Monarchy in literature. 9. Politics in literature. 10. Bible—In literature. I. Title.

PR3592.P7 G39 2002
821'.4—dc21

                                                                    2002018053

For Sarah and Rachel

Contents

Foreword: Scripture and Society

> Both read the Bible day & night,
> But thou readst black where I read white.
> —William Blake, "The Everlasting Gospel"

AMONG THE MANY POETS INFLUENCED BY MILTON IN LATER GENERATIONS, Blake is the most perceptive of the condition of the Bible in Milton's writings. The Bible is, of course, central to both writers; it is the real subject of most of their writings, and that is why a strong bond exists between them. I use the word condition, however, to call attention to the Bible as a cultural, political, and textual entity in Milton's three major poems. The final lines of Blake's "The Everlasting Gospel" quoted above tell us a great deal about this condition. They speak of the paradox of opposed interpretations generated by a single, common text. Blake's treatment of this paradox produced a poetry of dialectical tensions and conflicts that work to reclaim the Bible as a prophetic text for the creative imagination, the faculty uniquely emphasized by Blake and his contemporaries in part through the influence of Milton. In producing a poetry of conflict, Blake was emulating Milton, whose major poems reclaim the Bible as a text for the conscience, the faculty of singular importance for Milton and his readers. *Paradise Lost*, *Paradise Regained*, and *Samson Agonistes* recreate and interpret specific biblical narratives from Genesis, Luke, and Judges. They reflect, however, on how the whole of the Bible is both formed and possessed inwardly by its readers, and upon how the uses of scripture in opposed polemical discourses can both maintain and threaten that vital inwardness.

The Bible as a printed artifact consists of its own entirety, but it does not enter the conscience of each reader in this entirety.

9

The Bible is initially a broken and incomplete text. Its texture is aphoristic, consisting of sayings, precepts, and isolated teachings. In *Paradise Lost*, for example, a single prohibition is sufficient to the whole of prelapsarian life: "Of every tree of the garden thou mayest freely eat: But of the tree of the knowledge of good and evil, thou shalt not eat of it: for in the day that thou eatest thereof thou shalt surely die" (AV Gen. 2:16–17). But the meaning of the prohibition can be contested and suborned by a demonic adversary. In *Paradise Regained*, a specific biblical quotation is sufficient to stand against the adversary in the postlapsarian world: "Ye shall not tempt the Lord your God" (Deut. 6:16). The quotation functions, however, in a larger conflict that opposes metaphoric and literal, or in Paul's terms, spiritual and natural, hermeneutics, with the condition of the Bible, meaning its potential effect on political and religious liberty, at stake. In *Samson Agonistes*, the Bible is much more fragmented and dissonant. The Chorus reminds Samson of the "sayings of the wise" as he undertakes the painful reconstruction of his life narrative. Samson's central adversary is his own reckless and presumptuous nature, but Dalila, his ostensible adversary, proves as perceptive as Blake in her reflections on the "contrary blasts" of invective that inform the poem, and in her assessment of the black and white sides of historical interpretation where both she and Samson reside.

Milton situates the Bible, as an entity ultimately possessed in the conscience of each fit reader, in the midst of the hermeneutic conflicts that are at the core of each of his major poems. He does this first to reflect the conflicts that define the context in which he completed and published these poems. In 1644, *Areopagitica* claimed that the Bible is the type of its own metaphors for truth. These metaphors reflect the dynamic vitality of an inwardly possessed scripture: scripture is a perpetually streaming fountain, and a scattered body that is always regathered and recombined by its active readers. The vitality of scripture is in turn the type of a genuinely reformed society. Such a society is not a final utopia, but an ongoing social and political process guided by its own typological vision. In 1660, the Restoration of the monarchy frustrated Milton's hopes for a reformed society. The voices that celebrated the Restoration emphasized the outwardness rather than the inwardness of liberty. They did so by identifying scriptural precepts with the material displays of monarchy. For

Milton, this identification led the English people from an active envisioning of a reformed society to the passive reception of a political idol. The Bible undergoes an analogous degeneration in the hands of those who suborn it to the legitimization of power. Milton's adversaries at the time supposed that his response was merely a bitter man's declaration of partisanship in a time of defeat. I will argue in the following chapters that it was considerably more than that. Milton's major poems recreate the ideal vitality of scripture articulated in *Areopagitica* in order to make that vitality the unique possession of future generations of those readers he called the "children of reviving libertie" (*CM* 6:148–49). This recreation depends, not simply upon a loud declaration of his own partisan views, but on a careful recreation of the interpretive conflicts and oppositions of which his views formed one part. The maintenance of these conflicts and oppositions through the complex and contrary perspectives that inform his poems impels each reader toward a conscientious rather than complacent possession of scripture.

Readers perceive Milton's role in this system of oppositions as primarily prophetic. As a type of prophet, Milton is the single figure who stands against the corruptions and failings of his society. *Areopagitica* imagines a society in which all the Lord's people become prophets, but the major poems resume with the prophet's isolation. This study concentrates on another aspect of social and scriptural formation articulated in *Areopagitica* and recreated in the major poems: wisdom. *Areopagitica* identifies wisdom as the virtue of self-possession in the face of temptation. Raphael seeks to teach Adam this virtue before the Fall in *Paradise Lost*. Jesus uses wisdom to defeat Satan's "hellish wiles" in *Paradise Regained*. Samson's followers claim a "new acquist of wisdom" at the close of *Samson Agonistes*. As I will argue, wisdom is crucial to the inward possession of scripture and to the vision of a scriptural society. Wisdom is a distinctively aphoristic phase of the Bible. Canonically, its sayings and proverbs impel the active, inward reading that Milton requires of his readers. Generically, its representative texts—Proverbs and Ecclesiastes—are rich in the Royalist precepts that Milton opposed, but also conducive to the critical, intertextual dialogue that Milton valued. The dialogue of tradition and experience conveyed in these Old Testament texts anticipates the visionary mode of wisdom found in the Gospels. Jesus' sayings cohere around the vision of a Kingdom of God. In *Paradise Regained*, Milton proclaims this kingdom as a potential alternative to the actual manifestation of the restored monarchy. Where Royalist propaganda equates the Kingdom of God with its material manifestation, Milton establishes a critical conflict between the two kingdoms in order to prevent the inertia of political idolatry in his readers. The endless kingdom predicted by Jesus in *Paradise Regained* becomes Milton's final type of the ideal scriptural society his poems seek to sustain.

Milton's major poems are not ahistorical, or consistent with the image of a detached poet who withdrew from the conflicts of his time.[1] His major poems are not merely historical if that term only signifies their circulation within the biblical discourses that pervaded seventeenth-century political culture. Instead, as I will argue, Milton's major poems are radically counterhistorical in their critical engagement with, and opposition to, those discourses. They are so because the Bible is counterhistorical in its capacity to form and sustain communities that oppose and challenge overwhelming historic trends. Milton's poems testify to the counterhistorical capacity of the Bible. This capacity has far-reaching effects for our own culture which, however more secular and less biblical it may seem, is shaped profoundly by the legacy of conscience and criticism it has acquired from Milton's scriptural society.

Acknowledgments

I AM GRATEFUL TO DONALD MELL AND HIS STAFF AT THE UNIVERSITY OF Delaware Press for their consideration and support of this book. The readers who examined the manuscript on behalf of the press offered valuable suggestions that brought many improvements. I wish to thank Sharon Achinstein for her detailed and supportive commentary. I am grateful to Julien Yoseloff, Christine Retz and the staff at Associated University Presses for their care and attention in the production of this book. A grant from the Social Sciences and Humanities Research Council of Canada allowed me to pursue my research at the British Library, and to employ two fine research assistants: John Morris, and Edie Snook, whose master's thesis on Milton I had the honor of supervising. I wish to thank the graduate and undergraduate students I have encountered in my courses on Milton and the King James Bible over the years. Without the vital medium of classroom teaching this book would not have been possible. Among friends and colleagues I have been privileged to know and work with, I am particularly grateful for the encouraging words of James F. Forrest, Jim Mulvihill, Rick Bowers, Arlette Zinck, Garry Sherbert, Troni Grande, Bill Cameron and John Privett. I have also appreciated the good wishes of people who have responded to my ideas in various conference settings, especially John Shawcross, Neil Keeble, Vera Camden, Hideyuki Shitaka and Ken Simpson. Other friends and family members have been a source of much encouragement. Above all, my wife Anne has made everything possible. Since words cannot adequately express my debt to her, I join with her in dedicating this book to our beautiful and amazing daughters, Sarah and Rachel.

A portion of chapter three appeared in *Christianity and Literature* (42:2) 1993. A portion of chapter four appeared in *English Studies in Canada* (18:4) 1992. I thank the editors of these journals for permission to use these materials. A portion of chapter three is excerpted from "'Honied Words': Wisdom and Recognition in *Samson Agonistes*" from *Milton Studies* XXIX, Albert C. Labriola, Ed. © 1993, and is reprinted by permission of the University of Pittsburgh Press. A portion of chapter three appeared in *Literature and Theology* (9:4) 1995. I thank the editors of this journal and the Oxford University Press for permission to use this material.

Note On Texts and Abbreviations

REFERENCES TO DON M. WOLFE GEN. ED., *Collected Prose Works of John Milton*, 8 vols. (New Haven: Yale University Press, 1953–82) are abbreviated CPW with volume and page number. References to Frank Allen Paterson gen. ed., *The Works of John Milton*, 18 vols., (New York: Columbia University Press, 1931–38) are abbreviated *CM* with volume and page number. References to Milton's poems are to Merritt Hughes ed., *John Milton: Complete Poetry and Major Prose* (Indianapolis: Bobbs-Merrill, 1984). I have retained original spellings when quoting early modern texts.

The Endless Kingdom

1
The Righteous Ruler:
Wisdom and Restoration in Milton's England

> How God hath been compassed about by fastings and
> thanksgivings and other exercises and transactions, I
> think we have cause to lament.
> —Oliver Cromwell, speech of 4 July 1653

"The Effects of Wisdom": Scripture and Restoration

On Thursday, 28 June 1660, less than two years after Cromwell's death, John Spencer, bachelor of divinity and fellow of Corpus Christi College, climbed the steps to the pulpit in St. Mary's Church in Cambridge to deliver a sermon. This was a national day of celebration. It was "appointed a day of publick Thanksgiving to God for the happy restauration of His Majesty to his Kingdomes."[1] Spencer's text was Proverbs 29:2: "When the Righteous are in authority, the people rejoice, but when the Wicked bear rule, the people mourn." The text constructs a sharp opposition between the righteous and the wicked, and is typical of "antithetical" biblical proverbs that present contrasts between truth and error, good and evil, wisdom and folly. The text was ideal for Spencer's purpose. He planned to contrast the manifestation of divine wisdom in the restoration of the monarchy with the nation's unhappiness under the protectorate. He did not presume to know the character of the king he was praising: "every pencil especially at so great a distance is not permitted to draw a Kings picture."[2] But he was confident that, in the postdiluvian moment of June 1660, England had weathered "a floud, which covered the tops of our highest Mountains (Princes and Nobles)."

19

England had also made an exodus out of Egyptian bondage, since God had provided England with a Moses "to conduct us (in a happy degree) out of that wilderness condition the Nation was in." The returning monarch was also a new Solomon, the epitome of biblical wisdom and the presumed author of Proverbs and Ecclesiastes. The new Solomon was an incarnation of Proverbs 29:2. When the sermon was published in Cambridge five weeks later, Spencer embellished this point in his chosen title: *The Righteous Ruler*.

Where was Milton on that Thursday morning of 28 June 1660? Two weeks earlier, on 16 June, the Commons had ordered his arrest.[3] Milton had defended the regicide ten years earlier, and in recent months had written vehemently to oppose the Restoration on its eve. In the second published edition of *The Readie and Easie Way to Establish a Free Commonwealth,* he asked his fellow citizens: "Certainly then that people must needs be madd or strangely infatuated, that build the chief hope of thir common happiness or safetie on a single person; who, if he happen to be good, can do no more then another man; if to be bad, hath in his hands to do more evil without check than millions of other men" (*CM* 6:121). Many disagreed. Clement Ellis, in a sermon of thanksgiving for the Restoration, considered how "much of England's happinesse is bound up in the Prudence and Fortune of England's Kings."[4] Milton spoke more against the idea than the person of the monarch. But he was called a murderer by one "G.S.", a "philosopher by the fire," and self-proclaimed "lover of loyalty" who addressed his work to the king:

> This detestable, execrable Murther, committed by the worst of Parricides, accompanyed, with the disclaiming of your whole Royall stock, disinheriting your Majesties self, and the rest of the Royall Branches, driving you and them into Exile, with endeavouring to expunge and obliterate, your never to be forgotten just Title, tearing up, and pulling down the Pillars of Majesty, the Nobles, garbling and suspending from place of Power, all of the Commons House, that had any things of Honesty, or relenting of spirit toward the injur'd Father of three Nations, and his Royall Posterity, Acts horrible to be imagined, and yet with high hand most Villanously, Perfideously, and Perjuriously, prepetrated by Monsters of mankind, yet blasphemously dishonourers of God in making use of his name, and usurping the Title of Saints, in these never before parallel'd, nor ever sufficiently to be lamented, and

abbored Villanies, this Murther I say, and these Villanies were defended, justifyed, nay extolled and commended, by one Mr. John
Milton. . . .[5]

"G.S.," probably George Starkey,[6] hoped that his argument
would lead to Milton's execution. In the *Royal and Other Innocent Bloud Crying Aloud to Heaven For Due Vengeance*, published on 18 June 1660, he named Milton again, and called for
revenge upon the regicides: "Haslerig, Vane, Lenthall, and others
of that gang, had as deep hand in that Crimson fact, as any who
were present at sentence, or confirmed it under hand and Seal."
"Mr. Milton in answer to Salmasius gives the whole glory of this
Heroick action (as he call'd it) to the English Parliament."[7]
Starkey's title emulates the *Cry of the Royal Blood to Heaven,*
which Milton attacked in the *Second Defence* (1654), as if to
aspire to Milton's level of discourse. But Milton is of the race of
Cain, linked not only to an archetypal murderer, but to Satan
himself:

> Nor was this all, but as if Satan had taken possession of the
> Nation, and held it as his own private murthers (which were fre-
> quent and merciless,) were swallowed up in that abomination of
> desolation, the Murther of his Sacred Royall Majesty: Atheisticall
> profaness, sacriledg, and seditious heresy went (hand in hand)
> with the (almost) extirpation, of all our fundamentall Lawes; So
> that civill liberty, and true Christianity, were in hazard, (almost
> quite lost) together, indeed which were brought in, Arbitrary
> tyranny, and ruling by will and lust, (in the state) scandalous in
> piety, irreligious Sects, and blasphemous heresyes (in the Church;
> these with an Impudent brow, defied (I may say) heaven it self.[8]

The biblical types in this discourse of restored monarchy were
the polar opposite of what Milton would make of them in his
major poems. Milton, from the Royalist perspective, was aligned
with Satan, Cain, and the Philistines. Charles II, like the Jesus
of *Paradise Regained*, was entering into his kingdom at the age
of thirty: "The Anointed of the Lord, whom we fear'd to have
been taken in their nets, is return'd in peace, " said Clement
Ellis in a sermon first preached on the restored king's thirtieth
birthday.[9]

If the sermons of Spencer and Ellis were midsummer cele-
brations of restoration, with the tracts of Starkey lording gory

carnivals of retribution over the deposed oppressors, Milton's *The Readie and Easie Way* marked a "Shroving-time" before a long "Lent of Servitude . . . wherein to speak freely, and take our leaves of Libertie" (*CM* 6:111). He hoped that England would still seize its moment: "Now is the opportunitie, now the very season wherein we may obtain a free Commonwealth and establish it for ever in the land, without difficulty or much delay" (*CM* 6:125). Monarchy would reattach England to fortune's wheel, since a king might happen—or happen not—to be good and wise. A commonwealth, in contrast, could function, not as a synchronized and self-perpetuating utopian system, but as a progressive collaboration of the wisdom of its wiser citizens. However far it appears from the inclusive ideal of modern democracies, such a commonwealth would, from Milton's historically situated perspective, mark a higher level of political maturity for England. The Restoration, however, offered not to renew the vigorous youth of the nation, but to maintain the nation in a more helpless infancy, with the monarch serving as a nurturing parent subduing anarchy.

Clement Ellis deployed the monarchical metaphor of parent and child in his Restoration sermon: "We have known what it is to have Kings our nursing Fathers, and Queenes our nursing Mothers: and how happily those two Twins the Church and Commonwealth did thrive, ande grow, and flourish, when fed and cherished at such brests: and alas! we have to our sorrow found, what sad Daies those were, wherein there was no King in our Israel: dayes full of nothing but black clouds, raging winds, and fatall stormes; in which both God's house and Cesar's were blowne downe to the grounde."[10] Ellis alludes to Judges 21:25: "In those days there was no king in Israel: every man did that which was right in his own eyes." Milton's reading of biblical political theory would be very different from his contemporaries in both *Paradise Regained* and *Samson Agonistes*. Ellis views the absence of monarchy as a condition modulating between anarchy and democracy, and predicated on the selfishness of benighted human will: "nothing appear'd for many yeares together but the horrid face of rebellion and confusion, no Religion, no law, no Justice, no Charity, no Order, nay, nothing but the bare name of that, a meer pretence wherof was craftily imposed upon a deluded multitude as a sufficient warrant for their disobedience, & a sure basis for Anarchy, or what is neerest Kin to it, a Democracy, indeed nothing but the bare name of Liberty."[11]

Milton, who had claimed for himself an office beside that of a pulpit as early as *The Reason of Church Government*, never hesitated to derive political theory from scripture. The expression of political theory from the pulpit in sermons celebrating the Restoration can at times reveal discomfort. George Morley, bishop of Worcester, preaching at the coronation of Charles II on 23 April 1661, was defensive in the dedicatory epistle to the published sermon: "I hope that neither Your majesty, nor any other impartial Hearer or reader of it will blame me, for not keeping within the verge of mine own Profession, or for taking more liberty then ought to be made use of from the Pulpit."[12] This suggests that the bishop expected criticism for meddling "in matter of State an argument Excentrick to my Profession, and Improper for the Pulpit." In defending himself against this criticism, the bishop notes that he was commanded by the king to publish the sermon, and that his voice is submerged in a singular voice of popular acclamation: "after so long a series of several forms of Tyranny and Usurpation, Monarchy (which seemed to have been Put to Death with Your Majesty's blessed Father) was again Revived by Your Sacred Majesties Personal Inauguration in so solemn, so magnificent, and so glorious a manner, beginning with as loud shouts of Acclamations, as could be made here on Earth, and ending with much louder shouts and Acclamations from Heaven it self."[13] Morley's self-effacement, combined with the king's insistence that he publish a sermon that modulates into a political tract, suggests that the characterization of popular fervor at the Restoration is a mixture of truth and fiction, or an event exaggerated into the thing Milton most abhorred: a political illusion.

Morley was concerned that "by Repeating and Reviving some passed miscarriages, I had trespassed against the Act of Indemnity."[14] His repeating and reviving consists of a theoretical exposition of various political systems in order to show that monarchy, as the visible supremacy of a single individual, can alone achieve the coherence and stability people need. He polarizes all political systems in terms of plurality and unity, disintegration and wholeness. Monarchy is a valid synthesis of the body politic, while republicanism or democracy, two terms he does not distinguish, bring chaos: "though it be monstrous enough for one body Politick to have more heads then one; yet it is much more monstrous and unnatural, when that which should be the body is the head, or when the body and the head are but one confus'd, undistinguish'd mass or lump; there being in a popular State no difference between those that Govern, and those that are governed." [15] The public entertainment staged for Charles's coronation performed the opposition of monarchical concord and unnatural confusion, illustrating an alliance between pulpit and pageant. John Ogilby witnessed the presentation:

> On the North-side, on a Pedestal before the Arch, is a Woman personating REBELLION, mounted on a Hydra, in a Crimson Robe, torn, Snakes crawling on her Habit, and begirt with Serpents, her Hair snaky, a Crown of Fire on her Head, a bloody Sword in one Hand, a charming Rod in the other. Her Attendant CONFUSION, in a deformed Shape, a Garment of severall ill-matched Colours, and put on the wrong way; on her Head, Ruines of Castles; torn Crowns, and broken Scepters in each Hand. On the South Pedestal is a Representation of BRITTAIN'S MONARCHY, supported by LOYALTY, both Women: Monarchy in a large Purple Robe adorn'd with Diadems and Scepters, over which a loose Mantle, edg'd with blue and silver Fringe, resembling Water, the Map of Great Britain drawn on it; on her Head London, in her right hand Edinburgh; in her left Dublin; Loyalty all in White, three Scepters in her right hand, three Crowns in her left. [16]

In both pageant and sermon, the Restoration reinforced the identification of concord with a single, visible personage in the English political imagination. Milton argued for a plural government of wise and able people in *The Readie and Easie Way*; Morley allows that a "Polycracy" such as a "Senate of Aristocracy," meaning "the Nobility or some of the better sort," is at least a lesser evil than rule by a "multitude of the worst and basest of the people, as it is in a Democracy, or that which is commonly called a Republick." A "plurality of voyces" defies the law of God and nature, notwithstanding seditious arguments that "make use of Scripture . . . to wicked and ungodly ends." [17] Scripture, for Morley, is plain in its affirmation of monarchy: "for at the coming of Christ there was nothing but Monarchy in the World; so that Monarchy as it was Instituted by God at the Creation, so it seems to be restored by Christ at the Redemption of

Mankind, and to be recommended by both the Father and the Son as the best and onely form of Government for all Nations."[18]

Spencer, Ellis, Morley, Starkey and many others could not conceive of a unified body politic apart from monarchy. Ellis asked, "How long this famous Nation may possibly continue one Body, without one Head, How long those two great sides of this glorious Fabrick the Church and State, may stand firme and unshaken, as they ought to be, the beauty, the strength and support of each other, if not well knit together by these Corner-stones: Our ancient flourishing, and our late miserable and never sufficiently deplored condition, when compared together, will too manifestly evidence."[19] Morley observed that the nation was delivered "from the slavery we were in under the Tyranny of many" and restored "to our former freedome and happiness under one Lawful Hereditary Soveraign Prince."[20] Similar sermons were preached for the balance of the century on the anniversary of the Restoration. Bishop Symon Patrick, preaching before the king and queen in 1690 on the anniversary of Charles II's return to England, suggested that subsequent national misfortunes manifested the wisdom of providence: "What were the late Civil Wars, and the woful Effects of them, but the Calamities which God sent upon a sinful People, for our disobedience to him? And since, the wonderful Restoration of the Royal Family and Monarchy, What were the Pestilence, the Fire, and other Judgments, which presently ensued, but tokens of God's continued displeasure against us, for our abuse of his loving-kindness?"[21] The theme of divine judgment, modulating between the polarities of anarchy and monarchy, typifies the political imagination of these sermons.

For Milton, in contrast, the Restoration was a calamity. It meant the loss of "all those happinesses, which in a free state we shall immediatly be possessd of" (*CM* 6:134). The freedom lost was a potential and not an actual freedom, for Milton was certainly not idealizing the Protectorate that had gone before. England was, nevertheless, going backwards by choosing "a captain back for Egypt" (*CM* 6:149). It was time for England to gain maturity: "Shall we never grow old anough to be wise to make seasonable use of gravest autorities, experiences, examples?" (*CM* 6:136). His appeal for political maturity had no effect. Having written "with all hazard" to his personal safety, he was "sorry the effects of wisdom are so little seen among us"

(*CM* 6:148). He spent the summer of 1660 in hiding with friends, emerging in autumn only to suffer a brief imprisonment in November. He escaped a longer imprisonment—and even possible execution—through the intercessions of voices other than his own: "some that stood his friends both in Council and Parliament," Edward Phillips records.[22] Those some included Andrew Marvell.

Milton did not allow the Royalist pulpit to foreclose on the public, vocal space he had helped create in his polemical tracts, particularly *Areopagitica*, except when his personal safety required him to go into hiding. He sought a free and open encounter with his Royalist adversaries prior to Charles's return in his *Brief Notes upon a Late Sermon*. This tract attacked Matthew Griffith's sermon *The Fear of God and the King*, preached at the Mercer's Chapel on 25 March 1660, and registered for printing on 31 March. Milton's attack on Griffith drew a counterattack from Roger L'Estrange who, in 1663, would become Charles II's "Surveyor of the Imprimery and Printing Presses," a tenacious censor in other words. L'Estrange's *No Blinde Guides, In Answer to a Seditious Pamphlet of J. Milton's, Intituled Brief Notes upon a Late Sermon*, appeared on 20 April 1660. The entire exchange occurred in the five weeks before Charles returned to England.

While Griffith's sermon expresses support for the Royalist cause through biblical citations, its timing prior to the Restoration was ill-considered. Griffith addressed his prefatory epistle to General George Monck. Governor of Scotland under Cromwell, Monck entered London with his army in February 1660 and oversaw the reconstitution of the Parliament that would negotiate the return of Charles II. Restoration, Griffith argued in the midst of events, would be Monck's most illustrious deed: "You may by this one Act ennoble and aeternize your selfe more in the hearts and chronicles of these three Kingdoms; then by all your former Victories" for "It is a greater honour to make a King, then to be one."[23] Griffith casts Monck in the national sanctity of his namesake: as a modern St. George, he is destined by God to be England's "temporall Redeemer." As Parker has observed, Griffith's tactless attempt to commend Monck's possible intentions drew fears of popular reaction from Royalist sympathizers.[24] Unlike his more punctual colleagues who celebrated the Restoration after the fact, Griffith was briefly imprisoned for his Royalist fervor. The timing of the sermon also angered Milton, for while England would soon be awash in similar sermons after Charles's return, there was, Milton insisted, no legal king of England in March 1660.

Griffith's epistle to Monck rehearses the biblical themes of another of his sermons, *The Samaritan Revived*, preached at St. Paul's in 1642 and republished in 1660. He assumes the role of Physician to the "Body-Politick (consisting of both Church and State)."[25] He recalls that the body politic of 1642 declined not only from fever and pestilence, but also from "having received divers dangerous wounds" until it "began to gangrene."[26] The image evokes Thomas Edward's *Gangraena*, which viewed sectarianism as a disease in the body politic; Griffith eventually blames "the Anabaptists and the Quakers, whose principles are destructive of rule and settlements in which both our being, as men, and our well-being, as Christians, do under God, and his Christ, chiefly consist."[27]

Griffith's account of the 1640s qualifies him as divine physician as he describes the "Rise, and Progress of our national malady."[28] He compares himself to the Good Samaritan who "cur'd the wounded Traveller, by searching his wounds with wine, and suppleing them with oil."[29] He then identifies himself with Luke the physician by appropriating the opening of his gospel: "It seem'd good unto me, having had perfect understanding of things from the very first, to write unto thee in order (most excellent Theophilus) that thou might'st know the certainty of those things wherein thou hast been instructed."[30] He demands an equal agility from Monck, who must, as his principal listener, shift from being Theophilus to "Jethro's Magistrate," to Esther as she was counseled by Mordecai. As the person poised to restore monarchy, Monck is also Ezekiel in the valley of dry bones: "it must needs grieve you to see these three distressed kingdoms lye, like a body without a Head: so it may also chear you to consider that the Comforter hath impower'd you, (and in this nicke of time, you onely) to make these dead and dry bones live."[31] If Griffith is the physician, Monck, a unique vehicle of the Holy Spirit effecting the reconstitution of a diseased body politic, is the cure.

Milton scorns Griffith as a "Pulpit-Mountibanck" who "would seem to personate the Good Samaritan" and "suborn Saint Luke as his spokesman" (*CM* 6:151–52). He derisively reminds Griffith

of his imprisonment: "I leave your malignant narrative, as need-
ing no other confutation, then the just censure already pass'd
upon you by the Councel of State" (*CM* 6:163). This final sentence suggests why it was worthwhile for Milton to attack Griffith's "sophisticated and adulterate" suborning of scripture.
Griffith encouraged Monck towards restoration by equating it
with God's law; Milton reminded Monck that law had abolished
monarchy in England. That law, moreover, reflected the broader
right of people to choose their form of government: "This choice
of Government is so essential to thir freedom, that longer than
they have it, they are not free. In this land not only the late King
and his posteritie, but kingship it self hath been abrogated by a
law" (*CM* 6:158). Impressing these points upon Monck may have
been Milton's real purpose in responding to Griffith; he was
equally hostile to the deifying of monarchy through the suborna-
tion of scriptural texts.

Griffith's sermon text was Proverbs 24:21: "My son, fear God,
and the King, and meddle not with them that be seditious, or
desirous of change."[32] Griffith links God and the king in a bond
of popular fear: "God, and the King, at the first blush, seem to
stand in the Text, like those two Cherubims on the Mercy-seat
(Exod. 37.9.) looking on each other: yet with this difference, That
God is an heavenly King, and eternal, 1 Tim. 1.17. but the King
is an earthly, and dying God, Psal. 82.6—And yet in a qualified
sence, they are both Gods, and both Kings, and therefore both to
be feared."[33] Milton calls this equation a "vain vision" that "degrades God to a Cherub, and raises your King to be his collateral
in place" (*CM* 6:153). By noting that there was no king in England at the moment of Griffith's sermon, Milton can accuse
Griffith of exciting the people "to fear that which is not" and, in
an aside to Monck, that which "the present Government takes
no notice of" (*CM* 6:153).

Griffith presents a range of scriptural citations to connect God
and the king. Milton contests the citations in order. Citing
Judges 7:20, Griffith argues that the "sword of the Lord and
Gideon, is spoken of as but one two-handed sword; the Lord
gives it, and Gideon girds it to himself. . . . The King is Gods
Sword-bearer, and he bears no sword in vain."[34]   Milton observes that Gideon "not only was no King, but refused to be a
King or Monarch, when it was offered him" (*CM* 6:154). Griffith
cites Psalm 105:15 as a reference to kings: "touch not mine

anointed." Milton responds that "this is not spoken in behalf of Kings, but spoken to reprove Kings, that they should not touch his anointed Saints and Servants" (*CM* 6:155–56). Milton scorns Griffith's cryptic reference to 1 Samuel 8:7, a crucial part of scripture for monarchical and antimonarchical discourse, in which God accedes to Israel's request for a king. For Griffith, 1 Samuel 8:7 shows "how indissoluble is the conjunction of God and the King." [35] For Milton, the words "were not spoken to any who had resisted or rejected a King, but to them who much against the will of God had sought a King, and rejected a Commonwealth, wherin they might have lived happily under the Raign of God only, thir King" (*CM* 6:156). Milton's use of the word "commonwealth" echoes *The Readie and Easie Way*, written to prevent the Restoration. At the same time, Milton recognizes God as the true monarch of Israel, and hence of England. This recognition depends upon maintaining the widest possible disjunction between earthly and heavenly monarchs, and not the unquestioned conjunction that Griffith's sermon, and other Royalist sermons, uphold. Milton is appalled by Griffith's "notorious abuse of Scripture" (*CM* 6:156). He speaks beyond Griffith as an opponent to the people who may still have it in their power to prevent the Restoration:

> O people of an implicit faith no better then Romish, if these be thy prime teachers; who to thir credulous audience dare thus jugle with Scripture, to alleage those places for the proof of thir doctrin, which are the plane refutation: and this is all the Scripture which he brings to confirm his point. (*CM* 6:156–57)

This is a crucial moment in Milton's definition of the English political imagination on the eve of the Restoration. It is the credulity of an implicit faith rather than the resistance of a critical skepticism that will defeat the development of a genuinely scriptural society, from Milton's perspective. He would later call Eve "credulous" as she follows Satan to the Tree of Knowledge (9:644).

Opposed uses of common scriptural passages characterize what Christopher Hill calls the "biblical culture" of seventeenth-century England.[36] The Bible was not only a sacred text, but a viable medium for the interpenetration and opposition of political and religious discourses. As Hill remarks, the Bible in the seventeenth century was "a huge bran tub from which anything might be drawn. There are few ideas in whose support a biblical text cannot be found. Much could be read into and between the lines." Orthodox authorities and dissenting sectarians, comprising a range of political and religious factions, all "appealed to the Bible for support."[37]

The Bible was amenable to the defense and destruction of monarchy. Hill notes that the Old Testament "supplied evidence for attacks on Monarchy and Royal Courts." Thus in *Eikonoklastes*, "Charles I is described as worse than Ahab, Jeroboam, Rehoboam or Saul, comparable with the wilful apostate Ahaz, with Nimrod, Balak and Agag."[38] It was just as plausible, however, for supporters of monarchy to draw from a range of biblical figures to depict the condition of the monarchy at a given moment. Matthew Griffith makes ample use of the subjects of two of Milton's major poems to condemn the opponents of monarchy. Griffith can "multiply scripture instances" of sedition and the desire for change from the Old Testament: they include Cora, Dathan, Abiram, Absolom, Zimri, and Sheba. The "primary cause of sedition" is Satan, who used the "desire for change" to entice Adam and Eve in paradise.[39]

Hill's view of the Bible as a "bran tub" suggests that scripture is a convenient resource for opposed perspectives. While disparaging Presbyterian opponents of his argument, Milton implicitly acknowledges the problem in 1649 in *The Tenure of Kings and Magistrates*:

> Nor let any man be deluded by either the ignorance or the notorious hypocrisie and self-repugnance of our dancing Divines, who have the conscience and the boldness, to come with Scripture in thir mouthes, gloss'd and fitted for thir tunes with a double contradictory sense, transforming the sacred verity of God, to an Idol with two Faces, looking at once two several ways; and with the same quotations to charge others, which in the same case they made to justify themselves. (*CM* 5:5)

In 1660, opposed perspectives were equally purveyed as the genuine recognition of the hand of providence, but they remained opposed.

The political dilemma of the Bible in Milton's age—and perhaps in every age of modern history—is summarized by Northrop Frye: "The normal human reaction to a great cultural achievement like the Bible is to do with it what the Philistines did to Samson: reduce it to impotence, then lock it in a mill to grind our aggressions and prejudices. But perhaps its hair, like Samson's, could grow again even there."[40] The corollary of Frye's metaphor is that Milton, in a poem like *Samson Agonistes*, is not simply writing about the actions of individual characters found in the Bible, but about the Bible itself, including its entire cultural and political condition. With a conviction equal to many of his adversaries, Milton saw the Bible as a revolutionary manifesto of human liberty and political happiness. Why is its revolutionary significance not obvious? Milton, without question an intense partisan in the political argument of the seventeenth century, saw it as his purpose to make the Bible appear in such clarity. But Milton did not merely insist on his own version of political truth without recognizing that his opponents appealed to scripture to support their perspectives. His approach, formulated in *Areopagitica*, a paradigm of Milton's biblical poetics, was not to induce conformity but rather to stimulate the critical vitality of scripture in his own writings. The style of the treatise, figured as a perpetually "streaming fountain" and not a "muddy pool of conformity," models the dynamism of a renewed and reformed society (*CPW* 2:543). In 1644, when Milton published *Areopagitica*, the dynamic correspondence of textual and social vitality seemed almost possible to achieve. The Restoration of 1660 destroyed this correspondence for Milton, and so he chose to proclaim the endless kingdom primarily in the textual and critical space of the poetry he bequeathed to future generations, addressing, as he said in *The Readie and Easie Way*, "som perhaps whom God may raise of these stones to become children of reviving libertie" (*CM* 6:148–49).

Without the imposition of political authority, the Bible seemed to generate sectarian division and personal isolation rather than a stable society. Matthew Griffith's Restoration sermons draw from his experience of the 1640s, and are thus marked by the fear of schism and sectarianism that was a general anxiety of the time. For Griffith, the conjunction of God and the King in popular fear is the only guarantee of political cohesion and stability. The alternative would be anarchy. Milton, also writing from his experience of the 1640s, would concur that a mature society is more than an aggregate of isolated parts or members. Milton's embrace of contending perspectives in *Areopagitica*

leads to the vision of a "noble and puissant" nation that is
wholesome. How could such visions of political integrity be realized without the framework of a single church and the king who
was its head? The Restoration in 1660 answered that they could
not; nevertheless, Milton had laid the foundations of his post-
Restoration solutions to this dilemma as early as *Areopagitica*.
Interpretation can manifest the authority of scripture as each
speaker possesses it, and interpretive dialogue can in turn revi-
talize society. The vision of a society of energetic readers presented in *Areopagitica* combined with the scriptural premises of
the later prose works comprises the basis of Milton's scriptural
society.

These premises incorporate the theory of the double scripture
in the *Christian Doctrine*, the liberty of conscience in *The Readie
and Easie Way*, and the Pauline opposition of spiritual and natural perception in *A Treatise of Civil Power*. The transformation
of perception into criticism makes scriptural interpretation part
of a shared political dynamic. The site of this transformation is
conscience, the place of "inner knowing."[41] In *The Readie and
Easie Way*, Milton identifies "liberty of conscience" as that
"which above all other things ought to be to all men dearest and
most precious" (*CM* 6:142). Other freedoms depend upon conscience: the "whole freedom of man consists either in spiritual or
civil libertie. As for spiritual, who can be at rest, who can enjoy
anything in this world with contentment who hath not liberty to
serve God and to save his own soul according to the best light
which God hath planted in him to that purpose, by the reading
of his reveal'd will and the guidance of his Holy Spirit?" (*CM*
6:141). Conscience as the site of reading and interpretation, or
the cultivation of that "which God hath planted in him to that
purpose," anticipates the metaphor of the inner paradise which
Michael promises to Adam at the close of *Paradise Lost*. The
inner paradise is the text of scripture planted in the individual
conscience. The text of scripture is not an artifact, but the precursor of the individual's possession of what Milton calls the
"double scripture":

> We have, particularly under the gospel, a double scripture. There
> is the external scripture of the written word and the internal
> scripture of the Holy Spirit which he, according to God's promise,
> has engraved upon the hearts of believers, and which is certainly
> not to be neglected. (*CPW* 6:587)

Nowadays the external authority for our faith, in other words, the scriptures, is of very considerable importance and, generally speaking, it is the authority of which we first have experience. The pre-eminent and supreme authority, however, is the authority of the Spirit, which is internal, and the individual possession of each man. (*CPW* 6:587)

Milton's concept of the double scripture proceeds from the external authority of the artifact to the internal authority of the spirit in each conscience: "the external scripture, particularly the New Testament, has often been liable to corruption and is, in fact, corrupt. This has come about because it has been committed to the care of various untrustworthy authorities, has been collected together from an assortment of divergent manuscripts, and has survived in a medley of transcripts and editions. But no one can corrupt the Spirit which guides man to truth, and a spiritual man is not easily deceived" (*CPW* 6:587–88). Milton's purpose as a writer was to clarify the thesis of liberty he encountered in the Bible. He did this by encouraging readers to cultivate the inner scripture. The outward, material spaces of this cultivation were disappearing with the Restoration: John Spencer occupied the pulpit of St. Mary's Church in Cambridge on 28 June 1660 because he was required to proclaim the providential wisdom of the Restoration. Milton found no safe place to speak or write on that date outside of his own conscience and the elementary interpretive companionships that are the focus of his social vision in his major poems. Milton would designate church and pulpit as the conscience of each fit reader, and defer to the author of the inner scripture, the spirit that prefers "Before all Temples th'upright heart and pure."

The state placed controls upon scripture "with an accepted machinery for controlling its interpretation."[42] When John Spencer delivered *The Righteous Ruler* from the pulpit, he did so in a framework of state control, sermons of thanksgiving being required on that day. State control was no less of a factor in the 1640s and '50s, when Parliament abolished episcopacy and ejected many Anglican ministers from their livings. Spencer defended the reinstated framework of monarchical state control in his sermon, arguing that "God and religion justifie and abet Rule, Soveraignty, and Authority in the world: God doth by setting up such to rule; and religion doth, in that we see here, that righteous men (called thereto) do not decline it. God never intended that the Magistrates Sword should be turned into a plough-share."[43] Milton challenges the power of magistrates in relation to conscience and the Spirit: "if anyone imposes any kind of sanction or dogma upon believers against their will, whether he acts in the name of the church or of a Christian magistrate, he is placing a yoke not only upon man but upon the Holy Spirit itself" (CPW 6:590). In Civil Power he argues that God draws people "by the inward perswasive motions of his spirit and by his ministers; not by the outward compulsions of a magistrate and his officers" (CM 6:27).

The opposition between inner motion and outward compulsion connects the central scriptural texts of Civil Power to the difficult political questions of Milton's time. Civil Power elaborates upon 1 Corinthians 2:14–15: "the natural man receiveth not the things of the Spirit of God: for they are foolishness unto him: neither can he know them, because they are spiritually discerned." The biblical opposition of spiritual and natural perception is an aspect of political subjectivity for Milton. Northrop Frye argues that this opposition distinguishes those levels of the reader's consciousness that are socially conditioned from those levels that may achieve some critical perspective on social conditioning. The "natural" reader of 1 Corinthians 2:14 is "a product of ideological conditioning. . . . his faith is simply an adherence to the statements of belief provided for him by social authority, whether spiritual or temporal."[44] The spiritual reader, in contrast, struggles to gain critical perspective on the forces that condition the natural reader: "The New Testament sees the genuine human being as emerging from an embryonic state within nature and society into the fully human world of the individual, which is symbolized as a rebirth or second birth, in the phrase Jesus used to Nicodemus. Naturally this rebirth cannot mean any separation from one's natural and social context, except insofar as a greater maturity includes some knowledge of the conditioning that was formerly accepted uncritically."[45] The implication of individual subjects in the power structures they seek to criticize and transform is a commonplace of critical theory. Frye's interpretation of 1 Corinthians 2:14 is helpful, however, because it is influenced by Milton's concepts of social maturity and gospel liberty. The "spiritual" in Milton is synonymous with the critical revolt of reason against habitual forms and conditions of power. The ground of this revolt is the textual space of an internalized scripture in which the "spiritual" person can begin the heroic struggle of gaining a critical vantage point on the "natural" forces that constitute the fallen world.

The impasse between the outward forces of state-imposed uniformity in religion and the inward motions that produce a scattered isolation of individual consciences and sects is first addressed in *Areopagitica*. A genuinely reformed society must regulate itself by the dynamics of critical reading figured as a war between truth and falsehood: "As therefore the state of man now is; what wisdome can there be to choose, what continence to forbeare without the knowledge of evill? He that can apprehend and consider vice with all her baits and seeming pleasures, and yet abstain, and yet distinguish, and yet prefer that which is truly better, he is the true warfaring Christian" (*CPW* 2:515). As it would be in Milton's major poems, wisdom in the prose writings is a potent amalgam of faith, reason, and vision focused on moments of personal and political choice.

Areopagitica is an early formulation of what Milton would come to mean by the double scripture. We find in the *Christian Doctrine* a certain skepticism expressed towards the "single scripture" as a textual or material artifact: translations may vary, and texts may be corrupt; nevertheless, the "double scripture" makes possible the true possession of the spirit's text in the heart of each believer. The inner paradise possessed by Adam at the close of *Paradise Lost* is a metaphor for this inner critical and textual space. *Areopagitica* also deploys self-reflexive scriptural metaphors for the truth of scripture: truth is a "streaming fountain," for example, and also our "richest Marchandize" (*CPW* 2:543, 548). A particularly pervasive metaphor connecting the conscience of the reader, the reformation of the nation, and the text of scripture is the metaphor of the body. The comparison of truth to a "torn body" (*CPW* 2:550), and of books to the "pretious life-blood of a master spirit" (*CPW* 2:493) and to "meats and viands" (*CPW* 2:512), evokes the Eucharist with its fracturing and distributing of the broken body and blood of Christ. As Thomas Luxon observes, the "early Reformers had removed the body of Christ from the altar and relocated it in the Scriptures, redefining Christ's true body as a discursive body—the Word."[46] Milton appropriates the imagery of the Eucharist from the Catholic traditions he attacks and portrays in its place a Protestant epiphany of the Word as text rather than the Word made flesh. The sacrament is appropriated into a textual space where the reader alone is sovereign. The communion of Milton's reformed body politic is a communion of reading.

Areopagitica is effective in requiring the kind of reading its central eucharistic metaphor implies. The pieces of its scattered body are verbal units comprised of maxims and aphorisms, or short, pithy, and memorable phrases that strike the reader as forms of wisdom: "As good almost kill a Man as kill a good Book" (*CPW* 2:492); "reason is but choosing" (*CPW* 2:527); "opinion in good men is but knowledge in the making" (*CPW* 2:554); "faith and knowledge thrives by exercise" (*CPW* 2:543). These sententious phrases are linked in the continuous prose of a reasoned argument that moves through the phases of a formal Ciceronian oration. The writer's task of linking these aphorisms in prose provides a model for the reader's interpretive task of gathering up the scattered body of truth. Both tasks converge in a moment of political vision: "Methinks I see in my mind a noble and puissant Nation rousing herself like a strong man after sleep, and shaking her invincible locks. Methinks I see her as an Eagle muing her mighty youth, and kindling her undazzl'd eyes at the full midday beam; purging and unscaling her long-abused sight at the fountain of heav'nly radiance" (*CPW* 2:557–58). If "reason is but choosing," then wisdom is the epistemology of faith that emerges from critical reasoning. It is the discerning eye by which mature readers and mature societies see within themselves.

Milton's writings call attention to the activity of gathering up the scattered body of truth while exploring the political conditions under which that activity can be maintained. The three treatises written with some urgency and haste at the Restoration—*Means to Remove Hirelings, Civil Power,* and *The Readie and Easie Way*—formulate these conditions in terms of the primacy of individual conscience. *Civil Power* in particular can be read in a complementary relation to his earlier prose works, as Milton himself suggests: "Of civil libertie I have written heretofore by the appointment, and not without the approbation of civil power: of Christian liberty I write now" (*CM* 6:2). The thesis of *Civil Power* is conveyed in its subtitle: "That it is not lawfull for any power on earth to compell in matters of religion." The argument is based on the sharp opposition of spiritual power, identified with the inner conscience and the "persuasive motions" of faith, and corporal power, identified with external political authority that compels conscience. The argument develops the opposition of natural and spiritual perception. As in *Areopagitica*, Milton argues that a person can be a "heretic in the truth" by abandoning the dictates of personal conscience, while casting the choices facing England in terms of the historical tensions of the Reformation. Like most Protestant polemicists of his time, Milton is hostile to the Catholic Church as a model of earthly power; the elevation of church over scripture surrenders the principles of Reformation: "He then, who to his best apprehension follows the scripture, though against any point of doctrine by the whole church receiv'd, is not the heretic; but he who follows the church against his conscience and perswasion grounded on scripture" (*CM* 6:12–13).

Milton's emphasis on heresy as an aspect of the power of choice recalls the maxim that "reason is but choosing" from *Areopagitica*.[47] In outlining the principles of his ideal republic, James Harrington argued that a "commonwealth is nothing else but the national conscience. And if the conviction of a man's private conscience produce his private religion, the conviction of the national conscience must produce the national religion."[48] For Milton, a complete merger of individual and national consciences is a utopian condition. Constructive heresy maintains the distinction between individual and national consciences in order to affirm the ongoing differentiation of opinion that is germane to reformation.[49] If the synthesis of individual and national consciences were realized, then presumably citizens would move from a fragmented state comprised of heretics in the truth to a state in which all the lord's people are become prophets. Milton is emphatically not a utopian thinker: at any given time conscience is a place to envision the spiritual kingdom of Christ. As such, it must be distinguished from, rather than amalgamated with, the imperfect legislative paradigms under consideration by Parliament, and above all from any state apparatus comprised of corporal power: "This proves the kingdom of Christ not governd by outward force; as being none of this world, whose kingdoms are maintaind all by force onely" (*CM* 6:22). *Civil Power* channels the poetics of *Areopagitica* towards the politics of the kingdom of Christ by rejecting the kingdom's finite association with corporal power while identifying it with an infinitely progressive liberty of conscience, just as *Are-opagitica* presents its own ideal of gathering up the scattered body of truth as a process that will never, and perhaps can never, be completed: "We have not yet found them all, Lords and Commons, nor ever shall doe, till her Master's second comming" (*CPW* 2:549). In his three major poems, Milton is concerned to open a textual space analogous to conscience as the site of critical reading and political vision. In refusing to name that site under the fiction of a synchronic and sequestered "utopian polity," he identifies it completely with the scriptural locus of paradise, knowing that his readers will be perpetually and progressively in motion between its loss and restoration.

"THE BODY OF TRUTH": SCRIPTURE AND THEORY

This study will show how the premises of Milton's scriptural society are recreated in his three major poems. In order to accomplish this, I have selected a specific aspect of biblical rhetoric that demonstrates how the authority of scripture is maintained in the larger, biblical culture in which Milton lived and wrote, and how Milton uses scripture as the grounds upon which to contest that authority. That aspect is the biblical proverb, a form associated with the Old Testament texts of Proverbs and Ecclesiastes and with the teachings of the Gospels. The biblical proverb appears as a small aspect of biblical literature if treated in isolation; viewed within the fabric of seventeenth-century political and religious polemics, the proverb acquires hermeneutic and cognitive dimensions that show how opposed discourses converge and conflict. The sermons of John Spencer, George Morley, and Matthew Griffith, for example, all take citations from Proverbs as their sermon texts. Each sermon expands a central proverb into a recognition of the operation of providence in the restoration of the monarchy. Milton calls attention to proverbs and wisdom frequently in his major poems. The Son is identified with divine wisdom in *Paradise Lost*; Satan offers Eve demonic wisdom at the forbidden tree. The incarnate Jesus of *Paradise Regained* attacks the "politic maxims" of Satan with scriptural precepts that he expands into broader visions. Samson broods over the disjunction of wisdom and strength in servitude, while the Chorus reminds him of the "sayings of the wise." Biblical wisdom provides a language that assumes that providence is operative and apparent in history; it articulates the search for, and the recognition of, the hand of God in history, even when those who give voice to wisdom differ radically in their sense of what providence might be doing.

Wisdom in its broadest configuration is manifest in God's design of the universe. In Proverbs, wisdom is a divine attribute personified as a woman who is present with God at the creation of the world: "When he gave to the sea his decree, that the waters should not pass his commandment: when he appointed the foundations of the earth: Then I was by him, as one brought up with him: and I was daily his delight, rejoicing always before him; Rejoicing in the habitable part of his earth; and my delights were with the sons of men" (8:29–31). In *Paradise Lost*, Milton follows 1 Corinthians 1:24—"Christ the power of God, and the wisdom of God"—by making the Son the agent of divine creation in Book 7: "And thou my Word, begotten Son, by thee / This I perform, speak thou, and be it done" (7:164–65) and of the divine recreation of the fallen world in Book 3: "Son who art alone / My word, my wisdom, and effectual might" (3:169–70). The perception of God's wisdom in creation is evident in a sermon by Edward Stillingfleet:

> When God by his infinite Wisdom had contrived, and by a power and goodness, as infinite as his Wisdom, had perfected the creation of the visible world, there seemed to be nothing wanting to the glory of it, but a creature endued with reason and understanding, which might comprehend the design of his wisdom, enjoy the benefits of his goodness, and employ itself in the celebration of his power. The Beings purely intellectual were too highly raised by their own order and creation, to be the Lords of this inferiour world: and those whose natures could reach no higher than the objects of sense, were not capable of discovering the glorious perfections of the great Creator: and therefore could not be the fit Instruments of his praise and service. But a conjunction of both these together was thought necessary to make up such a sort of beings, which might at once command this lower world, and be the servants of him who made it. Not as though the great fabrick of the world were meerly raised for man to please his fancy in the contemplation of it, or to exercise his dominion over the creatures designed for his use and service; but that by frequent reflections on the author of his being, and the effects of his power and goodness, he might be brought to the greatest love and admiration of him.[50]

This passage, taken from a sermon preached before Charles II on Proverbs 14:9 "Fools mock at sin," could almost serve as a preface to *Paradise Lost*. It asserts that divine wisdom is apparent in the design and purpose of the created universe. The association of wisdom and providence manifest in creation gives us, as the angel Raphael suggests to Adam, an earth that is the true shadow of heaven. When we encounter the association of wisdom and providence in the material displays of political power, however, we are given what Milton would make of that association: his version of Hell.

The texts of biblical wisdom are uniquely attached to the discourse of monarchy because Solomon, the purported author of Proverbs and Ecclesiastes, was king of Israel. While specific proverbs on kingly authority support this attachment, seventeenth-century views of the generic and canonical characteristics of Proverbs and Ecclesiastes also bear this out. George Morley begins his coronation sermon on Proverbs 28:2 with reflections on Solomon's canon. God permitted Solomon's speculative writings on natural philosophy to be lost, Morley notes, but preserved the writings on divinity, morality, politics, and economics "in order to the making of us honest Men, good subjects, good neighbours, and good Christians." He calls Ecclesiastes "an holy Satyre against the world and worldly things, written on purpose to wean us from them, by shewing us the vanity and vexation of them." Proverbs is a "Divine Miscellany or mixture of Theological, Moral, Political and Oeconomical Aphorisms or Observations."[51] The spheres of theology and politics merge in the biblical aphorism, as the observation of Proverbs 28:2 is "partly Political, and partly Theological; for as it observes many Princes in a Land to be a National Calamity, so it is Political; but as it observes, That Calamity to be a National Judgement, or a Judgement of God upon the Land, for the sins of the people of that Land, so it is Theological."[52] In his effort to read contemporary events as both providential and political, Morley constructs a Solomon who is equally king, theologian, and preacher. The site of the fusion of political and divine authority becomes his own coronation sermon.

Joseph Hall's *Salomon's Divine Arts*, published in 1609, also examines the structure and purpose of Proverbs in terms that merge wisdom with monarchical authority. Calling Solomon the "Royallest Philosopher and wisest King,"[53] Hall divides

Solomon's text into the three areas of ethics, politics, and economics. These categories are in turn subdivided into specific attributes of wisdom, such as the ethical virtues of felicity, prudence, justice, and temperance. Politics is divided into the roles of King, counselor, courtier, and subject, thus constructing a hierarchical monarchical court out of the biblical text. "Fear God and the King," which would become Matthew Griffith's text decades later, reinforces the degrees of authority that align monarchy and divinity at the apex. If Hall's work seeks to inculcate virtue and character, it really functions as a commonplace book, as he admits: "I have only endeavoured to be the common-place-booke of that great king, and to referre his divine rules to their heads, for more ease of finding, for better memory, for readier use."[54]

Proverbs is particularly amenable to use as a commonplace book. An example of an entirely scriptural commonplace book is Edward Browne's *Rules for Kings, and Good Counsell for Subjects: Being a Collection of certaine places of holy Scripture, directing the one to Governe, and the other to obeye* (1642). This book compiles lists of biblical citations under monarchical headings: "Speake not Evill of the King"; "Exalt not thy selfe against the King": "The King Loveth Judgment"; "Gods Care of his Annoynted"; "The Punishment of his Adversaries," and others. Supporting texts are listed by chapter and verse and recommended to the reader's attention. The general heading of each commonplace category, offered by the compiler as a remedy for "a time when humane learning, and the discipline and precepts of men are so much despised, as in these our days," filters each precept through Royal power, and thereby reduces scriptural precepts to a rigid conformity.[55]

In both form and content, wisdom literature is a particularly copious provider of topics of monarchical authority. Ecclesiastes 8:2–4, for example, joins the voice of God with the voice of the King: "I counsel thee to keep the king's commandment, and that in regard of the oath of God. . . . Where the word of a king is, there is power: and who may say unto him, What doest thou?" William Pemble comments on this passage in *Salomons Recantation and Repentance*:

> From the danger of disobedience: it is not safe to oppose a King, because it is not easie to over-master him: and therefore hee that resists and incurres his displeasure, is sure to smart for it. The

Kings power is of a large extent, [he doth what pleaseth him] he
will have his pleasure performed, either by thee obeying or upon
thee in punishing thy rebellion, vers. 3. The reasons are: His words
and commands are alwaies joyned with power and authority, and
therefore will over-sway all power opposed against it. . . . His actions cannot be censured and scanned by his subjects [Who may
say unto him, what dost thou?] his faults are liable to Gods, not
mans judgment, so that it is not in the subjects power, nor belongs
to their duty to call him to examination.[56]

Commenting on the same passage, Thomas Granger, a Lin-
colnshire minister who published a substantial commentary on
Ecclesiastes in 1621, argues that the laws of kings must be
grounded in the laws of God: "so is Gods Law the Kings Law, and
his word the Kings word, as he taketh it into his custody to
impose it, and to inforce the obedience thereof under God upon
all men, and to punish under God the breakers thereof. . . .
Therefore must wee chearefully, readily, willingly, faithfully obey
the same, as if wee had received it immediately from the mouth
of God."[57] Thomas Fuller develops the fear of punishment further: "Hence it is if one chance to conceive ill of his sovereign,
though within the cabinet of his soul, presently his own heart
grows jealous of his own heart, and he could wish the tongue cut
out of his tell-tale thoughts lest they should accuse themselves.
And though sometimes rebels (atheists against the God on
earth) may labour to obliterate loyalty in them, yet even then
their conscience, the king's attorney, frames articles against
them, and they stand in daily fear lest Darius Longimanus
(such a one is every king) should reach them, and revenge himself."[58]

In 1685, Symon Patrick, then dean of Peterborough and one of
the king's chaplains, used Ecclesiastes to affirm order: "For this
Tractate is truly Royal, and worthy to be read perpetually, in
this most turbulent Age, both by high and low: That from hence
Subjects may learn to perform Obedience, and the greatest observance both in word and deed toward their Princes; chusing
rather to bear and suffer any thing, than to attempt Rebellion
against them: and Kings may also remember, that they ought to
govern their Kingdoms, according to the Rules of Law and
Equity, and not according to their own will and pleasure; God
having committed them the Scepter of Justice, Clemency, and
Welfare of their Subjects; not the Scepter of Cruelty, Tyranny,

and Destruction." Concerning Ecclesiastes 8:2–4, Patrick argues: "be obedient to the King, and that in regard (or because of the matter) of the Oath, to which God is a Witness, and a severe Revenger of the breach of it. From which a modern Interpreter doth not much vary: whose words it will not be unprofitable to set down in this place; which run thus in English. Regard the Kings mouth. Do whatsoever comes out of his mouth."[59]

These conflations of monarchical and divine authority are anathema to Milton. Scriptural precepts that convey unchallenged assumptions turn perception into political idolatry. Wisdom transforms perception into criticism: it constructs a vantage point on the effects of generations of political habit and conditioning. In *The Tenure of Kings and Magistrates,* Milton reflects on this kind of conditioning: "If men within themselves would be govern'd by reason, and not generally give up thir understanding to a double tyrannie, of Custom from without, and blind affections within, they would discerne better, what it is to favour and uphold the Tyrant of a Nation" (*CM* 5:1). *Areopagitica* is also an attack on the scriptural reinforcement of political conditioning. The static configuration of scriptural texts used as commonplaces makes scriptural truth a model of conformity; *Areopagitica* imagines the revitalization of scriptural interpretation and social reformation as corresponding types. After 1660, Milton had to recreate the opposition between Royalist fervor and conscientious resistance in his poetry in order to promulgate his scriptural ideals. In its themes and rhetorical patterns, biblical wisdom is an important site at which to view this opposition.

The identification of wisdom and providence in Royalist discourse explains why Milton would use biblical wisdom literature to recreate his ideals of oppositional reading in his major poems. How he uses biblical wisdom raises theoretical questions. In order to explore these questions, we need to compare Milton's practice to contemporary theories of wisdom literature. Three theorists of biblical literature will facilitate this comparison. First, Carole Fontaine's theory of proverb performance facilitates an evaluation of the structure and context of proverbial discourse. Second, James Williams's theory of aphoristic order and counterorder provides a model of oppositional reading and interpretation that invites comparison with Milton's practice. Third, Northrop Frye's typological perspective on reading the biblical canon allows us to locate wisdom in relation to law, prophecy, and other phases of scriptural revelation; moreover, Frye's idea of the counterhistorical direction of the biblical message allows us to consider wisdom in opposition to the historical realities and directions that frustrated Milton's hopes for the English people. Fontaine and Williams derive their theories from the Bible, while Frye considers the influence of the Bible on western literature. We should bear in mind that those who wrote, formed and shaped the texts of the biblical canon in the first millennium B.C. created verbal messages and structures that would profoundly shape the perceptions of biblically influenced cultures for centuries. These theories remind us of our contemporary situation as readers of Milton; they also serve to augment and focus distinctively seventeenth-century perspectives on the Bible, helping us discover what is normative and what is original in Milton's poetic practice.

The choice of the right proverb for the right life situation is an affirmation of social and verbal order. The power of interpretation emphasized in biblical wisdom implies a concomitant control over one's own experience and destiny: the power of choice. Theorists of the proverb, both Renaissance and contemporary, emphasize both aspects of power in the etymology of the Hebrew word for proverb. In her theory of "proverb performance," for example, Carole Fontaine argues that the citation of a proverb helps people to analyze social or literary situations. Fontaine points out that the Hebrew word for proverb—*mashal* or "saying"—has "two basic meanings: 'to be similar to' and 'to rule over'."[60] Proverbs, she argues, make "visible the relationships inherent in the events they have observed" by expressing "a connection between a psychological attitude and the subsequent effects of that orientation. Once this similitude is understood, the proverb then allows people to rule over such situations wherever they are encountered." Proverbs "are not simply observational, but rather, persuasive sayings that exert social control."[61]

Fontaine's theory, with its insights into the etymology of "mashal," resonates with the observations of the seventeenth-century commentator Robert Allen. In the *Concordances of the Holy Proverbs of King Solomon*, published in 1612, Allen writes:

> King Salomons Proverbs or Parables only, are worthy to be called, as they are in the Hebrew tongue Meshalim of the verbe Mashal, which signifieth to beare a chief rule, or to have a singular domin-

ion or soveraignty above other. For these sentences of this most wise King, are of like excellency, with the King himselfe: they are of special dignity and preheminence, even predominant, and of very rare excellency, as it were bright shining diamonds, or glistering Starres, to adorne and beautify speeches of more large discourse.[62]

Milton incorporates this idea of sovereignty in his definition of wisdom as a virtue in *Christian Doctrine*. Wisdom is the "Virtue by which we earnestly seek out God's will, cling to it with all diligence once we have understood it, and govern all our actions by its rule (*CPW* 6:647)." The theory of the proverb performance further suggests that the utterance of the right proverb in the right situation is analogous to naming the situation: it could even be viewed as an analogy, within the context of fallen epistemology, of Adam's prelapsarian verbal power in his naming of the creatures. Jesus wields this power in *Paradise Regained* by seeing through Satan's facades, and vanquishing "by wisdom hellish wiles."

The concept of *mashal* also calls attention to the context and occasion of proverbial discourse. The occasion or timing of a proverbial utterance allows the speaker to identify and define a life situation by its correspondence to the chosen proverb. The proverb identifies and defines a situation by rendering it explicable to its hearers or readers. The explanation of a situation occurs by virtue of the familiarity of the proverb, and by the apparent capacity of the proverb to contain the situation within limited moral and rhetorical boundaries. Furthermore, a scriptural rather than folkloric or literary proverb can acquire the force of divine wisdom and providential perspective, especially if it is issued from the pulpit. The effect of the proverb in defining a situation is a function of its content. As Fontaine suggests, content consists of both the rhetorical structure and the poetic image that combine to convey the message of the proverb.[63] Antithetical or contrastive proverb structures, which oppose truth and error, good and evil, darkness and light, wisdom and folly, construct and condition analogous, antithetical political perceptions in their hearers or readers rather than passively witness political events.

The Royalist sermons of John Spencer, George Morley, and Matthew Griffith all elaborate on sermon texts taken from Proverbs. Their context and occasion is the Restoration of the monarchy; their purpose is to approve of the Restoration by supporting it from biblical wisdom. By examining the specific sermon texts used in each case, we can treat the sermons theoretically as "proverb performances," and thereby determine the kind of political epistemology they inculcate in their listeners. In each case, the sermon text is a proverb structured by contrast or antithesis. Spencer used Proverbs 29:2: "When the Righteous are in authority, the people rejoice, but when the Wicked bear rule, the people mourn." Morley used Proverbs 28:2: "For the Transgression of a Land, many are the Princes thereof; But by a Man of understanding and knowledge shall the state thereof be prolonged." Griffith used Proverbs 24:21: "My son, fear God, and the King, and meddle not with them that be seditious, or desirous of change." Each constructs a binary opposition that instills a rigid political perception. The first two divide the antitheses by the conjunction "but" while the third uses the conjunction "and" to create a contrast. For Spencer it is the contrast between the righteous and the wicked; for Morley it is transgression contrasted with understanding; for Griffith it is monarchy contrasted with sedition. A contrast common to all three, however, is the opposition of unity and multiplicity, a feature most apparent in Proverbs 28:2. All three assert that the stability of the body politic is only possible when it is unified under the image of a single monarch. Sedition, transgression, change, and volatility are associated with a plurality of leaders, voices, and perspectives. The contrastive, antithetical structure of each proverb conveys as strong a political message as any of the specific images the proverbs deploy.

The use of wisdom to inculcate a Royalist political perception challenged Milton to find scriptural grounds upon which to counter this form of authority. A further theoretical view of biblical wisdom allows us to see how an oppositional mode of reading is encouraged from scripture. Wisdom can oppose concepts of order with articulations of an alternative "counterorder." If the wisdom of order were merely a stable and self-replicating system then scripture could only recommend the uncritical conformity Milton condemns in *Areopagitica*: the unquestioned reception of received wisdom would make society a "muddy pool of conformity" rather than a perpetually "streaming fountain" of new questions and ideas. The unchallenged control of traditional wisdom would create a dystopia. *Areopagitica* offers a rhetorical model of the dynamic critical reading it seeks to impress upon society; moreover, it identifies that model with scripture, since the streaming fountain is Milton's metaphor for biblical truth. The treatise is therefore a theoretical as well as rhetorical model of oppositional biblical discourse. Milton wanted to portray the Bible as more than what Hill calls a "bran tub" conveniently supportive of any opinion. The characteristic that makes the Bible a revolutionary rather than conformist text consists in its own internal maintenance of the critical, dialogic, oppositional reading Milton idealizes in *Areopagitica*. The Bible's character- istic questioning spirit revitalizes, and indeed replicates, further critical reflection in each part of its canon. Biblical wisdom con- tains within its own corpus an analogous critical dynamic that Williams calls the wisdom of counterorder. Counterorder is not equivalent to disorder, or to the simple negation of order. In- stead, order and counterorder abide in a dialectical tension, with the wisdom of counterorder offering a coherent and necessary critique of the wisdom of order. It thereby provides a legitimate grounds for challenging the wisdom of authority and tradition. The wisdom of counterorder challenges the priorities of tradi- tional order in two ways: first, it affirms the authority and the legitimacy of the voice of the individual in critical opposition to the collective voice of tradition; second, it affirms lived experi- ence as a legitimate empirical basis for the criticism of received tradition.

The relationship between Ecclesiastes and Proverbs, juxta- posed as these books are in the biblical canon, is a central model for this critical dialogue. The "preacher" in Ecclesiastes continu- ally emphasizes lived experience, and its honest contradiction of received wisdom, as the scope of his empirical vision: "I re- turned, and saw under the sun, that the race is not to the swift, nor the battle to the strong, neither yet bread to the wise, nor yet riches to men of understanding, nor yet favor to men of skill; but time and chance happeneth to them all" (Eccl. 9:11). This passage responds to proverbs that identify prosperity with righ- teousness. Strength, wisdom, and understanding are not always materially vindicated in the fallen world. The maintenance of a clear, objective, and critical eye is therefore the persistent theme in Ecclesiastes: "Better is the sight of the eye than the wander- ing of desire." The "sight of the eye," I argue, signifies the tren- chant critical vision that typifies the character of Jesus in *Paradise Regained*.

The image of the Preacher as an energetic critic occurs in seventeenth-century commentaries that read Ecclesiastes as a treatise on personal and political happiness. The Preacher makes a diligent search for the sources of true happiness according to this reading. In a commentary published in 1669, Edward Reynolds, bishop of Norwich, summarized Ecclesiastes as "the Curious and Critical inquiry [the Preacher] made after true happinesse, and what contribution all things under the Sun could afford thereunto."[64] Moreover, when "he had set himself to make a most Critical and Accurate search into all things here below," he "doth conclude of them all in general, and of the most excellent of them all in particular, namely of wisdome and knowledge, that they are not onely Vanity, and so unable to satisfy the Soul, but are further Vexation of Spirit, as causing much grief and sorrow to that heart which is immoderately conversant about them."[65] The form that critical counterorder takes in Ecclesiastes is its rejection of the things of this world, which include not only its luxuries and pleasures, but even its forms of knowledge. This apparent *contemptus mundi* is not the chronic pessimism many readers have attributed to this text, but rather a vigorous realism: the Preacher is "not a weary pessimist tired of life: he is a vigorous realist determined to smash his way through every locked door of repression in his mind."[66] Yet even this attack on worldly vanity can be rendered politically innocuous if it is displaced, as it easily can be, into a resigned, otherworldly perspective that evades the responsibilities of the present world. Milton transforms this attack on worldly vanity by politicizing it in Jesus' survey and rejection of worldly forms of power and knowledge in *Paradise Regained*. By giving the theme of worldly vanity a political charge, he opens the potential for the transformation of the world which is otherwise discouraged. What Bishop Reynolds calls a "most Critical and Accurate search into all things here below" also typifies the character of Jesus in *Paradise Regained*, but with a radical political commitment the bishop would not anticipate.

While Ecclesiastes epitomizes the biblical idea of wisdom as a critical exchange between tradition and experience, it is only one version of counterorder. A second version, representing an alternative to the empirical eye of experience, is the eye of vision. Visionary wisdom occurs in the great theophany at the conclusion of Job, and in visions of a renovated society in the

prophets. Visionary rather than experiential wisdom is epitomized for Milton in the idea of the "kingdom of God" that connects the various sayings and proverbs of Jesus in the New
Testament. As Williams observes, the wisdom of counterorder
challenges tradition either through personal experience that
may contradict the wisdom of order, as in Ecclesiastes, or
through the vision of a renovated order, as in the Beatitudes. In
both cases, the proverb of counterorder "moves the mind to look
into a small aspect of an accepted order or to deconstruct the received state of things on the basis of a vision that requires a
counterorder." [67] This critical impulse is transformative. In its typological symbolism, the Sermon on the Mount, for example,
which begins with aphoristic beatitudes, presents a structural
symmetry to the Ten Commandments received on Mount Sinai
in Exodus, with each beatitude corresponding to a commandment.[68] The sermon establishes this symmetry to proclaim the
transformation—not rejection—of the prior tradition into the
"kingdom of God," which Milton, in *Areopagitica*, *Civil Power*,
and the major poems, interprets as a social and political gospel.

Wisdom focuses on the reader. As such, it can make the reader
more aware of the nature of the inward, double scripture. As
Williams argues, "aphoristic thought does not proceed systematically, but empirically. It directs itself to the fragments of experience as they occur, so that the mind is compelled to make its
own connections among phenomena."[69] Scattered aphorisms
demand a critical *re-cognition* of tradition by the reader. The
cognitive dimension helps to overcome the idols of mental conditioning and to encourage what Frye terms a "program of continuous mental energy." The cognitive aspects of aphoristic
discourse make reading a more self-conscious activity. Robert
Cawdray makes a similar case in the sphere of his Protestant
polemics. The authors of his commonplaces, he states, "learnedly
beautifie their matter . . . stirring up thereby, mens drowsie
minds, and awaking slouthfull, negligent, carelesse, sluggish,
and retchlesse people, to the confident consideration and acknowledgement of the truth; and to the following and imbracing
of vertue and godlinesse."[70] Cawdray's chosen authors, not surprisingly, show a "zeale likewise of advancing true Religion, and
of banishing all Idolatrie and superstition."[71]

Proverbs also emphasize reading by demanding a degree of interpretive skill in each reader. Robert Alter argues that "the

transmission of wisdom depends on an adeptness at literary formulation, and the reception of wisdom . . . requires an answering
finesse in reading the poems with discrimination."[72] Thus in the
apocryphal book of Sirach, the reader is exhorted to "seek out
the secrets of grave sentences, and be conversant in dark para-
bles" (39:3). The cognitive aspects of the aphorism are evident in
the four generic kinds of biblical proverb. The plain precept is a
straightforward exhortation valued for its plainness and per-
spicuity: "Get wisdom, get understanding: forget it not; neither
decline from the words of my mouth" (Prov. 4:4). The antithetical
proverb contrasts good and evil, truth and error, virtue and vice,
and so demarcates ultimate borders between life and death: "He
that keepeth his mouth keepeth his life: but he that openeth
wide his lips shall have destruction" (Prov. 13:3). Proverbs based
on similitudes or metaphors tend more deliberately to exercise
interpretive skill: "Burning lips and a wicked heart are like a
potsherd covered with silver dross" (Prov. 26:23). The paradoxi-
cal proverbs used by Jesus in the Gospels extend the cognitive
range of counterorder because their logic and integrity are recognizable only in the context of the alternative social vision they
advance: "So the last shall be first, and the first last: for many be
called, but few chosen" (Matt. 20:16).

Milton's prose style in *Areopagitica* links aphoristic sentences;
the tract thereby enacts its own metaphor for the reading process by gathering up the scattered body of truth. Short, pithy
phrases like "reason is but choosing" or "as good almost kill a
Man as kill a good Book" strike the reader as keys to the argument of *Areopagitica*, and tend to be extracted by the reader's
memory from the line of continuous rhetorical persuasion, however indispensable that line remains.[73] The cognitive integration
of constellated aphorisms converges in moments of recognition:
Milton exhorts his readers to see a "Nation rousing herself like a
strong man after sleep" (*CPW* 2:557–58). This vision of an awakening, reading nation gives a political charge to Cawdray's idea
of "stirring up thereby, mens drowsie minds, and awaking
slouthfull, negligent, carelesse, sluggish, and retchlesse people,
to the confident consideration and acknowledgement of the
truth." Milton's program of gathering the scattered body of truth
into a vision of an awakening nation responds to the nation's
anxiety over the perceived disintegration of the body politic:
"There be who perpetually complain of schisms and sects, and

make it such a calamity that any man dissents from their maxims. . . . They are the troublers, they are the dividers of unity, who neglect and permit not others to unite those dissever'd peeces which are yet wanting to the body of Truth" (*CPW* 2:550–51).

Not everyone shared Milton's confidence. The fear of schism, or the sense that political and religious turmoil comprised disorder rather than counterorder, pervaded the century. Dod and Cleaver, for example, illustrate this anxiety in their use of Proverbs 13:13 to accuse the Brownist sect of separatism: "Howsoever they pretend to stand for sinceritie, they resist it: and taking upon them to be champions for Christ his kingdome, they fight against it: and though their arguments deeme to be grounded on the word, yet beeing well sifted they prove mere fallacies, and have no agreement with the meaning of the holy Ghost, in the word. They are strongly illuded by Sathan, and made his agents, as much as may be, to pervert the right wayes of the Lord."[74] Charles Herle, a Presbyterian divine who retired to Winwick, Lancashire, after opposing the execution of Charles I, sensed that chaos and disintegration were the only alternatives to traditional order. In arguing that one "office" of wisdom is the "confutation" of error, Herle cites and confutes in succession the "Arrian Errors old and new," the "Arminian Errors of Universal Grace, Free-will, Final falling away from saving grace," the "Socinian Errors, that deny any need of satisfaction to Divine Justice by Christ's death," the errors of antinomians "who but distinguish . . . between a Principle and a Rule," as well as the assorted errors of Anabaptists and Familists.[75] Herle observes that "Man is naturally a Congregative Creature, and society is very apt to disband again and to corrupt into Parties, and parties as apt again to multiply and widen differences."[76] "I confess," Herle adds later, that "the present errors and strange delusions of many, look't upon formerly as forward Professors, is matter of no less wonder, than grief."[77]

Finding sectarian division more salutary, Milton points out in *Areopagitica* that Christianity itself began as a sect. At risk is the isolation of each believer in an idiosyncratic theology, a risk Milton accepts in reaching out to "all the churches" in his *Christian Doctrine*. Nevertheless, *Areopagitica* and *Civil Power*, are consistent in preferring freedom of conscience, even with the risk of the chaotic sectarian contradictions that entails, to an imposed or "forced" uniformity always typified for Milton by the Catholic Church. The aphoristic body of truth is a rhetorical analogue for the tensions and reformations within Milton's society. The proliferation of the sects points out that wisdom, even with its encyclopedic range of topics, is also finite and partial in its perceptions and comprehensions of the totality of God and creation. Each person sees, as Blake later said, only portions of the infinite. A proverb may be a key to understanding a larger narrative or rhetorical argument, but it cannot be the single or comprehensive key. At most, it can join with other "dissever'd peeces" of the body to crystallize into the kind of vision Milton attains in *Areopagitica*.

Genuine wisdom, therefore, acknowledges that the dimensions of reality are too great to be comprehended in any single statement or individual perspective. As Williams notes, "ancient aphoristic wisdom is an attempt to master the complexities of experience, but reality is a plethora of beings and events that cannot be systematically comprehended. Analogies that enable one to find one's way may carry the mind toward an ever increasing mystery of things, but neither the world's secrets nor the divine reality can be finally comprehended."[78] Milton was, by temperament, a totalizer: the genre of the "diffuse" epic implies the writer's attempt to offer a comprehensive justification of "the ways of God to man." Yet in its heterocosmic survey of literary kinds, its perspectival cosmology, its accommodated theology, and its postlapsarian epistemology, *Paradise Lost* always acknowledges that reality is a rich and copious manifold of dimensions and perspectives. This acknowledgment is maintained in juxtapositions of the infinite and the finite, the macrocosm and the microcosm. Hence, at the greatest extent of their survey of creation, Raphael counsels Adam in humility:

> Heav'n is for thee too high
> To know what passes there; be lowly wise:
> Think only what concerns thee and thy being.
> (8:172–74)

The finitude of human perspective raises the question of the relationship of the proverb, as both a nonnarrative verbal unit and a vehicle of perception or insight, to the larger narrative "worlds" Milton constructs in his poems. The same relationship is explored in the Bible, where law, wisdom, prophecy, and gospel

maintain a dialogue within a narrative framework that emphasizes growth and journeying as consistent parameters of history
and community. Frye notes that law is general and wisdom is
particular: proverbial wisdom therefore portrays the "individualizing of law," or the internalization of the law in the mind of an
individual character who must apply "it to specific and variable
situations."[79] In the *Basilikon Doron*, James I corroborates this
view by describing wisdom as a "commentarie" on the law in the
mind of the reader who is his son and heir:

> Would ye then know your sinne by the Lawe? reade the bookes of
> Moses containing it. Would ye have a commentarie thereupon?
> Reade the prophets, and likewise the bookes of the Proverbes and
> Ecclesiastes, written by that great patterne of wisedome, Salomon,
> which will not only serve you for instruction, how to walk in obedi-
> ence of the Lawe of God, but is also full of golden sentences, and
> morall precepts, in all things that can concerne your conversation
> in the world, as among all the prophane Philosophers and Poets,
> ye shall not finde so rich a storehouse of precepts and naturall
> wisedome, agreeing with the will and divine wisedome of God.[80]

George Herbert also corroborates this idea in "The Holy Scriptures II," where he suggests that one's life is a commentary on
scripture: "Such are thy secrets, which my life makes good / And
comments on thee. . . ."[81] Both King James and Herbert recover
for us the perspective of the Bible as a dynamic, intertextual
commentary as described by Jane Melbourne: "For Milton . . .
the Bible was one book, not a collection of books, its parts inter-
woven in ways that commented upon each other to produce a
unified text. Read in this manner, the Bible provides a system of
symbols, shared by readers and writers, that represents larger
complexes of meaning than words."[82]

The larger complex of scripture consists of typological and
canonical relationships. Frye views the biblical canon as a progressive revelation comprising a sequence of phases:

> The content of the Bible is traditionally described as "revelation,"
> and there seems to be a sequence or dialectical progression in this
> revelation, as the Christian Bible proceeds from the beginning to
> the end of its story. I see a sequence of seven main phases: cre-
> ation, revolution or exodus (Israel in Egypt), law, wisdom,
> prophecy, gospel, and apocalypse. Five of these phases have their
> center of gravity in the Old Testament and two in the New. Each

phase is not an improvement on its predecessor but a wider perspective on it. That is, this sequence of phases is another aspect of
Biblical typology, each phase being a type of the one following it
and an antitype of the one preceding it.[83]

Wisdom is a phase of revelation contained within the canonical
framework of the Bible. The sequence of progressive revelation in
the canon of scripture combines with the intertextual pattern of
collated scriptural texts to form a dynamic and integrated sense
of the inward possession of scripture. The dimensions of this possession can be further aligned with the temporal dimensions of
past, present, and future in the hermeneutic situations Milton
creates for his readers and his characters. Adam, for example, experiences the Bible as a vision of the future at the end of *Paradise
Lost*, but the reader experiences this vision as part of the past.
Samson looks with regret to the past while Jesus looks with anticipation to the future. In both *Samson Agonistes* and *Paradise
Regained*, the perspective gained from the linear sequence of
episodes or temptations is both enhanced and complicated by the
intertextual and collated readings undertaken by characters
within each episode or temptation. Intertextual reading as a progressive sequence is ultimately typological.

The discontinuous nature of aphoristic wisdom combined with
the typological and temporal phases of revelation shed light on
Milton's "double scripture" and the kind of reading it requires.
Law is a general frame of reference; wisdom individualizes and
internalizes law by "applying it to specific and variable situations."[84] As Dod and Cleaver remark, the Ten Commandments
are "the words of God, because they be written and engraven in
every man's conscience."[85] Revolution consists of historic events,
as in the milieu of Judges and *Samson Agonistes*, while prophecy
is revolution internalized by the individual and expressed as a
solitary voice confronting injustice, as in the prophets, the
gospels, and *Paradise Regained*. While Milton emphasizes the
internal or double scripture in part because of a mistrust of biblical sources and translations, he also posits, as a result of his
emphasis on the inner possession of scripture through reading,
an ultimate synthesis of the dialectically synergized phases of
law and revolution, prophecy and wisdom. A convergence of
these phases is implied in the gospels, since Jesus is both a
teacher and a revolutionary, but an ultimate convergence could

only be defined as apocalyptic. Such an apocalypse is not the material appearance of God's kingdom anticipated by Milton's millenarian contemporaries, nor is it the general thanksgiving offered by those who celebrated the Restoration as a material theophany. The material correspondence of poetic text and historic event belongs to what Frank Kermode calls "naive apocalypticism."[86] As an alternative to this naiveté, Milton pursues what Frye calls the literary or "readerly" apocalypse, the vision of the "total meaning of scripture" conveyed in Revelation through the completion of the double scripture as the reader's imaginative and political possession.

The apocalypse posits the possibility of envisioning this total meaning, while aphoristic wisdom reminds us that human perceptions and interpretations are limited, partial, and often provisional. Apocalypse and wisdom appear to juxtapose the mind of God, where a vision of the totality of scripture may reside, with the mind of the reader. Hence, while Milton uses wisdom literature to characterize the reader's search for meaning, he also makes the apocalypse of Revelation a subgenre of each of the three major poems, a point most apparent in Michael's prophecy at the close of *Paradise Lost*, in the discussion of Pareus's commentaries in the preface to *Samson Agonistes*, and in Jesus' final triumph over Satan at the climax of *Paradise Regained*. Milton's literary or "readerly" apocalypse seeks a restoration of the reader's spiritual perspective—in opposition to the material spectacle of the Restoration of 1660—by offering the poems as sites of critical vision. The site of critical vision is both the "paradise within" Michael speaks of in *Paradise Lost*, and, ultimately, the "endless kingdom" Jesus speaks of in *Paradise Regained*.

"On David's Throne": Scripture and Resistance

Milton's Jesus stands as a critical counterpoint to the confusion of divine and royal images presented at the Restoration. Divine wisdom in the Royalist discourse Milton opposed was, in the events of 1660, thought to be more actual than potential; triumphal pageants, monarchical displays, and acts of retribution comprised the material *anagnorisis* or recognition scene of a tragic drama that began in the 1640s. John Spencer's *The*

Righteous Ruler effects this recognition by proclaiming the wisdom and justice of providence in the event of the Restoration. The obviously polarized difference between Spencer's sense of providence and Milton's in the weeks following the Restoration serves to illustrate the dynamic of critical conflict already idealized in *Areopagitica*. But the writer who envisioned the awakening of his nation "like a strong man after sleep" in 1644 could not have foreseen that his would be the fugitive and ostracized voice in 1660, his own works "killed," by being banned or burned, as part of the reassertion of Royalist discourse. That Milton saw his task as partly one of recovering a political and religious voice from Royalist Restoration discourse is dramatized in the invocations in *Paradise Lost*.

One striking example of this recovery occurs in Milton's very use of the word "Restoration." As Neil Keeble points out, for Milton "the Restoration and its culture epitomized the hostile wilderness of this world through which the saints pass and the temptations with which they are beset. It was . . . part of a continuity, merely another revolution in the seventeenth-century sense of that word, and not, as figured by the dominant ideology, a divine mercy, unique, unprecedented, inexplicable."[87] In contrast, in Royalist works such as Anthonie Sadler's *Mercy in a Miracle*, another thanksgiving day sermon, the opponents of Restoration are compared to biblical agents of treachery and sedition:

> God's King, found Jehoiada, his Restorer, in dispite of Athaliahs Treachery. Yea, and so hath our now dread Soveraign, Charles the Second; he hath (in dispite of the Treachery, the Cruelty, and Heresy of all his Enemies) found the King of Kings, his Helper, to defend him; and his Defender, to Preserve him; and his Preserver, to restore him; and his Restorer, to establish him, in the Throne of his Kingdome, and the Hearts of his People. . . . Oh! what will not the Lord do for those that serve him? Because the King putteth his Trust in the Lord, in the Mercy of the most High, he shall not miscarry. He shall not, no, he did not: for by a few single (singular) persons, such a King is so Restor'd; that all Christendome admires: and such a Restoration, is so establisht; that all the world's amaz'd.[88]

Clement Ellis observed that "The Restauration of this Royall person, and in him of Israel's happiness, was a work more pecu-

liarly & properly the Lord's whereby he was wonderfully pleased
to exhibit to the world, as it were, under his hand and seal, a
most signall testimoniall of David's Just and Righteous cause."[89]
Opponents of Restoration were, for Ellis, opponents of divine
providence itself: "But now when they behold the Lord making
bare his own arme from heaven, & shewing himself mindfull of
David in his lowest condition, bringing all the subtile devices of
the long prosperous sinner to none effect, & without the help of
man, even against all the projects of man, restoring his Anointed
to his own how can they chuse, but seeing, be amazed & wonder,
be silenced, and condemning themselves. . . ."[90] Milton was
aligned with biblical traitors, blasphemers, and enemies of God.
Since "restoration" became the prominent Royalist term for the
event of 1660, Milton's conspicuous use of it in the invocation to
Paradise Lost—"till one greater Man / Restore us"— recovers the
word by opposing the kingdom of Christ to the kingdom of the
Stuarts. As Keeble further observes, Milton's use of "restore" in
the invocation "dismisses the events of recent history as of no
consequence to true (eternal) restoration."[91]

Milton opposed the Royalists' conflation of earthly and heavenly kingdoms as visibly and materially manifest in the
Restoration with an "endless kingdom" conceived and sustained
in the elementary community formed in the textual and critical
space of reading. A community of readers is spiritually formed
rather than materially conditioned. Biblical wisdom literature
gave Milton one poetic model for the social and political dynamics he envisions in *Areopagitica* and *Civil Power* and expresses
in his three major poems as the spiritual exercise of this elementary community. Milton felt "compass'd round" by the sermons of Spencer and Ellis, and the tracts of George Starkey, at
the Restoration. While *Paradise Lost* is not a direct answer to
any one of these writers, it is a comprehensive answer to what
the Restoration meant to all of them. Spencer, for example, is an
apt example of the ironies and paradoxes of the biblical culture
of seventeenth-century England, given that he celebrates all
that Milton deplored in a sermon celebrating God's apparent
vindication of the Stuart monarchy. The occasion of his
sermon—a national day of thanksgiving for the Restoration—
typified and hence synchronized his celebratory argument in the
political consciousness of the English people. Milton eventually
achieved a cultural and poetic magnitude that overshadows

Spencer's brief sermon, but Spencer, on that Thursday morning in 1660, spoke with the political and historical magnitude of the Restoration entirely on his side. Meanwhile, in *Britain's Triumph*, George Starkey gleefully scorned Milton's blindness as Charles II entered London:

> But who appears here with the *Curtain drawn*?
> What *Milton*! are you come to see the sight?
> Oh *Image-breaker*! poor Knave! had he sawn
> That which the fame of, made him crye out-right,
>   He'ad taken counsel of *Achitophell*,
>   Swung himself weary, and so gone to Hell.[92]

Milton's emergence from the shadow of the Restoration, and the personal and political vilification it entailed, is part of the meaning of his work.

Milton's vocation as a prophet has been documented by Joseph Wittreich, William Kerrigan, and others.[93] A prophet is one who confronts society directly, often with indictments of its mediocrities and injustices. The rudiments of wisdom, as they are transmitted from generation to generation, speak to the formation rather than confrontation of societies in the first instance, calling our attention in particular to the educative function of poetry.[94] Dayton Haskin has shown us how the process of gathering and connecting different biblical places, of "closing up truth with truth," is not only basic to Milton's scriptural hermeneutics but also integral to the biblical culture of seventeenth-century England. As Haskin observes, Milton "aims to discover in the general tenor of the Scriptures the deep structure of God's language, which generates all the various particular texts."[95] Milton's *Christian Doctrine*, for example, with its assemblage of scattered proof texts, "is his attempt to collate texts *in unum corpus*, a textual body of the Word of God that will not be complete short of the Second Coming."[96] *Areopagitica* and *Civil Power* defend the right of each individual to engage in the process of interpretation according to conscience. This principle is tested and affirmed in the three major poems that follow the Restoration. The formation of individuals into communities through the collaboration of their reason and conscience produces an analogy to the textual sphere of Milton's Bible as it is perceived through the interpretive dynamics of wisdom. The Bible is a book that demands associating, linking, joining readers conscious of the motions inherent in reading, and aware of reading as a defining feature of a mature society.

The analogy between individual reading and the formation of community points us in two directions that ultimately converge. The first direction points inward to the interior worlds of conscience and imagination Milton expands and exercises in his poetry. From this direction, we can better understand how Milton's major poems serve to awaken and educate his readers to the tasks and the powers of reading. The vitality of the inner world is sustained through Milton's emulation of the critical, questioning spirit of the Bible as it is typified in Job, Ecclesiastes, and other texts. The second direction leads outward to the world of history and political events that are the scene of conflict and engagement in Milton's poetry. The critical impulse to understand Milton's use of the Bible in his major poems leads us to recognize their relationship to the "biblical culture" of seventeenth-century England documented by Christopher Hill. The recovery of Milton in his engagement with the events of his time leads to a better appreciation of his literary and cultural legacy. It is in the historical as well as the aesthetic framework that we come to realize that the biblical culture of Milton's times was in many ways the crucible in which the modern critical imperative—our modern sense of the need for criticism in a mature society—was forged.

These inner and outer worlds can have but one point of convergence, and that is in the here and now. In her comparison of Milton and Dietrich Bonhoeffer, Joan Bennett demonstrates the commitment of Milton's religious thinking to the personal and political renovation of the present.[97] Like the Bible, which is suborned in all ages by prejudice, yet persistent at all times in its underlying emancipatory potential, the "work of building the holy society" begins in the present.[98] Recalling the overwhelming discourse of reestablished monarchy he opposed in 1660, Milton chose to end his major poems with reestablished relationships that signify the potential of an endless kingdom. Milton's vision of an endless kingdom is predicted by Mary and Jesus in *Paradise Regained* :

> A messenger from God foretold thy birth
> Conceiv'd in me a Virgin; he foretold

Thou shouldst be great and sit on *David's* Throne,
And of thy Kingdom there should be no end.

                                        (1:238–41)

Know therefore when my season comes to sit
On *David's* Throne, it shall be like a tree
Spreading and overshadowing all the Earth,
Or as a stone that shall to pieces dash
All Monarchies besides throughout the world,
And of my Kingdom there shall be no end.

                                        (4:146–51)

The prediction is based on Mary's Magnificat in Luke, which prophesies an endless kingdom founded on the ruins of earthly monarchies. The endless kingdom envisioned by Mary and Jesus offers a different kind of restoration from that celebrated on 28 June 1660 by John Spencer in *The Righteous Ruler.* Milton's "endless kingdom" is not a utopian fantasy that dreams of an end to history. It defers rather than expects the reign of Christ and his saints anticipated by the Fifth Monarchists and other millenarian sects of the time, for Milton's three major poems are written in the experience of defeat and reflect a poetically and politically mature conception of apocalyptics. Milton writes for a community that feels excluded from history by the events of 1660, and he writes to allow that community to envision its own restoration to the narrative of providential history. The kingdom projected in *Paradise Regained* is endless because it maintains within the continuum of history the critical dynamic of gathering up the scattered body of truth described in *Areopagitica*. It does not abolish or supersede this dynamic in utopian or millenarian expectations; it relocates these expectations in the mind of the reader by conceiving of what Frye terms a "readerly apocalypse," a possession of poetic and political consciousness made possible by the opening of a textual and critical "kingdom without end."

Milton's reconstitution of a poetic and political consciousness helps to address the critical question of his supposed quietism or withdrawal from political engagement after the Restoration. The image of Milton that emerges in many recent critical studies counters the view that Milton perfected the major poems in serene detachment from the turbulence that marked his times.[99] Milton's purpose was not to transcend or withdraw from the political circumstances of the production of his poems, but to oppose the circumstances that appear to contain and defeat the expectations he articulates. The alternatives between historical engagement and ahistorical withdrawal overlook a third term in the dynamic that better represents Milton's use of scripture. Each poem is a site in which conscience and reading reconstitute the endless kingdom in a manner that is dynamically counterhistorical, and not ahistorical, in relation to the historical events and impulses it criticizes and resists. Frye makes this claim for the mythic direction of the gospels; myth "is neither historical nor anti-historical: it is counterhistorical. Jesus is not presented as a historical figure, but as a figure who drops into history from another dimension of reality, and thereby shows what the limitations of the historical perspective are."[100] The limitations of the historical perspective are embodied in Satan in *Paradise Regained*. Milton's Jesus is counterhistorical because he embodies the possibilities of a criticism that can oppose the forces of history that, through Satan, surround him.

The central figures in the major poems inhabit a space of nonnarrative dialogue and deliberation in which wisdom is a prominent theme. Adam and Raphael, for example, hold a symposium that anticipates temptation; Jesus withdraws into the seclusion of the desert to undergo trial; Samson and his visitors analyze past events on the assumption that Samson is exiled from history in his defeat. The resumption, or restoration, of action occurs after the confluence of prophecy, the scriptural perspective of the narrative framework of history, and wisdom, the scriptural perspective on the individual's power of choice and hence power to act and participate in history. Michael's revelation of the "paradise within," Jesus' standing on the pinnacle, and Samson's "rousing motions" point toward this pivotal identification of wisdom and prophecy in Milton's poetics. Milton causes the fragments of biblical discourse representative of the different phases of revelation to cohere in structural moments of *anagnorisis*, completing the individual's internalization of the double scripture and envisioning a restored community.

Wisdom is the maintenance of action as potential: it depends upon vigilant self-criticism. For this reason, reading and interpretation revolutionize the reader's sense of what makes actions meaningful by supplanting the satanic norms and conventions of acting in the world. Confrontations between the individual conscience and worldly authority are a basic configuration in Milton's three major poems. These confrontations consist of protracted dialogues rather than overt actions. The dialogues assume a certain detachment from history. Both the fallen Adam and Jesus seek the scriptural terms on which they will enter the sphere of history, while Samson assumes that his humiliation has exiled him from history. In each case, the dialogues seek forms of order that can counter the demonic order of fallen history. As such, the dialogues offer a rhetorical analogue to the counterhistorical direction of biblical myth. In *Paradise Regained* in particular, the dialogues generate the sayings of the endless kingdom the poem envisions, linking the critical counterorder of Ecclesiastes to the visionary counterorder of the Gospels. As a locus of critical possibilities, Jesus' endless kingdom is ultimately a typological metaphor for scripture itself as the textual space that is internalized and recreated in the conscience of individual readers. The endless kingdom is neither transcendent nor deferred, ahistorical nor detached: it counters, in every moment of history, the worldly kingdoms Satan presents.

2

"Happier Life":
Wisdom and Perception in *Paradise Lost*

Did true Righteousness, for instance, prevail in this Christian Kingdom, what an happy People might we be? As happy, as we have made our selves notorious to all the World, for the Punishments God hath inflicted on us.
—Bishop Symon Patrick, 16 April 1690

"No star interpos'd": The Opticks of Wisdom

MILTON'S SUBJECT IN *PARADISE LOST* IS THE LOSS OF EDEN, AND WITH it the loss of happiness. Happiness is within the power of Adam and Eve to maintain in the prelapsarian world. The forbidden tree is not a fatal trap or perverse flaw in creation, but rather a symbol of the conscious priorities of happiness.[1] Happiness is integral to the purpose of creation, and therefore an effect of divine wisdom. Since temptation jeopardizes happiness, Milton plays upon the words "hap" and "happiness" as Satan roams the garden seeking a random opportunity for temptation in Book 9.[2] Satan seeks "where hap may find / The Serpent sleeping" (9:160–61). He seeks both Adam and Eve, but "wish'd his hap might find / *Eve* separate" (9:421–22). Eve in her separateness is described as "hapless" (9:403). "Hap" signifies a fortuitous occasion and the apparent randomness that might bring it about. Happiness, in contrast, is not the product of chance but an "inward possession" to maintain. Milton considers the Fall as a gambling away of happiness by investing it in an external power. This is precisely how Milton viewed Restoration in *The Readie and Easie Way*: "Certainly then that

63

people must needs be madd or strangely infatuated, that build the chief hope of thir common happiness or safetie on a single person: who if he happen to be good, can do no more then another man, if to be bad, hath in his hands to do more evil without check than millions of other men" (*CM* 6:121). National happiness invested in a hereditary monarchy is a matter of pure luck.

Satan promises Eve a "happier life" if she eats the forbidden fruit. The inward possession of true happiness requires critical resistance to Satan's temptation. Ecclesiastes is a model of this resistance. In its opposition to worldly vanity, Ecclesiastes was read by many seventeenth-century commentators as a treatise on the nature of happiness. In his substantial commentary on Ecclesiastes, Thomas Granger remarks that the "maine purpose of Solomon in this booke, is, to shew wherein the blessed estate, and happie condition of man in this vale of miserie consisteth."[3] For Symon Patrick, Ecclesiastes teaches "in what our genuine, true and solid felicity lies, both in this life and the next."[4] Theodore Beza calls Ecclesiastes "Solomons Sermon made to the people, teaching every man how to order his life, so as they may come to true and everlasting happiness."[5] For Milton, the rejection of worldly vanity that leads to happiness requires engagement and not withdrawal. He uses the theme of happiness in Ecclesiastes to portray this engagement in open encounters between truth and error, such as the argument between Abdiel and Satan in Book 5, and the fraudulent and dissembling appropriations of wisdom that characterize Satan's temptation of Eve in Book 9. In portraying both open encounter and seductive disguise, Milton draws from Ecclesiastes to examine the loss of happiness with the Fall, and to demonstrate the perception needed to maintain it in the first place.

Knoppers calls attention to the reassertion of public, royal spectacle at the Restoration. The ritualized spectacles that mediated royal power included triumphal entries, coronations, and processions as well as public executions and desecrations of the graves and corpses of opponents, using the "theater of punishment as dark twin to the celebratory pomp."[6] Print was an ally in the deployment of spectacle: some published tracts included visual illustrations linking the regicides with Satan; some others depicted the bodies of Cromwell, Bradshaw, and Ireton disinterred and desecrated at Tyburn. National anniversaries would also prescribe topics for sermons. Joy was instituted on the anniversary of Charles II's coronation; lamentation was observed in the "Fast Day" sermons prescribed for the anniversary of Charles I's death.

Spencer's *The Righteous Ruler*, among the earliest official reassertions of Stuart power from both the pulpit and the press, identifies national happiness with the Restoration. We have seen that Spencer based his sermon on Proverbs, and that he held the "dark twin" of the failed rebellion in sinister proximity to the filial replica of Charles I. As a sermon proclaiming the divine wisdom of Restoration, Spencer's sermon contains the same thematic elements as Milton's theodicy. Spencer asserts eternal providence: "we are never more confounded and humbled into a sense of our own shortness, then when long entertaining our thoughts about the mysteries of Divine Providence. Now Providence is thus mysterious especially (as the wise man notes) because of the strange checquer-work therein, the wonderful vicissitudes, and mixtures of happy and adverse occurrences. A thing frequently noted in Scripture. . . ."[7] The providence of Restoration is an extension of the original creating fiat that brings order out of chaos:

> That method which God observed in making of the World, he sometimes observeth in governing of it; he permits things to run first into a kind of Chaos and confusion, that so his Saints (like the Morning-starrs) may sing praises to God, when they see his Wisdom and Power issuing all things at last into excellent order, beauty, and composure.[8]

As a proverb performance, the contrastive, antithetical structure of Proverbs 29:2, which was Spencer's sermon text, projects a contrastive political epistemology. The dark confusion of the interregnum serves as a dark contrast for the brilliant clarity of Restoration. Hence there is a "bright and dark side of this pillar of divine Providence."[9] Divine wisdom is the source of happiness, but it requires the outward circumstances of a reinstated order: "The case proposed, when the Righteous are in authority, God and religion justifie and abet Rule, Soveraignty, and Authority in the World: God doth by setting up such to rule; and Religion doth, in that we see here, that righteous men (called thereto) do not decline it."[10] The reestablishment of monarchical government resonates with the creation of the earth: "When the foundations of earth were laid, *the Morning stars sang for joy,* Job 38:7, all our foundations of Government, Religion, Law, Parliaments, were out of Course; now that we see God laying them again, should we not express a joyful sense of the Mercy, and like good members of the body politick, rejoice in the welfare of the whole?"[11] Spencer also uses Proverbs 8:15— "By me Kings reign"—to vindicate monarchy in its divine identity: "O methinks those words, *by me Kings reign, Prov. 8,* should strike reverence and religion into every Atheist against those whom the Scripture stiles Gods among men."[12] He further instructs his hearers to see and recognize God's judgment on rebels: "These three sins, high ingratitude, oppression, and rebellion, very seldom have their dooms adjourned to another world, because they so much thwart Gods government of this. None of all those people guilty of rebellion in Scripture, went to their graves in peace."[13] Dates and anniversaries are impressed into the English psyche as Spencer recalls the regicide: "the Papists seem to have now a 30th of January to return us for a 5th of November."[14] The cycle of anniversaries, whether joyous for some and traumatic for others, would even make the calendar a "checquer-work" of dark and light moments in the national memory.

The "strange checquer-work" continued to be cast in its light and dark aspects in sermons for the balance of the century. In a fast sermon based on Proverbs 14:34, preached before the king and queen on 16 April 1690, the anniversary of Charles II's return to England, Symon Patrick, then bishop of Chichester, observed: "What were the late Civil Wars, and the woful Effects of them, but the Calamities which God sent upon a sinful People, for our disobedience to him? And since, the wonderful Restoration of the Royal Family and Monarchy, What were the Pestilence, the Fire, and other Judgments, which presently ensued, but tokens of God's continued displeasure against us, for our abuse of his loving-kindness?"[15]

Clear-sightedness is a central theme in Ecclesiastes. For Beza, wisdom and folly are as sight and blindness: "For wise men are truely sighted, so beholding things present with the eyes of the head, that they consider them also with the eyes of the minde, and doe also providently foresee things to come: but fooles can see no better at mid day then blind men."[16] Milton was aware of those who saw his blindness as the consequence of God's anger. John Heydon remarked that "If Milton beginning to write an Answer to the late Kings Book against Monarchy, was at the second word, by the power of God strucken blind: What shall fall upon them that endeavour to destroy his Son; verily they that fight against him, fight against Providence."[17] George Starkey mocked Milton's inability to see the triumphal return of Charles II: "What *Milton!* are you come to see the sight?"[18] Starkey expected the "sight" would impel Milton to despair and suicide rather than to the writing of three great poems. In Milton's poetic theodicy, the correspondence of inner and outer sight ended long before 1660. It ended with the loss of Eden. As a response to those who saw that correspondence renewed in the Restoration, Milton turned his reader's attention to the interior, invisible, spiritual world that found no material or objective confirmation in the events of 1660.

Blindness may have given Milton a unique experience of the disjunction of the material and the spiritual worlds. In the invocation to Book 3, Milton develops his argument in terms of sight and speech. Wisdom "at one entrance" is "quite shut out": blindness deprives the poet of the "Book of knowledge fair," the book of nature. The poet's purpose, however, is to open and illuminate interior worlds of both poetic and political liberty:

> So much the rather thou Celestial Light
> Shine inward, and the mind through all her powers
> Irradiate, there plant eyes, all mist from thence
> Purge and disperse, that I may see and tell
> Of things invisible to mortal sight.
>
> (3:51–55)

Milton's coordination of the visual and verbal aspects of his theodicy promotes the spiritual above the material. Milton undertakes to "see and tell / Of things invisible to mortal sight." Such "things" are spiritually discerned, not materially apparent. Discernment, however, is not a demonizing of those who had demonized Milton at a time when the "Good Old Cause" was lost; instead, it is an elevation of the faculties of critical judgment in every fit reader so that the critical dynamic expressed as both a poetic and political manifesto in *Areopagitica* could endure as long as fast sermons, thanksgivings, and anniversaries of the Restoration, if not longer. Spencer's sermon conditions the acceptance of the spiritual and the material in the restored monarchy. Milton's is the voice of counterorder: he seeks critical perspective on the forces that conditioned the popular acceptance of a tradition he opposed.

Political conditioning and resistance help us to understand the function of sight and vision in *Paradise Lost*. In Book 9, when Eve falls, she feels vulnerable to visual policing:

> And I perhaps am secret; Heav'n is high,
> High and remote to see from thence distinct
> Each thing on Earth; and other care perhaps
> May have diverted from continual watch
> Our great Forbidder, safe with all his Spies
> About him.
>
> (9:811–16)

In Book 12, a recovered inwardness and self-possession replace her paranoia as she awakens from her dream of the redeemer:

> For God is also in sleep, and Dreams advise,
> Which he hath sent propitious, some great good
> Presaging, since with sorrow and heart's distress
> Wearied I fell asleep.
>
> (12:611–14).

In his fall, Adam descends from rational clear-sightedness to the lower orders of sensual perception. In Book 9, his lust for Eve conflates sight with carnality, yielding a confused rather than discerning wisdom: "Eve, now I see thou art exact of taste / And elegant, of Sapience no small part" (9: 1017–18). In Book 12, his vision recovers through Michael's narrative which takes as its vantage point the highest mountain, or "top / of Speculation," in Eden. Satan, the agent of temptation, is also the primary focalizer for every reader entering the poem. The poem begins with Satan peering into the baleful shadows of Hell; in Book 2, Satan becomes a monarchical idol seated "High on a Throne of Royal State." As a political icon, Satan reconciles our perceptions of Hell with our perceptions of the fallen world. He seeks, moreover, to expand rather than to redeem the fallen world. As a primary focalizer, Satan tests each reader's capacity to distinguish spiritual from material vision at the outset of the poem and in the scenes of temptation.

Milton would agree with most commentators that wisdom was the eye of understanding: his task as poet was to open that eye and exercise its perceptions in each reader. John Spencer understood this task just as well as Milton: "Gods government of the World is full of Riddles and Mysteries; the Temple out of which the Angels (the Ministers of Divine Providence) proceed, is said to be *full of smoak, Rev. 15.8,* and we never find the eyes of our Understanding to ake & smart so much, as when long detained in this smoakie Temple."[19] Milton was not content in the smoky temples of mystery; he preferred the purgation and dispersion of all such mists just as he preferred "th'upright heart" before all other temples. For this reason, *Paradise Lost* addresses the "optics" as well as the voice of wisdom.

Charles Herle expounds the optics of wisdom in *Wisdom's Tripos.* Christian wisdom, a higher form of wisdom than the "vanity" of "Worldly Policy" or the practicality of "moral prudence," is no less than "Nature's Soul, the Soul's Eye, the Eye's Light, the Light's Sun."[20] Herle compares the soul's eye to the body's eye:

Now in the Eye's distinct sight of any Object, three things are required: 1. A right disposition of the Organ or Instrument. 2. A right position of the Object. 3. A right interposition of the medium or deferent. In this right disposition of the Organ, two things are required: 1. A vacancy from any prepossession by the Idea or visible species of any other object. *Cast out the beam out of thine own eye* (says our Saviour) *so shalt thou see clearly.* 2. An intention or fixedness of the sight on the object: a slight retortion or glance will not serve turn to see anything distinctly. 'Tis so in the eye of the soul too; nothing precipitates more into a prejudice, than prepossession by some other object: A man having separated himself, (says Solomon [Prov. 18:1]) seeketh and intermeddleth with wisdom.[21]

The absence of "preposession" is necessary to accurate perception for both the eye of the body and the eye of the soul. By making Satan the "focalizer" of the opening books of *Paradise Lost*, Milton concedes that his reader is already "prepossessed" by Satan, or subject to perceptual distortion. Milton invokes Galileo in the simile of the Tuscan artist with his "optic glass" in order to make us conscious of the play of distortion in his representation of Satan and Hell:

his ponderous shield
Ethereal temper, massy, large and round,
Behind him cast; the broad circumference
Hung on his shoulders like the Moon, whose Orb
Through Optic Glass the *Tuscan* Artist views
At Ev'ning from the top of Fesole,
Or in *Valdarno,* to descry new Lands,
Rivers or Mountains in her spotty Globe.
His spear, to equal which the tallest Pine
Hewn on *Norwegian* hills, to be the Mast
Of some great Ammiral, were but a wand.

(1:284–94)

Herle compares interposition to a curtain or a mist "drawn between the eye and object":

'tis neither the right disposition of the one, or right position of the other. . . . 'tis no less so too in the Soul's sight; if the object be Divine Truth, let the medium not be conjectural and ambiguous, but the clear evidence and demonstration of the Spirit: nor may we here piecen out the medium, to eek out faith with, with sence or fancy, Opinion, Faction, or Interest; Flesh and blood will not help to reveal it. Such mediums will but make up such an Optick glass, as if we look through it, the Devil will have the holding it: Would we look through it on the things of the World, he will be sure to hold us the multiplying end, and represent them great at hand; but if on the things of Heaven he cunningly shifts the Glass, and turns the contracting end to the eye, representing them a great way off, inconsiderable and uncertain.[22]

Herle's observations show how interposition and perception can become political metaphors. A solar eclipse, for example, occurs when the moon interposes between the earth and the sun, the "eye of nature." A solar eclipse occurred in 1652. William Ramesay argued at the time that an eclipse was adverse to monarchs: "The Sun is Eclipsed just in the very point of his exaltations; Let the Kings and rulers of the earth repent them of their oppression and Tyranny. . . . Know that when the Sun is eclipsed in [Aries] it portendeth the death of Kings."[23] Nicholas Culpepper predicted famine and pestilence in his *Catastrophe Magnatum Or, The Fall of Monarchie, A Caveat to Magistrates deduced From the Eclipse of the Sunne.*[24] In *The Shepherds Prognostication Fore-Telling the Sad and Strange*

Eclipse of the Sun, Laurence Price asserted that the "eclipse sig-nifieth and betokeneth the fatall overthrow of some great kings and princes and men in authority, within the limites of Chris-tian dominions, with many other troubles and sad disasters that will happen this yeare in our Cities, and Countries."[25] Eight years later, however, John Spencer compared the entire Protec-torate to a solar eclipse obscuring the righteousness of monar-chy: "As for the Nation, never was that more eclipsed and fuller of darkness, then, when, (like the Moon) in most direct opposi-tion against our Sun (our lawful Sovereign). . . . Very guilty indeed the Nation hath formerly been of opposition against Kings."[26] Spencer may have been echoing the eclipse imagery found in the *Eikon Basilike,* where the persona of Charles I pre-dicts the imminent eclipse and eventual restoration of monar-chy: "Happily, when men have tried the horrours and malignant influence, which will certainly follow My enforced darknesse and Eclypse (occasioned by the *interposition* and shaddow of that bodie which (as the moon) receiveth its chiefest light from Me) they will at length more esteem and welcome the restored glory and blessing of the Suns light."[27]

Milton knew the imagery of the *Eikon Basilike. In Paradise Lost,* he treats the eclipse as an instance of "interposition," re-claiming the image for the dissenting political perspective in a visual representation of Satan that gave the censors pause:[28]

>   his form had yet not lost
> All her original brightness, nor appear'd
> Less than Arch-Angel ruin'd, and th'excess
> Of Glory obscur'd: As when the Sun new ris'n
> Looks through the Horizontal misty Air
> Shorn of his Beams, or from behind the Moon
> In dim Eclipse disastrous twilight sheds
> On half the Nations, and with fear of change
> Perplexes Monarchs.
>
> (1:591–99)

Milton not only calls attention to Satan as an object of percep-tion but also to Satan as an agent of "interposition" and "prepos-session." Temptation, for example, requires the interposition of Satan between Eve and the forbidden tree. When Raphael de-scends to earth in Book 4, Milton invites us to imagine angelic perception without satanic "interposition":

> From hence, no cloud, or, to obstruct his sight,
> Star interpos'd, however small he sees,
> Not unconform to other shining Globes,
> Earth and the Gard'n of God, with Cedars crown'd
> Above all Hills. As when by night the Glass
> Of *Galileo,* less assur'd, observes
> Imagin'd Lands and Regions in the Moon.
>
> (5:257–63)

The absence of interposition—"no star interpos'd"—alludes to Satan under the name of Lucifer, the morning star, reminding us of his initial function in the poem as interposer and pre-possessor of the reader's perceptions.[29]

The dialogue in Heaven between the Father and the Son becomes the highest paradigm of the association of vision and narration, seeing and telling, in the poem. It is here that the Father calls the Son "My word, my wisdom" (3:170), echoing Paul's identification of Christ as the wisdom of God in 1 Corinthians 2:7. Milton's reference to the Pauline concept of wisdom designates the Son as the prime agent of divine creation and redemption in the poem. The synthesis of vision and narration begins when God surveys the cosmos and observes Satan moving toward earth to destroy it. God's speech amalgamates vision and narration to the extent that God perceives, and hence narrates, in the dimension of time as well as space. God's perception is temporal as well as spatial when he foresees and foretells Satan's initial success: Satan "shall pervert; / For Man will heark'n to his glozing lies" (3:92–93). God's speech, troubling to some readers in its seemingly self-exonerating logic, is necessary to the overall scheme of the poem because it offers, in the context of wisdom and perception, divine counterparts to demonic prepossession and interposition established in Books 1 and 2. These divine counterparts are predestination, expressed in God's vision of the future, and intercession expressed in the Son's offer to redeem humanity.

The Son's response to the Father's speech selects and extends the role of mercy:

> O Father, gracious was that word which clos'd
> Thy sovran sentence, that Man should find grace;
> For which both Heav'n and Earth shall high extol
> Thy praises, with th'innumerable sound

Of Hymns and sacred Songs, wherewith thy Throne
Encompass'd shall resound thee ever blest.

(3:144–49)

The Son's response incorporates components of the scriptural
canon, including the Psalms, or in Hebrew the book of "praises,"
and also wisdom. The phrase "sovran sentence" at first suggests
a judicial sentence of punishment or an edict to end disputes between parties and factions. Richard Hooker uses the latter sense
to appeal for closure in ecclesiastical disputes: "But of this we
are right sure, that nature, scripture, and experience itself, have
all taught the world to seek for the ending of contentions by sub-
mitting itself unto some judicial and definitive sentence."[30] Uses
of "sentence" in the seventeenth century include the authorita-
tive pronouncement on questions, the passing of judicial sentences in court cases, and the sentence as a cognate term for the
proverb or aphorism. I argue that the third sense of "sentence"
functions in the Father's first speech insofar as wisdom consists
of the internalization and realization of the Father's words in
the figure of the Son. The Hebrew etymology of *mashal* bears
this out, since it derives from the verb "to rule over" both in the
general sense of law and in the individual application of
wisdom. As William McKane has shown, the "most generally
canvassed explanation of *masal* is 'sovereign saying' or 'word of
power.'"[31] Robert Allen, we recall, notes its "singular dominion or
soveraignty." The opening phase of the dialogue therefore portrays the typological progression from the generality of law to
the individuality of wisdom in the relationship between Father
and Son in the poem.

It is immediately after this response that the Father names
the Son "My word, my wisdom." The completion of the "sovran
sentence" in filial wisdom is still not situated in a narrative of
redemptive history. How will God's purpose be fulfilled after the
Fall?

wilt thou thyself
Abolish thy Creation, and unmake,
For him, what for thy glory thou hast made?
So should thy goodness and thy greatness both
Be question'd and blasphemed without defence.

(3:162–66)

Milton uses the balance of the dialogue to locate wisdom in a narrative-historical framework. The Father asks: "Which of ye will be mortal to redeem / Man's mortal crime, and just th'unjust to save, / Dwells in all Heaven charity so dear?" (3:214–16). The Son's offer to redeem humanity is a prophetic narrative of his own incarnation, death, and resurrection, drawing from Paul's account of the destruction of death in 1 Corinthians 15, and concluding in an apocalyptic image of "the multitude of my redeem'd" entering Heaven at the end of time. The narrative response completes the typological integration of the biblical canon proceeding from the relationship between law and wisdom portrayed in the first part of the dialogue, to the inclusion of prophecy as the coming of the messiah:

> Account mee man; I for his sake will leave
> Thy bosom, and this glory next to thee
> Freely put off, and for him lastly die.
>
> (3:238–40)

The next phase is Gospel, or the death and resurrection of Christ as narrated by the evangelists and interpreted in the epistles:

> Though now to Death I yield, and am his due
> All that of me can die, yet that debt paid,
> Thou wilt not leave me in the loathsome grave
> His prey, nor suffer my unspotted Soul
> For ever with corruption there to dwell;
> But I shall rise Victorious, and subdue
> My vanquisher, spoil'd of his vaunted spoil.
>
> (3:245–51)

The final phase is the apocalypse, or the completion of history in Revelation with its vision of the gathering of a redeemed multitude into a transcendent kingdom:

> Then with the multitude of my redeem'd
> Shall enter Heav'n long absent, and return,
> Father, to see thy face, wherein no cloud
> Of anger shall remain, but peace assur'd,
> And reconcilement; wrath shall be no more
> Thenceforth, but in thy presence Joy entire.
>
> (3:260–65)

The sequential integration of the scriptural canon in the Son's response to the Father demonstrates Milton's expectations of his readers: restoration means a restored participation in providential history in spite of the accusations that Milton and others were hostile to the workings of providence. Scripture can still be freely internalized, interpreted, and expressed in the heart of each fit reader, in spite of the impositions of state authorities, just as it is in the scriptural synthesis of the Son's heroic speech in heaven, his "commentary" on God's law in his heroic actions on earth, and his restoration of the "paradise within" synchronically repossessed by Adam and the reader at the end of the poem.

TRIUMPHAL MARCHES: ROYAL AND RADICAL DISPLAYS

Satan as preceptor mediates the reader's perceptions to make them compliant with the conditions of the fallen world. The task of the poet-narrator is to characterize these perceptions and disrupt them in order to encourage a clear and regenerate vision. In the biblical culture of seventeenth-century England, such undiscerning perception was typified by the use of scriptural language for indiscriminate invective. Terms such as sedition, treason, libel, rebellion, and blasphemy could be hurled at various groups and individuals. Milton recovers these terms of abuse so as to distinguish them from the virtues that political invective can efface.

We have seen how this mode of invective works in the case of sedition. L'Estrange called Milton's *Brief Notes Upon A Late Sermon* a "seditious pamphlet": Griffith preached from Proverbs 24:21: "meddle not with them that be seditious." Blasphemy is a particularly charged term because it equates an individual literally with God; for Milton, the identification of God and the king in the English political imagination was a point of attack. James Nayler, a leader of the Quakers, stood trial for blasphemy. His crime was to reenact Christ's Palm Sunday entry into Jerusalem at the Redcliffe Gate in Bristol, in pouring rain, on 24 October 1656. George Starkey's poem *"Britains Triumph,"* in contrast, celebrates Charles II's triumphant return to London using the imagery of Jesus' entry into Jerusalem on Palm Sunday. The messianic aura surrounding Charles' return is an ironic counterpoint to the trial and brutal punishment of James Nayler. Taken together, the two events demonstrate the polarity of cultural and political images Milton responds to in his major poems.[32]

The term blasphemy served the purpose of indiscriminate invective. "G.S.," probably George Starkey, saw Milton's defense of the regicide as both murder and blasphemy. Milton, Starkey insisted, was an accomplice in "Acts horrible to be imagined" perpetrated by "Monsters of mankind" and blasphemous "dishonourers of God."[33] In *An Antidote Against the Poysonous Weeds of Heretical Blasphemies* (1650), John Brinsley treats blasphemy as an "epidemic contagion in these times."[34] John Brayne defines it as the "High Rebellion of Man against God,"[35] and as an attack on the "law and government of God." Biblical types of blasphemy included Shimei, a kinsman of Saul's, who cursed King David when David was in flight from Absalom's rebellion (2 Samuel 19:21). Aligning Shimei with opponents of monarchy, Dryden called Shimei "The wretch who Heaven's anointed dar'd to curse."[36] Starkey also calls Milton a Shimei: "if God ever come to awaken your Conscience in mercy or in judgement, you will find such a like reproof in your breast, as cursing Shimei had from Solomon."[37] Milton, Starkey exclaims, "belched forth . . . filthy Expressions" against the king, "of whom those who are truly pious (fearing God and the King) give a different character."[38] Milton had indeed scoffed at the "parallels" between Charles I and Solomon in *The First Defence* (*CM* 7:141–43) and at the treatment of kings as "Demigods" in *The Readie and Easie Way* (*CM* 6:120); he now had to show why this was not blasphemy.

In *Christian Doctrine* Milton defines blasphemy as the polar opposite of "hallowing" God's name.[39] The desire to hallow God's name is "zeal." Hence, an "eager desire to sanctify the divine name, together with a feeling of indignation against things which tend to the violation or contempt of religion, is called Zeal" while the "opposite of this is to talk about God's name in an impious and shameful way, which is commonly called blasphemy" (*CPW* 6:697–98). In *Paradise Lost,* God's goodness and greatness are not "question'd and blasphemed without defence (3:166): the defender of God's name is Abdiel, who defies Satan and his legions at the outset of the war in Heaven. Abdiel, whose name means "servant of God," is Milton's portrait of the virtue of zeal:

> Thus far [Satan's] bold discourse without control
> Had audience, when among the Seraphim
> *Abdiel,* than whom none with more zeal ador'd
> The Deity, and divine commands obey'd,
> Stood up, and in a flame of zeal severe
> The current of his fury thus oppos'd.
> O argument blasphemous, false and proud!
> Words which no ear ever to hear in Heav'n
> Expected, least of all from thee, ingrate,
> In place thyself so high above thy Peers.
>
> (5:803–12)

Read allegorically, "Zeal" recognizes the Son as God's regent, and opposes "Blasphemy's" affectation of divine superiority. There is, however, a broader political scope to this encounter than the opposition of virtue and vice. The opposition also radically separates the kingdom of God from the prototypical kingdoms of the world, and the wisdom of God from worldly wisdom. The Father's commendation of Abdiel attains this political scope:

> Servant of God, well done, well hast thou fought
> The better fight, who single hast maintain'd
> Against revolted multitudes the Cause
> Of Truth, in word mightier than they in Arms;
> And for the testimony of Truth hast borne
> Universal reproach, far worse to bear
> Than violence: for this was all thy care
> To stand approv'd in sight of God, though Worlds
> Judg'd thee perverse.
>
> (6:29–37)

"Universal reproach" and the judgment of "Worlds" measure the political scope of this episode. Neil Keeble observes that Abdiel's heroic resistance does not attain the scale conveyed in God's speech: he is not judged by "Worlds." But his isolated defiance of Satan parallels the situation of religious nonconformists after the Restoration. Royalist discourse after 1660 characterized enemies of the established church and the reconstituted monarchy as rebels against God. The episode produces what Keeble calls a "lexical reversal," as the supposed "rebel" Satan is shown to be, in fact, the agent of persecution and oppression backed by force of arms and titular authority.[40] Milton's Abdiel portrays conscientious resistance for all dissenters.

In a conflict between conscience and external force, Abdiel's resistance is ultimately not out of proportion to God's universal commendation; rather, in his own universal scale of perception, God sees in Abdiel those attributes of the kingdom of Christ articulated in *Civil Power*:

> Christ rejects outward force in the government of his church . . . to shew us the divine excellence of his spiritual kingdom, able without worldly force to subdue all the powers and kingdoms of this world, which are upheld by outward force only: by which to uphold religion otherwise then to defend the religious from outward violence, is no service to Christ or his kingdom, but rather a disparagement, and degrades it from a divine and spiritual kingdom to a kingdom of this world. (*CM* 6:22)

Abdiel possesses what Milton, quoting Paul in 1 Corinthians 2:16, calls the "mind of Christ" as a guide to conscience in its revolt against the external imposition of authority.

Nayler unfortunately identified himself with the person rather than the mind of Christ in his reenactment of Palm Sunday in Bristol. The Blasphemy Act applied to anyone claiming "him or her self, or any other meer Creature, to be very God, or to be Infinite or Almighty, or in Honor, Excellency, Majesty and Power to be equal, and the same with the true God."[41] Nayler's punishment was a savage display of retribution.[42] He was "Whipt at a Carts-taile, from Westminster to the Royall-Exchange in London, December the eighteenth 1656 and there to stand in the Pillory, and to have the letter B set upon his forehead, and to be burnt through the toung with a hot Iron, and to be kept in prison during life, without being allowed any sustenance, but what he shall earne with his owne Labor."[43] Escaping death by a narrow vote of Parliament, he was afterwards committed to prison without writing material. He was eventually released and partially reconciled with his fellow Quakers before his death in 1660.

This terrible episode was not, however, Nayler's first trial for blasphemy, but only his first conviction. He stood trial with Francis Howgill at the Appleby Sessions in Westmorland in January 1653, for preaching that the risen Christ was a spiritual and not a corporal entity. Though the judges registered no verdict, Nayler spent twenty weeks in prison. It was during his imprisonment at Appleby that Nayler wrote *A Discovery of the*

First Wisdom from beneath, and the Second Wisdom from above
(1653). The treatise presents wisdom as the virtue of perception
necessary to reading the "things of God." Nayler's treatise is as
much a political statement as a spiritual consolation, for it seeks
to encourage his supporters. Politics for Nayler meant differing
from the world, as he asserts in his subtitle: he will elucidate the
"true worship of God after the Spirit. And the false worship of
the world, who lives in outward Forms, useth Customes and Traditions, not knowing the only True God that dwelleth in his
Saints, and rules by his Spirit of Power, which causeth them to
differ from the world." Differing from the world in turn means
differing from the world's lexicon. Hence, Nayler defines blasphemy as the opposition of conscience, which for Nayler meant
the inner light of the spirit, and authority, which Nayler calls
the "precepts of men." Nayler also uses the Pauline oppositions
of natural and spiritual perception (1 Corinthians 2:14–15) to
force the distinction. Nayler associates Paul's spiritual perception with the Quaker concept of inner light: "you who desire to
be fed with that which is Eternall, lay aside all your wisdom
which is naturall, for the naturall man receives not the Spiritu-
all things of God for that wisdom shall never know God which
stands in the will of man, but darkens the pure light in you."[44]
He associates natural perception with the confusion of good and
evil in a manner that invites comparison with Satan's "evil, be
thou my good": "that wisdom which ariseth out of the earth op-
poseth that which is from above, and calls evil good, and good
evil."[45] The light of Christ makes evil appear as evil, while
earthly or natural wisdom "makes a cover for it that it may
abide still."[46]

Nayler's natural man, who is controlled by the serpent who
tempted Eve, conforms to imposed practices. The natural man

> worships God at a distance, but knows him not, nor where he is,
> but by relation from others, either by word or writing; and as he
> receives his knowledge of him from men so his worship towards
> him is taught by the precepts of men; and if men, on whom he de-
> pends, command him to go to the Steeple-house; he goes; if they
> command him to pray; he prayes; if they command him to sing, he
> sings, if they bid him hear, kneel, sit, stand, fast, or feast, he doth
> it and here he hath fellowship with men. . . . And thus in vain
> doth he worship, receiving for Doctrines the commandements of

men, and so uphould and plead for a customary worship in a form
of tradition, which he is resolved to practice as long as he lives. . .
and if any go any further, or witness any more than he knows, he
accounts it blasphemy and cries out against it, as a thing not to
be suffered, and with carnall weapons would force all to his light;
but who have eyes open see him to be blind.[47]

The natural man is the product of political conditioning. The
second or "spiritual man," in contrast, "knowes what he worships, and he worships in spirit, and he prayes in the spirit, and
with understanding also, and not in a form and custom."[48]
Carnal or devilish wisdom, like the serpent who tempted Eve, si-
lences the spiritual voice "that he may not speak under pain of
imprisoning or killing the body in whom he speakes, and if that
will not prevail, then thou perswadest people not to beleeve that
it is he that speaks in his own, calling it Blasphemy. . . ."[49] The
real blasphemer for Nayler is the "subtil Serpent" in its hostility
to heavenly wisdom. The natural man loses his voice in conformity to imposed rites, and allows his voice to be appropriated by
Satan:

> O Thou subtil Serpent, why dost thou so rage at the voice of the
> Lord, when he speakes in his own, whom he hath redeemed and
> why art thou so mad against his Image where it is renewed and
> doth appear in whom he hath begotten to himself? Thou hast long
> uttered thy voice, in open streets, by blasphemous swearing, curs-
> ing, lying, slandering, railing, false accusing, scorning, and all
> manner of evil speaking. . . .[50]

The spiritual man discerns the voice of Christ within. Nayler's
treatise, as an extensive elaboration of 1 Corinthians 2:14–15,
educates its reader, as Milton does from his own perspective, in
the importance of perception and discernment as modes of
wisdom. Espousing his doctrine that Father and Son are united
in the heart of each believer, Nayler asserts that this inner spirit
is expressed as voice: "he speakes in them and by them, and they
know his voice from all other voices in themselves and others."[51]
The carnal wisdom of the serpent cannot discern the voice of the
spirit: "the Serpents brood can no more own his voice now, when
he speakes, then formerly he could do, when he spoke in flesh."[52]
The separation of carnal and spiritual wisdom leads to Nayler's
uncompromising resistance to the wisdom of the world. He

evokes this resistance in the apocalyptic biblical images Milton employs in *Paradise Lost*: "what concord hath Christ with Belial, or the believer and the unbeliever?"[53] He further prophesies against all the worldly forces that he sees embodied in Satan: "But wo unto thee and thy kingdom, for the day of thy torment is upon thee: for now Michael our Prince, who stands up for the children and people of God, is arisen against thee, who will break thee and thy Image in pieces, and thou shalt be cast out of heaven, and thy Angels into the earth, and thou shalt be chained in the bottomless pit, and shalt deceive the nations no more."[54]

While Nayler's concepts of voice and spirit are distinctively Quaker in their emphasis on the inner light, he shares Milton's sense of the irony of labeling dissenting voices as blasphemous, especially when these are so readily distinguished from blasphemy defined as "all manner of evil speaking." For Nayler and Milton, the misrepresentation of blasphemy is a precondition of religious persecution; Nayler cautions "all who shall be found persecutors, persecuting the righteous, not suffering that Spirit to speak. . . ."[55] If the voice of the spirit cannot be silenced, it can always be labeled blasphemous.

Neither Charles II nor Nayler was the "one greater Man" who restores us in the invocation to *Paradise Lost*; why was one figure less blasphemous than the other? As I will eventually argue, Satan's temptation of Eve succeeds in part as a confusing appropriation of her voice. In mingling his voice with hers, Satan also confuses her self-image with the godlike image that appropriates divinity in blasphemous terms. In *Paradise Regained*, Satan's appeals to Jesus to merge his voice and identity with Alexander, Caesar, or even Socrates, meet with Jesus' steady resistance founded on the separation of spiritual and natural perceptions. James Nayler may have temporarily confused his identity with Christ's in his journey to Bristol; from Milton's vantage point, there is also blasphemy in shouting hosannas to the restored monarch in 1660.

Examples of implicitly blasphemous propaganda appeared in due season. Starkey's *Britains Triumph,* a commemoration Charles's triumphal return to London, vilifies Milton and many others of his cause while casting a messianic aura around Charles II. Starkey gleefully displaces the frustrated expectations of the Fifth Monarchists onto Charles:

> The rest who thought that *Christ* would come as *King,*
> And reign among them, but mistook the time,
> Which they were confident would be this Spring,
> And were providing for to welcome him,
>   It is but fit they should both weep and bleed,
>   Who were so confident, yet lost their *Creed.*
>   (st. 63, 16)

Focusing also on Christ's Palm Sunday entry into Jerusalem, Starkey echoes Luke 19:40—"And he answered and said unto them, I tell you that, if these should hold their peace, the stones would immediately cry out":

> Long live King *CHARLES,* the very stones would cry
> Should men be silent, yea the very Drums,
> Trumpets and Guns, to all the standers by,
> (Sometimes, though seldom, as to passe it comes,
>   I know not by what fate) seem'd to Proclaim,
>   (The best of Monarchs) great King *Charles's* name.
>   (st. 44, 12)

Milton had also used stones to represent liberty in *The Readie and Easie Way*, "som perhaps whom God may raise of these stones to become children of reviving libertie" (*CM* 6:148–49). Milton echoes Luke 3:8—"Bring forth therefore fruits worthy of repentance, and begin not to say within yourselves, We have Abraham to our father: for I say unto you, That God is able of these stones to raise up children unto Abraham." Milton puts faith in future generations while lamenting the immediate loss of liberty. Living more in the moment, Starkey's sense of happy occasion is as ruthless as it is sycophantic: he intermingles coercion and military force, as threatening drums speak for any who remain silent, while looking forward to the spectacle of cruel punishments for those who should "weep and bleed." Palm Sunday and punishment may have reminded many, not only of Nayler, but of the regicides and other accused traitors—potentially even Milton at that date—who were awaiting their horrible fates.

Aware of the messianic fervor of Restoration discourse, Milton associates blasphemy not with cursing but with the affectation of divinity. Satan blasphemes against God because he affects divinity to gain power over his followers. Affectation of divinity is an important component of the temptation of Eve in Book 9; the temptation is equally blasphemous in its motivation: the subjugation of others. The encounter between Abdiel and Satan, as a war of words involving blasphemy, conscience, and the revolt of reason against the spectacle of physical force, portrays and resolves the intermingling of praise, blasphemy, and triumphal march that make James Nayler and Charles II a study in contrast. For both Milton and Nayler, Satan is the supreme blasphemer. But where Nayler's Satan is heard in the profanity of street cries, Milton's is an eloquent associate of monarchical triumph. Satan's blasphemy is thus at first visual as he assumes the place of the Son of God in a Royal posture:

> *Satan* to his Royal seat
> High on a Hill, far blazing, as a Mount
> Rais'd on a Mount, with Pyramids and Tow'rs
> From Diamond Quarries hewn, and Rocks of Gold,
> The Palace of great *Lucifer,* (so call
> That Structure in the Dialect of men
> Interpreted) which not long after, he
> *Affecting all equality with God*,
> In imitation of that Mount whereon
> *Messiah* was declar'd in sight of Heav'n.
>
> (5:756–65, emphasis mine)

The blasphemy of affecting Godhead in Satan's Royal self-presentation is also the subject of his speech. His aristocratic sense of injured merit requires the assertion of a divine-right theory of privilege and superiority over the Father's new revelation, the Son: "Who can in reason then or right assume / Monarchy over such as live by right / His equals" (5:794–96). Abdiel, in contrast, forces distinctions between creator and creature:

> But grant it thee unjust,
> That equal over equals Monarch Reign:
> Thyself though great and glorious thou dost count,
> Or all Angelic Nature join'd in one,
> Equal to him begotten Son, by whom
> As by his Word the mighty Father made
> All things, ev'n thee. . . .
>
> (5:831–37)

Like the natural and the spiritual man in 1 Corinthians 2:14–15 as characterized in Nayler's treatise, or inner and outer

authority in *Civil Power*, Abdiel's distinction between creator
and creature characterizes the revolt of his own reason against
the idolatrous charisma of Satan. Satan, in contrast, uses selective amnesia to elide any distinction between himself and his
creator:

> We know no time when we were not as now;
> Know none before us, self-begot, self-rais'd
> By our own quick'ning power. . . .
>
> (5:859–61)

Satan defines his aristocratic merit as an ancient right that
shrouds rather than exposes its origins in divine grace. His
attack on God—ironically, for those modern readers who still
consider Satan a "rebel"—is calculated to *restore* and not destroy a hereditary system of titles and privileges.

In distinguishing between the creator and the creature,
Abdiel rehearses the premise of *Civil Power* by asserting the
sovereignty of God and individual conscience. Elisions between
secular and spiritual authority, sanctioned by disconcerting
scriptural places such as Romans 13:1—"Let every soul be subject to the higher powers"—invite a critical response bold
enough to separate "tyrants and persecuters" (*CM* 6:14) from
forms of authority that meet the standards of conscience and
reason. The elision of spiritual and secular power is notably developed in commentaries on Ecclesiastes 8:2: "I counsel thee to
keep the king's commandment, and that in regard of the oath of
God" and on Ecclesiastes 10:20: "Curse not the king." "Curse not
the King" became a particularly intimidating text, as commentators argued that kings are subject to God alone. Acknowledging that the laws of princes may prove malleable and at
variance with the law of God, Thomas Granger observes that
the divinity that hedges kings requires scrutiny: "For in regard
of superiority, splendor, and administration of humane things,
they are tearmed gods. But sometimes this title, state, and
power is turned into greatest vanitie. It becommeth vaine, first
in respect of those that are governed, when a Prince seeketh
rather the hurt then the good of the people, as when he falleth
to covetousnesse, and oppression, when he exalteth, dejecteth,
graceth, disgraceth, according to his owne lust, not regarding
the worthinesse or unworthinesse of the persons, whereby
vertue is put to rebuke and silence, and all manner of vice flour-

isheth, as weeds in an unclean or untilled soyle."[56] Yet the ideal is an alignment of external law and internal conscience:

> This is godly wisedome, godly policie. For the maine intendment, spirit, and life of mans law is the preservation and keeping of Gods law, that those that have not an inward conscience and fear, yea love wrought within them by the preaching of the word, or light of naturall principles before the word commeth, that those may have an outward conscience, to which they shall be inforced by the power of the magistrate, to make brutish men civill, and civil men religious, if God give grace, and religious men to continue religious.[57]

Thomas Fuller unequivocally suggests that a king is a "mortal God": "He holds his crown immediately from the God of heaven. Yea, the character of loyalty to kings so deeply impressed in subjects' hearts, shows that only God's finger wrote it there."[58] Fuller also designates the conscience as the "king's attorney," making it the king's voice and possession.

Parliament went to savage lengths to distinguish the person of James Nayler from the person of Jesus Christ; subsequently, and perhaps for Milton, ironically, the public associated the person of Charles II with Christ in the messianic fervor of the Restoration. Used indiscriminately, blasphemy was a symptom of the selective confusion of the material and the spiritual in its conflation of conscience with atheism and rebellion. The dynamic of dissent in *Paradise Lost* concerns the selection of voices: God selects Raphael's voice for his purpose, and Raphael in turn selects Abdiel's as it intervenes in Satan's triumphal march. The distinction of voices is part of the political purpose of *Paradise Lost*. In his portrait of Abdiel, Milton rejects the equation of rebellion with atheism, treason, and blasphemy per se; Abdiel models dissent, not as the profession of any sectarian creed, but as the revolt of reason against Satan's blasphemous self-image.[59] The Fall of Adam and Eve is, in contrast, a moment of conformity: in *Paradise Lost*, the Fall is the failure of the dissenting conscience to distinguish its own voice.

A PARADISE WITHIN: THE TYPOLOGY OF READING

Although Satan moves from open encounters with his adversaries to fraudulent coercion in the destruction of paradise,

Milton continues to gloss encounters with temptation by paraphrasing the tenets of *Areopagitica*. These tenets operate in the separation scene in Book 9, when Adam and Eve agree, after a charged and tense debate, to divide their morning labors. Unwilling to compel Eve to remain with him, Adam advises her to remain in his presence for security and protection. Eve replies:

> And what is Faith, Love, Virtue unassay'd
> Alone, without exterior help sustain'd?
> Let us not then suspect our happy State
> Left so imperfet by the Maker wise,
> As not secure to single or combin'd.
> Frail is our happiness, if this be so,
> And *Eden* were no *Eden* thus expos'd.
>
> (9:335–41)

This paraphrases *Areopagitica*: "I cannot praise a fugitive and cloister'd virtue, unexercis'd & unbreath'd, that never sallies out and sees her adversary, but slinks out of the race, where that immortall garland is to be run for, not without dust and heat. Assuredly we bring not innocence into the world, we bring impurity much rather: that which purifies us is triall, and triall is by what is contrary" (*CPW* 2:515). Knowing the outcome of Eve's decision, readers may look for ironic flaws in this echo of *Areopagitica* in the context of the separation scene. Adam points out, for example, that trial should not be sought for its own sake. *Areopagitica* reflects assumptions about the fallen state—the world "as it now is"—but Eve's state is still prelapsarian and innocent—the world as it was then. For some readers, the separation scene intensifies the patriarchal bias of the epic: if Eve's fall is a foregone conclusion then her reasoning must be specious and immature. But if Eve cannot resist temptation alone, the argument of the epic risks lapsing into notions of fate rather than providence. Eve's capacity to resist is necessary to the integrity of the poem.

The separation scene illustrates the critical dynamic of biblical wisdom. Its central theme is social formation and growth predicated on wisdom. Adam offers the precept that "solitude sometimes is best society" (9:249), acknowledging that, while change may be delectable, there are inherent orders and rhythms in human existence; nevertheless, the tension between "solitude" and "society" that governs their debate establishes the critical dynamic of order and counterorder germane to biblical wisdom. The debate points to Eve's need for a vantage point or "space" of legitimate critical reflection. Eve therefore represents the individual voice of counterorder: although she anticipates and does not possess experience, she voices a critical response to the collective voice of order represented by Raphael and Adam, meaning the "society" of men and angels from which excluded is Eve in order to give Adam the role of teacher in their domestic society. The separation scene may be the picture of social health: it depicts the critical dynamic of order and counterorder conveyed in biblical wisdom and developed broadly in the thesis of liberty in *Areopagitica* and *Civil Power*. The separation scene also reaches the impasse discovered in both treatises in its realization of the futility of compulsion or constraint, the mere forcing of individual conscience. Perhaps the real irony of the scene is that this critical dynamic is achieved in society rather than in solitude. Eve does not discover solitude in separating from Adam; after a brief solitude, she accepts Satan's offer of an alternative society comprised of mortal gods: Eve exchanges the "endless kingdom" of critical dialogue for an incipient monarchy. Satan's temptation appropriates the concepts of criticism, counterorder, theodicy, social formation, and, above all, happiness in promising Eve a "happier life" beyond the Fall.

As Knoppers has shown, Milton's treatment of the Fall "employs a language of joy that would have political resonances in Restoration England."[60] Tracts that celebrated the Restoration proclaimed it an occasion of celebration, a return even of the golden age. Milton's task was to challenge this "politics of joy" by portraying the choice England made as another Fall: it was an abdication of the potential for personal and political liberty. The connection between happiness and wisdom is evident on the title page of Spencer's *The Righteous Ruler*: 28 June 1660 was "appointed a day of publick Thanksgiving to God for the happy restauration of His Majesty to his Kingdomes." Happiness was the product of wisdom. When Adam speaks of "our happy state" in the separation scene, he attributes happiness to the wisdom of the creator who is the only real sovereign:

> O Woman, best are all things as the will
> Of God ordain'd them, his creating hand
> Nothing imperfet or deficient left

Of all that he Created, much less Man,
Or aught that might his happy State secure,
Secure from outward force; within himself
The danger lies, yet lies within his power:
Against his will he can receive no harm.

(9:343–50)

Happy "state" suggests a political as well as a personal condition based, until the Fall, upon the proper relations of inner spiritual power and outward force examined in *Areopagitica* and *Civil Power*.

Commentators on Ecclesiastes emphasize the theme of happiness or "felicity." Granger reads Ecclesiastes as a comprehensive guide to happiness, calling it *"Solomon's Ethiks,* his tractate *de summo bono*, of the chiefe, and compleat felicity, and the world's vanity, and therefore the very roote, seede, or kernell of all happy knowledge, both of good, and evill in all things, naturall, politicall, ecclesiasticall."[61] As the foundation of happiness, wisdom always opposes worldly vanity: "But Solomon here by speciall instruction and direction of the spirit of God, layeth downe such felicity as the world by their wisedome, could not comprehend."[62] Milton achieves a politically engaged rather than quietist resonance with the theme of happiness. The theme of political felicity is contained in Eve's exchange of one society for another in her Fall, but the rhetorical features of Ecclesiastes shed specific light on the structure of Eve's temptation, and so point to some of the reasons for Satan's success. The wisdom of Ecclesiastes is the wisdom of experience. While it is critical of some of the received formulas of justice and righteousness found in Proverbs, especially where those formulas are contradicted by lived experience, it remains a profession of experiential wisdom conveyed from an older to a younger generation. This transmission of wisdom is the most rudimentary structure of Eve's temptation: the Serpent claims to have already *experienced* the effects of the forbidden fruit, and he recommends the experience to Eve. The apparent benefits of the experience can be seen in the acquisition of speech and reason: Eve can expect what Adam later calls "Proportional ascent" (9:936).

Can we describe in detail the resonances between the language of happiness in Satan's temptation of Eve and the "politics of joy" that reverberate through Restoration discourse? A specific rhetorical technique of the wisdom of experience illustrates Milton's adaptation of Ecclesiastes, the scriptural text that questions received wisdom, in Satan's rhetoric in the temptation, making the temptation a demonic parody of genuine wisdom. The technique is "prolepsis." Granger defines prolepsis as the "prevention of an objection." Prolepsis is the rhetorical technique of anticipating the audience's objections to the speaker's argument.[63] These objections can be rendered explicitly as rhetorical questions and then answered, or the question can be implied but left unstated while the objection is addressed. Prolepsis is an appropriate technique in Ecclesiastes for two reasons. First, it offers yet another model of the critical dynamic that vitalizes the wisdom tradition since prolepsis, by its nature, accommodates a contrary or critical response. Second, the figure "prevents" objections in the seventeenth-century sense of the word: it goes before the objection by anticipating it. In this respect the figure offers a compressed, rhetorical model of the transmission of wisdom from generation to generation, since the experience and wisdom of one generation chronologically precedes the next.

In *Salomon's Recantation*, William Pemble sees prolepsis as the purpose of Ecclesiastes 1. The Preacher anticipates that his reader might question his wisdom: "A confirmation of the truth and justice of this censure by a Prolepsis; you may be deceived, your knowledge haply is weak, slight and ordinary, and this judgment ill-grounded, & c. Salomon answers, Nay, they are best able to judge of things that best know them. But upon due examination of his owne heart, and all the excellent endowments thereof, he findes that as he had all royal dignities, richnesse, and greatnesse of outward state, so he had gotten more wisdome than the greatest that went before him in his kingdome."[64] Ecclesiastes 2:13 also contains a prolepsis: "Then I saw that wisdom excelleth folly, a far as light excelleth darkness." Granger explicates the proleptic objection in this manner: "Thou seemest to put no difference betweene wisedome, and madnesse, and folly, in that thou canst finde no profit, no content in any of them, but onely vanity and vexation." The answer: "Although that true felicity is not to be found in wisedome, neither in the wisedome of this World, nor in the literall knowledge of the Gospell, yet it altogether

excelleth folly, yea, is contrary to folly. The proposition he il-
lustrateth by a comparison of things contrary. Even as light
excelleth darknesse, not in degrees, but in nature, having no
fellowship or communion with it, but mortifieth it, as light excelleth darknesse, and water extinguisheth fire."[65] Prolepsis
demonstrates, in the context of the dialogue between order
and counterorder, the vital questioning spirit that characterizes the Old Testament.

Satan's rhetoric of temptation therefore appropriates and controls one of the most vital features of scripture: its critical, questioning spirit. Satan even puts on the virtues of Abdiel by
affecting "Zeal and Love" (9:665) and the "Zeal of Right" (9:676).
The structure of the temptation scene as organized by the proleptic rhetoric of Ecclesiastes also calls attention to the movement from dialogue to monologue in the encounter between Eve
and the Serpent. After listening to the Serpent's personal testi-
mony, Eve recovers the critical stance needed to withstand
temptation:

> Serpent, thy overpraising leaves in doubt
> The virtue of that Fruit, in thee first prov'd:
> But say, where grows the Tree, from hence how far?
>
> (9:615–17)

The second question joins curiosity to her critical perspective,
and thus anticipates her coming to the tree. Once there, she remembers the divine prohibition, again using the conjunction
"but" to reiterate the tension between curiosity and obedience:

> But of this Tree we may not taste nor touch;
> God so commanded, and left that Command
> Sole Daughter of his voice; the rest, we live
> Law to ourselves, our Reason is our Law.
>
> (9:651–54)

Recognizing both the internalization of law as wisdom, the
"Sole Daughter of his voice," and the principle of growth and
discovery that makes Adam and Eve self-sufficient in their
obedience to God's sole command, Satan assimilates the critical responses and objections that emerge in *dialogue* with Eve
by converting them into a *monologue* that embellishes the proleptic rhetoric of wisdom. As in *Areopagitica*, dialogue main-

tains and expands the free space of critical exchange; as in *The Readie and Easie Way*, monologue forecloses on that space by replacing it with a verbal performance and a visual spectacle that induces conformity and assent. Prolepsis, as Satan uses it, affects dialogue in the context of a monologue. The affectation of dialogue takes the form of unanswered, rhetorical questions, nine in all, that clearly anticipate, articulate, and satisfy the objections that Eve might speak in her own voice. Satan's rhetoric scatters many "reasons" for eating the fruit rather than isolating one definitive reason, but his speech continues to appropriate the most vital features of the discourse of wisdom: discernment, critical perception, and the questioning spirit that animates the wisdom of counterorder. The scattering of reasons even vitalizes reading as linking and connecting, as in aphoristic discourse, but now in a demonic framework, and as a performance that Eve passively witnesses without active participation. Satan presents the fruit as the focus of a critical counterorder that responds to the divine prohibition, and hence as the *summum bonum* or height of felicity explored in Ecclesiastes: Eve should not be deterred from "achieving what might lead / To happier life, knowledge of Good and Evil" (9:696–97).

The core of the temptation, predicated on the promise of a "happier life," is Satan's dismantling of the integral features of Milton's theodicy, the justice and benevolence of God. The temptation itself is a kind of demonic theodicy:

> Of good, how just? of evil, if what is evil
> Be real, why not known, since easier shunn'd?
> God therefore cannot hurt ye, and be just;
> Not just, not God; not fear'd then, nor obey'd.
>> (9:698–701)

After separating the attributes of the Creator, Satan proceeds to obscure the difference between creator and creature by positing a plurality of gods:

> So ye shall die perhaps, by putting off
> Human, to put on Gods, death to be wisht,
> Though threat'n'd, which no worse than this can bring.
> And what are Gods that Man may not become
> As they, participating God-like food?

> The Gods are first, and that advantage use
> On our belief, that all from them proceeds;
> I question it. . . .

(9:713–20)

The first phase of the temptation presents counterorder as criticism based on experience; the second, following from the disintegration of theodicy, presents counterorder as the vision of a new social order, a higher society of "human Gods." This reestablishes the theme of blasphemy as it recalls Satan's earlier affectation of godhead in his encounter with Abdiel. The resonances between divinity, monarchy, and wisdom in Royalist discourse become clearer at this point: Thomas Fuller called the king a "Mortal God." For Milton, Satan's new order is merely an old order, and its acceptance—or restoration—is a travesty against the more empowering social order first established in Eden.

In her monologue following Satan's temptation speech, Eve internalizes and assimilates the technique of prolepsis by emulating Satan's use of the interrogative seven times. The number has clear numerological significance: the Fall unmakes paradise. The turning inward of her own questioning faculty represents Eve's self-authoring freedom, also one of the most vital of human attributes. The Fall portrays this attribute in its destructive mode: "to herself she mus'd" (9:744) the narrator says of her monologue, echoing the Father's disappointed prediction: they fall, "Authors to themselves in all." (3:122). The fruit, she supposes, is wisdom at one entrance quite shut out: "what forbids he but to know, / Forbids us good, forbids us to be wise? / Such prohibitions bind not" (9:758–60). As Charles Herle observed, the Fall is essentially the human affectation of divine wisdom.[66]

The wisdom of counterorder issues from experience that questions traditional wisdom and from the vision that imagines a new social order. Both aspects of counterorder appear in Eve's response to her own fall. She credits experience with contradicting her expectations:

> Experience, next to thee I owe,
> Best guide; not following thee, I had remain'd
> In ignorance, thou op'n'st Wisdom's way,
> And giv'st access, though secret she retire.

(9:807–10)

The reformation of her bond with Adam entails the prospect of a new order:

> But to *Adam* in what sort
> Shall I appear? shall I to him make known
> As yet my change, and give him to partake
> Full happiness with mee, or rather not.
> But keep the odds of Knowledge in my power
> Without Copartner?
>
> (9:816–21)

The prospect of this new order, based on a new sense of power over Adam and on the possibility of death without Adam, brings with it the reassertion of anxiety. At the moment of her own fall, Eve conceives of the wisdom of counterorder as an emancipation from fear and anxiety:

> What fear I then, rather what to know to fear
> Under this ignorance of Good and Evil,
> Of God and Death, of law or Penalty?
>
> (9:773–75)

Her sense of emancipation from the law echoes many of Paul's reflections on law and gospel. Romans 7:5–6, for example, states: "For when we were in the flesh, the motions of sins, which were by the law, did work in our members to bring forth fruit unto death. But now we are delivered from the law, that being dead wherein we were held; that we should serve in newness of spirit, and not in the oldness of the letter." The divine prohibition was, however, the only law in Eden; its internalization in Eve's consciousness, the only dimension of the double scripture necessary to prelapsarian life, was also her wisdom. Just as Satan's temptation speech dissociates the elements of theodicy, so does Eve's meditation dissociate the canonical relationships between law and gospel by abrogating rather than internalizing God's sole command.

These specifically New Testament rather than Old Testament echoes remind the reader that the Bible presents a plan of redemption for the postlapsarian world. The Son's prophetic narrative of the redemptive plan in Book 3 is a coherent model of the double scripture as a sequence of the canonical phases of revelation. The clear, though ironic, resonances between Eve's speech and Paul's epistles in the crucial interval between Eve's fall and Adam's cause the reader to speculate on what Adam could or should have done on Eve's behalf without falling himself. Dennis Danielson calls this effect the "telescope of typology" because it reminds the reader that Adam and Eve correspond to Jesus and Mary, the second Adam and second Eve, who will appear in the postlapsarian scheme of redemption.[67] I would add that the telescope of typology is pointed to the future, and therefore represents another form of proleptic anticipation. In his appropriation of the technique of prolepsis, Satan subtly approximates the godlike qualities of foreknowledge, election, and predestination in his "prevenient" experience of the fruit. But Satan's use of prolepsis in the rhetoric of temptation is local, deliberately negating any temporal perspective beyond the immediate moment. Typology is analogous to the proleptic rhetoric of anticipation because it focuses on time, and offers a broader, more comprehensive view of time than the immediacy of temptation. The preliminary evocation of typology acknowledges the reality of the Fall while offering a visionary and speculative alternative to Satan's appropriation of the discourse of wisdom.

Wisdom as the eye of reason will gradually open through typological vision, but Adam's fall also completes the more rigid contrast between spiritual and corporeal vision developed in the invocation to Book 3. Book 9 is structured as a tragic drama in five acts. Milton uses the structural feature of recognition or *anagnorisis* integral to tragic drama to signal the completion of the Fall. Recognition is also ironic, however, because Adam now sees Eve with the eye of lust: "Eve, now I see thou art exact of taste, / And elegant, of Sapience no small part" (9:1017–18). While sapience or wisdom is ordering and discriminating, Adam confuses the echelons of sense by equating sight and taste. This lapse into corporeal vision and brute sense requires the eventual transition from classical tragic structure in Book 9 to biblical tragedy modeled on Revelation in Books 11–12, and from an ironic *anagnorisis* to the restored spiritual vision of the apocalypse.

As Paul Reichert has shown, Satan tempts Eve by associating her with the vision of heavenly wisdom or the divine Sophia.[68] The Serpent considers her a "Goddess among gods," and suggests that the desire of the beasts is simply to gaze upon her form. In *Wisdomes Character and Counterfeit* (1656), Nathaniel Hardy, a Presbyterian minister who remained loyal to the monarchy, depicts true wisdom as the "Queen of Graces": "Her Parentage is sublime, she being of a noble, royall, yea Divine extraction, for she is the wisdome from above. Her person is altogether lovely in every part. The candour of purity adorneth her breasts, the honey of peace drops from her lips, and amiable gentlenesse smileth in her countenance, the jewell of tractablenesse hangs at her eares, bracelets of mercy and good fruits deck her hands, and she walketh upon the two even feet of impartiality and sincerity, who can look upon her, and not be ravished by her?"[69] The association of Eve with transcendent wisdom returns us to the problems of the feminine typology of wisdom, and in particular to its apparent division of the human feminine from the divine feminine, and its polarization of the human feminine into woman wisdom (Prov. 8:22–27) and woman stranger (Prov. 5:1–3). As we have seen, Satan's temptation succeeds by confusing rather than distinguishing the divine and the human, as he advises Eve to put off her humanity and assume divinity. During Adam's fall, Milton criticizes the veneration of the feminine by treating Adam's fall as a parody of the code of courtly love: Eve is delighted that Adam will, in falling, undertake such a "glorious trial of exceeding Love" (9:960). In Book 10, however, during the traumatic interval between the Fall and the expulsion from Eden, Milton recovers the more human typology of feminine wisdom in his portrayal of Eve. After patiently enduring Adam's venomous and irrational recrimination, Eve fulfills the typological role of domestic counselor by recommending courses of action. The first recommendation is intercession, which Adam should have thought of before his fall. Eve offers to return to the "place of judgment," there to

> importune Heaven, that all
> The sentence from thy head remov'd may light
> On me. . . .
>
> (10:933–35)

Her second recommendation is sexual abstinence, which circumvents the sentence of death by preventing the birth of future generations:

Childless thou art, Childless remain: So Death
Shall be deceiv'd his glut, and with us two
Be forc'd to satisfy his Rav'nous Maw.

(10:989–91)

Her third recommendation is suicide: "Let us seek Death, or he not found, supply / With our own hands his Office on ourselves" (10:1001–2). Eve's three recommendations are Christlike in character: they contemplate sacrificial, intercessory, and mediatorial acts that may frustrate or overcome death, though through ironic turns of logic: the Son's sacrifice in Book 3 ransoms people before they exist; Eve's suggestion of suicide forestalls the sufferings of people who would then never exist. In spite of these ironies, Eve initiates the redemptive countermovement to the Fall in the poem (a countermovement already realized in the Son's prophetic narrative in Book 3). Even Adam's swift appropriation of these ideas—"I to that place / Would speed before thee, and be louder heard" (10:953–54)—does not obscure their origin with Eve. Her ideas, however morbid, are as selfless as they are ingenious, and therefore represent forms of wisdom.

The Fall occurs when Eve seeks elevation to that superhuman society of gods offered by Satan. The Restoration for Milton was equally a reinstatement of the superhuman mystique of monarchy. Milton establishes clear resonances between the language of happiness Satan uses in his temptation of Eve and the language of happiness in Restoration discourse; he also adapts these resonances to the rhetoric of biblical wisdom. Eve succumbs to conformity and assent through witnessing the spectacle of Satan's performance, and is encouraged to conceive of herself in spectacular terms of divine pageantry without the harsh spectacle of punishment that augments power: "God therefore cannot hurt ye, and be just" (9:699). Satan's explication of the divine prohibition is designed to make Eve view herself as a divine monarch. It thereby makes the Bible into a mirror rather than, recalling Danielson's metaphor, a telescope. Satan invites Eve to view herself narcissistically in the mirror of scripture. An innocent narcissism is evoked in the autobiographical narrative of Eve's awakening by the pool in Book 4, a narrative Satan overheard in hiding. The temptation moves from the innocent narcissism of nature in Book 4 to the culpable narcissism of scripture in Book 9, achieving a correspondence with the public invitation to view Charles II as a mirror of the messiah. It is the general cultural and political use of the Bible as a narcissistic mirror that Milton counters in *Paradise Lost*.

The solution to biblical narcissism lies in the capacity to read for others as well as for one's self. What Milton seeks to recover and restore is a society of human readers characterized by those other selves who are biblical types. This readerly restoration is constructed at the close of the poem when Milton models Eve's speech of rededication to Adam on the dialogue between Ruth and Naomi. As Barbara Lewalski has noted, Ruth's "loving and faithful promise to follow Naomi to another homeland" is echoed by Eve at the close of *Paradise Lost* (apart from the final note of guilt in Eve's postlapsarian speech):[70]

> And Ruth said; Entreat me not to leave thee, or to return from following after thee: for whither thou goest, I will go; and where thou lodgest, I will lodge. (Ruth 1:16)

> with thee to go,
> Is to stay here; without thee here to stay,
> Is to go hence unwilling; thou to mee
> Art all things under Heav'n, all places thou,
> Who for my wilful crime art banisht hence.
> (12:615–19)

Naomi resembles Job in her sufferings at the start of Ruth, but both women perceptively negotiate their place in the social order in a narrative that moves from isolation to community. Ruth concludes with a genealogy that includes the birth of David in the Hebrew canon and anticipates the birth of Jesus in the Christian canon (Ruth is named in Matthew's genealogy of Jesus). The use of the genealogy in Ruth may have influenced Milton's use of Eve's dream of a future messiah at the close of *Paradise Lost*; moreover, the profession of loyalty between Ruth and Naomi is a powerful affirmation of spiritual and social values that transcend the forces of more mundane wisdom and material concern. Mundane wisdom, or common sense alone, would have led Ruth to abandon Naomi; instead, their bond becomes a social and spiritual microcosm of the biblical promises of restored life and community. In the same manner, Milton predicates the promises of restoration in

Paradise Lost on the reaffirmation of the basic human relationship between Adam and Eve. As Adam and Eve join hands at the expulsion, the anticipation of sharing and relating their separate and qualitatively distinct revelations makes their elementary union the emblem of the scriptural society Milton sought to encourage and sustain in the wilderness.

3

"Contrary Blasts":
Wisdom and Opposition in *Samson Agonistes*

None of all those persons guilty of rebellion in Scripture went
to their Graves in peace . . . we shall seldom find any men
(like blinded Sampson) endeavoring to pull down the pillars
upon which Gods house stands, (for such are Kings) but they
themselves (like him) perished in the ruine.
—John Spencer, *The Righteous Ruler,* 28 June 1660

"Privation of Light": Opposition and Interpretation

In a sermon preached to Parliament on 10 May 1660, John Price,
chaplain to General Monck, considered the opponents of Monck's
reconstitution of the Parliament that would negotiate the restoration of the monarchy, to be, like the captive Samson, benighted
and godforsaken:

Darkness is defined to be a privation of light: so now those, as they
thought, smiling providences, and the light of Gods countenance
are departed from them and withdrawn. They thought themselves
to be the Israelites, that must needs have the cloud by day, and the
pillar of fire by night to direct them; they thought that prosperity
should have for ever spread its wings over their tabernacles, &
that they had chained victory to their scabbards; but now they are
swallowed up in night and horror, and are put out in obscure darknesse, Prov. 20.20.[1]

Price predicted confusion for the defeated cause: "They shall
be ashamed of what they have done, and shall find no arguments to defend themselves, they have nothing to plead, for in-
iquity stops its mouth. . . . They shall be amazed at the

judgments of God, who hath over taken and ensnared them in their own doings. . . . They thought Sampson-like to have gone out as at other times, but their strength was departed."[2] Price accuses his enemies of self-delusion in their identification with biblical types such as Samson: to be "Sampson-like" is to be a false Samson and a false Israelite. Price asserts that the "light of Gods countenance" is "departed from them and withdrawn." The ending of *Samson Agonistes* opposes Price's assertion:

> And which is best, and happiest yet, all this
> With God not parted from him as was fear'd,
> But favoring and assisting to the end.
>
> (1718–20)

> Oft he seems to hide his face,
> But unexpectedly returns
> And to his faithful Champion hath in place
> Bore witness gloriously.
>
> (1749–52)

Other voices cast Milton and all of the king's enemies as the Philistines who persecuted Samson. In the *Royal and Other Innocent Bloud Crying Aloud to Heaven For Due Vengeance*, published on 18 June 1660, Milton is among those who helped fasten the yoke of servitude to Samson:

> It hath seemed good to the Divine providence, which we may truly call wonderfull, so to over-rule of late, the counsels of our former oppressors, who by strange success, and almost incredible dexterity in villany, had almost involved both our Church and state in unavoidable ruine; grinding without compassion, these (once free) but at length wofully enthralled Nations, fastning on their neck, an Iron, uneasy yoak of servitude, making them (with Samson) basely to grind, and abide captivity, and curbing them with rigor, who before repined at, grew weary of, and rejected the milder scepter, and so to ensnare them in their contrivances, that their plots (like potters vessells) were broken upon the wheele, nor produced any thing but confusion and distraction to themselves, together with unsetledness in the Nation.[3]

In *Areopagitica*, Milton had envisioned "a noble and puissant Nation rousing herself like a strong man after sleep," an image of the renewed power of Samson (*CPW* 2:557–58). *Areopagitica*, however, pertains to the potential of a reformed English society through the open conflict of contending voices and perspectives. While *Areopagitica* includes a range of nonbiblical texts in its vision, it includes them by connecting them to the overarching authority of the Bible. The Bible provides the range and variety of metaphors that characterize and envision a reformed society in its movement towards truth. These metaphors include the revived Samson, the scattered body, and the perpetually streaming fountain. The Bible is the real subject of *Areopagitica*. It is also the subject of the three major poems as Milton develops the typological analogy between the central, sacred text and the society it could project and reform. In *Samson Agonistes* and *Paradise Regained*, however, we encounter a suddenly intensified biblicism. This intensification is particularly evident in Jesus' rejection of the wisdom of Athens in *Paradise Regained*; it is also apparent in the exclusively biblical decorum required by the setting of *Samson Agonistes*. This new intensity may have reflected Milton's awareness that others used the Bible with an equal intensity to label radicals or dissenters as seditious. Opponents of Restoration were labeled atheists, traitors, and even murderers in sermons and pamphlets, as Milton was himself. Milton's method in *Samson Agonistes* is not a simple, partisan refutation of these charges in equally biblical language. His Samson, and also, as I will argue, his Dalila, are positioned between the "contrary blasts" of contending perspectives, realizing both the psychological pain and political turmoil of mutual accusation. Milton does not simply read white where others read black: he represents the polarities and conflicts of the biblical culture in which he wrote in order to recreate the energy and purpose of his original vision in *Areopagitica* in a new, more hostile context.

Hostile parties could identify with biblical figures such as Samson. As they lived "under change of times," however, the degree of openness with which they made these identifications could vary. Matthew Griffith compared Charles I to the restored Samson: the seditious "look upon him (as the Philistines did upon Samson without his hair, in which his strength lay) with scorn and contempt, as if he were as weak and worthless as other men: but let them remember how God renewed Samsons strength, to revenge himself at last" (61). The Restoration is God's revenge on those who humiliated Samson. In *Samson Ag-*

onistes, and also in *Paradise Regained*, there is a pronounced theme of silence and circumspection as the heroes become guarded in their speech and cautious of revealing their intentions. Secrecy is particularly important for Samson as he failed to maintain the secret of his strength under the "seal of silence."

Biblical references could serve as coded messages directed to a knowing audience. Bunyan offers a memorable example as he writes to his followers from prison: "I have sent you here enclosed, a drop of that honey, that I have taken out of the Carcase of a lion (Judges xiv. 5–8). I have eaten thereof my self also, and am much refreshed thereby. (Temptations when we meet them at first, are as the Lyon that roared upon Sampson; but if we overcome them, the next time we see them, we shall find a Nest of Honey within them.) The Philistines understand me not."[4] Bunyan's image comes from the middle of Samson's career before his meeting with Dalila, his blinding, and his final destiny in the temple of Dagon. Read in the context of the Judges narrative, the killing of the lion could signify strength without "a double share / Of wisdom." The riddle Samson fashions—"Out of the eater came forth meat, and out of the strong came forth sweetness" (Jgs. 14:14)—is a mere parody of the Word, often compared to honey in scripture, that would make the biblical Samson as wise as he is strong.[5] Like the ancient authors who invested theological significance in the story of Samson as they wrote it, Bunyan invests his own theological purpose in Samson's riddle in order to portray himself as a leader whose strength consists in patient suffering and faith. Samson's fight with the lion is made to fit the emblematic meaning Bunyan ascribes to it even as he uses it to separate his readers from the "Philistines" who are his captors. In like manner, in *Samson Agonistes*, Samson's final statements to the Chorus before he leaves for the Temple of Dagon approximate Bunyan's strategy. Like Bunyan, Milton's Samson speaks covertly and circumspectly above the heads of his captors to his own community. His riddling powers attain a new gravity and wisdom through his bitter experience of defeat and captivity.

In spite of the marked difference between the impulsive hero of the Judges narrative and the solemn figure of Milton's poem, Samson's meaning, and the meaning of Samson, retains a troubling uncertainty for readers in Milton's treatment of Samson's final hours and violent death. Readers explore the meaning of the poem in the space between the biblical Samson and the Miltonic Samson. The biblical Samson is produced by the Bible and, for Milton's contemporaries, by the range of uses to which Samson is put in Restoration discourse. The Miltonic Samson is a potent distillation of the biblical Samson combined with Milton's own interpretation and use of the story. The Samson of Judges acts, as Robert Alter remarks, as "a blind, uncontrolled force, leaving a terrible swath of destruction behind it, finally consuming itself together with whatever stands in its way."[6] Gerhard von Rad regards the Samson of Judges as a failed leader who perishes "in the great conflict between *eros* and *charisma*."[7] The Miltonic Samson contains much of the chaos described by Alter and von Rad in the fatal disjunction between strength and wisdom. He approaches, however, a resolved equilibrium of strength and wisdom by examining the limitations of martial heroism and by acknowledging the failures of charismatic political leadership, the two parameters of politics that proved so traumatic for Milton's contemporaries before and after the Restoration.

Samson, Manoa, and the Chorus seek evidence—that criterion of faith upon which Samson's heroism is based in Hebrews 11— that the "guiding hand" of providence is operating in Samson's final hours. The "privation of light," and the sense of "Gods countenance . . . departed from them and withdrawn," comprise the matter that Samson broods over in *Samson Agonistes*. This sense of privation is relieved by the close of the poem, as Manoa recognizes a God "not parted from him, as was fear'd, / But favoring and assisting to the end" (1719–20). Milton's poem begins with a Samson overwhelmed by accusations and recriminations analogous to the political discourse of Price and others who compared the opponents of Restoration to the defeated enemies of providence. It ends with a cathartic, therapeutic perspective in a "new acquist / Of true experience" in the manifestation of "highest wisdom" (1755–56; 1747). If the poem proceeds from the stark political opposition of victor and vanquished, and the inferences made about providence from that opposition, it moves towards emotional and intellectual clarity and perspective. Here again, the relationship between Milton's purpose is not one of simple inversion or self-vindication; instead, he dramatizes contending perspectives, in both their full complexity and inevitable partiality, to effect a clarity of perspective. Taking his audience as the final focus of that perspective, Milton assumes that both the trauma and the healing of a biblically based tragic poem are integral to the composure of his society of readers.

The Harapha episode shows an idiosyncratic use of opposed interpretations of scripture to reflect the political polarities of Milton's time. Harapha, a Philistine giant and warrior who is entirely Milton's invention, expands the range of biblical reference in the poem beyond the immediacy of the Judges narrative Milton recreates. The expansion is in part proleptic: Samson identifies Harapha as the "Father of five Sons / All of Gigantic size, *Goliah* chief" (1248–49). This reference predicts the defeat of Goliath by David, of Philistine by Israelite. Harapha's genealogy supports a proleptic typology linking Samson to David in 1 Samuel 17 and eventually to Christ in Hebrews 11:32. Harapha's stature as a giant is equally retrospective in its expansion of scriptural reference in the poem. He claims descent from

> stock renown'd
> As *Og* and *Anak* and the *Emims* old
> That *Kiriathaim* held.
>
> (1079–81)

Harapha's claim alludes to the postdiluvian giants of Deuteronomy 2–3, and ultimately the antediluvian giants of Genesis 6:4, the offspring of the union between the "sons of God" and the "daughters of men," who provoke God's wrath and the Flood. Harapha accuses Samson of gaining his strength, not from a divine charisma, but from the supernatural influence of the transgressive union of demons and humans:

> Thou durst not thus disparage glorious arms
> Which greatest Heroes have in battle worn,
> Thir ornament and safety, had not spells
> And black enchantments, some Magician's Art
> Arm'd thee or charm'd thee strong, which thou from Heaven
> Feign'd'st at thy birth was giv'n thee in thy hair.
>
> (1130–35)

The pseudepigraphical Book of Enoch associates the "sons of God" of Genesis with magic powers: the fallen angels "took unto themselves wives, and each chose for himself one, and they began to go into them and to defile themselves with them, and they taught them charms and enchantments."[8] Justin Martyr also develops the association of giants with magic arts:

> [God] appointed His angels, whom he placed over mankind, to look after men and all things under heaven. But the angels violated their charge, fell into sin with women and begot children who are called demons. Moreover, they subsequently subjected the human race to themselves, partly by magic writings, partly by the fear they instilled into them and the punishments they inflicted upon them, and partly by instructing them in the use of sacrifices, incense, and libations, which they really needed after becoming slaves of their lustful passions.[9]

Milton's use of Genesis 6:4 as a subtext for Samson's encounter with Harapha serves to exacerbate Samson's shame and despair. Samson feels that he may have been the slave of lustful passions. He is viewed by the Philistines as an enemy of civilization and humanity. The subtext of the Flood also links Samson to Cain, the first murderer, and the progenitor of all unnatural creatures hostile to God, including the murdering Grendel in *Beowulf*. These scriptural subtexts enhance the characterization of Samson, from Harapha's perspective, as what Alter again calls "a blind, uncontrolled force, leaving a terrible swath of destruction behind it, finally consuming itself together with whatever stands in its way."[10] The pseudepigraphical and patristic commentaries that develop these associations with Genesis resonate in turn with the political discourse of the Restoration contemporary with the writing of the poem. George Starkey had compared Milton to Cain. John Spencer and Clement Ellis saw members of the defeated cause as forces of chaos and anarchy.

The giants who perished due to a lack of wisdom were the carnal adversaries of God's spiritual purpose. John Spencer compared the Restoration to the renewed postdiluvian world in Genesis: "We have seen the Dove and the olive-branch of mercy & peace, and settlement after so many tossings and tempests mearly approaching us. . ."[11] The interregnum was, in contrast, the Flood itself: "National calamities are frequently in sacred Writ compared to a floud: and such were the evils (civil and spiritual) England long laboured under. . . ."[12] The Flood makes a political statement by suggesting that God's righteous anger was turned upon Cromwell and his supporters, though Cromwell is never named in the sermon. At the same time, the metaphor implies that monarchy is God's foreordained idea for England, as its restoration succeeds political turmoil, with royalty and aristocracy reemerging like sunlit mountain peaks as the waters recede. The Flood could even be evoked from more distant biblical references. George Starkey, the physician-pamphleteer who mocked Milton's blindness in *Britains Triumph*, called for revenge upon opponents of monarchy in the *Royal and Other Innocent Bloud Crying Aloud to Heaven For Due Vengeance* (London, 1660). The title casts the opponents Starkey identifies as Cains and Charles I as Abel. His readers would note that the race of Cain produced monsters and giants that roamed the earth, transgressing moral borders, and provoking God to flood the earth in anger.

Samson's response to Harapha's charge begins to reclaim his character by orienting it around the scriptural locus of his own nativity:

> I know no spells, use no forbidden Arts;
> My trust is in the living God who gave me
> At my Nativity this strength, diffius'd
> No less through all my sinews, joints and bones,
> Than thine, while I preserv'd these locks unshorn,
> The pledge of my unviolated vow.
> For proof hereof, if *Dagon* be thy god,
> Go to his Temple, invoke his aid
> With solemnest devotion, spread before him
> How highly it concerns his glory now
> To frustrate and dissolve these Magic Spells,
> Which I to be the power of *Israel*'s God
> Avow.
>
> (1139–51)

Samson distinguishes the narrative of his nativity from the narrative of the mingling of fallen angels and humans in Genesis 6:4 through a profession of faith, the "evidence of things not seen." If this profession places trust in the authenticity of his divine charisma, it also accepts blame for his failure to live up to that charisma. Milton evokes the ambiguous, at times unresolved history of the term "sons of God" in Genesis 6:4 in

order to challenge and reaffirm the divine commission predicted by the angel at Samson's nativity. Milton's use of this
exegetical crux in the encounter between Samson and Harapha may appear to demonize the Philistines, and, by implication, Milton's monarchist adversaries after the Restoration.
But this is not the case. By using Samson's adversaries to
"mirror" Samson's state, Milton ensures that our critical perceptions are not reduced to the simple labels sometimes
proffered by the Chorus. Harapha, who sees Samson as a tem-
pestuous obstacle to his own civilization, links Samson's nativity to the hermeneutic problems of Genesis 6:4 in order to cast
doubt on the wisdom of God in both the macrocosm of creation
and the microcosm of Samson's birth. In the encounter with
Harapha, Milton situates Samson between contending exegetical perspectives on Genesis 6:4 in order to portray Samson
himself as a point of exegetical contention. The Samson who
stands before the Philistine lords in the temple, his body a site
of intersection for many interpretive views, becomes an
emblem of this contention. In evoking Genesis 6:4, Milton provokes careful consideration of the nature and meaning of being
a "son of God." The underlying question for Samson, posed in
the prologue, concerns the facts of his birth: "Why was my
breeding order'd and prescrib'd / as of a person separate to
God?" (30–31).

The Flood divides the world into agents of chaos and agents
of order, with the latter reduced to a saving remnant. The treatment of the Flood in *Paradise Lost* 11 is extensive because
Noah and his family mark the end of the "generations of
Adam," and because the episode teaches central lessons to
Adam about the sanctity of place and the renewal of covenant
and creation. Although the import of the Flood is not explicit
here, and must be excavated from the cryptic and fragmented
biblical allusions that are characteristic of the dialogue in this
poem, the importance of the Flood in *Samson Agonistes* bears
upon the polarized political discourse of Restoration England as
illustrated, for example, in Spencer's sermon, with its contrast
between good and evil causes and enlightened and blinded
people. *Samson Agonistes* internalizes the tragic "us-against-
them" polarities recorded by Spencer and others by entertaining the possibility that Samson's cause was simply chaos.
Harapha's perspective tests and reaffirms Samson's under-

standing of the wisdom of God in creation, and hence the
grounds of Milton's theodicy. All of these ideas, embedded in
Harapha's evocation of the antediluvian giants, show Milton's
willingness to name the deepest fears felt by the defeated side.
He also answers these fears. In the encounter with Harapha,
Samson's reaffirmation of the divine strength given to him at
birth is an expression of trust which implicitly rejects any association with the fallen angels of Genesis 6:4, and ultimately
views those "sons of God" as morally responsible humans.
Samson's reaffirmation, as a decisive interpretive distinction,
enhances the dimension of theodicy in the poem by affirming
the premise of free will, while enacting the prediction made by
the angel in Judges 13:5: "the child shall be a Nazirite unto God
from the womb."

Lacking the divine vantage point of the heavenly councils that
occur in *Paradise Lost* and *Paradise Regained*, *Samson Agonistes* emphasizes a system of manifold and contending human
perspectives. As Herle implies in his summary critique of the
various sects that comprised the fractious religious milieu of
seventeenth-century England, wisdom consists in knowing that
human perspectives are partial and limited. The contending perspectives that constitute this tragic poem elicit hermeneutic indeterminacy amongst Milton's perceptive contemporary readers.
This view is put forward by Derek Wood, who argues that Milton
leaves his reader in moral and interpretive indeterminacy: "Possible meanings intercross in the intertextual space on which
Samson is written, but the writer's voice is silent, and he points
to no one of these paths."[13] Noam Flinker, referring to the Harapha episode in particular, concludes that the "values of Christ
and Satan beckon with almost equal force to Samson and Harapha, and the modern observer is hard-pressed to decide just how
to view the enigma."[14] Even at this stark extreme of *Samson Agonistes*, however, Milton continues to reaffirm the vision of *Areopagitica* as the model for his scriptural society. The scriptural
tempest of accusation and recrimination found in the poem
merges with a trial of reading as vital and elevating as that
found in the treatise, and recreates in a new context the image
of "a noble and puissant nation rousing herself like a strong
man after sleep, and shaking her invincible locks" (*CPW*
2:557–58).

"FOUND IN THE CLOSE": THE WISDOM OF TRAGEDY

Preaching from Psalms 118:22–23—"The stone which the builders refused is become the head stone of the corner; This is the Lord's doing; it is marvellous in our eyes"[15]—Clement Ellis proclaimed monarchy the cornerstone of the English nation, and argued that its enemies fight against providence and destroy themselves:

> touch but the Lord's anointed, and you disjoint all, the whole King-dome shatters into confusion; all falls into pieces, and all the wit of man is not able to bind it up again. . . . whosoever wildly pushes at these sacred stones, he onely runs his head against an hard Rock, which though he should have the unhappy strength to shake a little, yet he shall be sure withall to dash out his own brains; at least he must expect to receive such a wound, as cannot easily be healed but he is like to bleed into a too late repentance: He that fights against powers set up by God, can onely beat the skin off his own fingers."[16]

God's replacement of the cornerstone reestablishes justice, liberty, and true religion in England:

> But there is no fighting against Heaven, the same wise hand which fitted this Second stone is an Omnipotent hand too, and hath fixed it. Even that same Royall stone, which (with shame we may speak it) for so many years together had layen in the dust, neglected by the People, Hated by the Builders, beat upon by stormes and Tempests; and hath felt the heavy hammers of his implacable Enemies; is now sent home again, more solid and firme for all that Hammering, more sound and undecayed by reason of that long obscurity, more welcome and acceptable after so long an absence. With whom is restored a lost Justice, a long time smoother'd amongst numberlesse Interests and Factions: a lost Liberty, so long shackled by a most intolerable Tyranny and Usurpation; a lost religion, so long buried in grossest Atheisme, onely with a fair flourish of Hypocricy, and an inscription of Holinesse over her grave. . . .[17]

The interregnum was a period of chaos and confusion: "we have to our sorrow found, what sad Daies those were, wherein there was no King in our Israel: dayes full of nothing but black clouds, raging winds, and fatall stormes; in which both God's house and Cesar's were blowne downe to the grounde; all honest and Loyall men driven out of the Land, or dispersed, and scatter'd, and hurled into the little narrow Corners of the earth, making privacy and poverty their sanctuary: nothing appear'd for many yeares together but the horrid face of rebellion and confusion. . . ."[18] Ellis compares the interregnum to the period of the Judges, the source of the Samson story, and particularly its ominous final sentence: "In those days there was no King in Israel, and every man did what was right in his own eyes" (Jgs. 17:6). Judges is positioned in the biblical canon between the leadership of Moses and Joshua and the coming of the monarchy under David and Solomon.

In considering Judges as a reflection of the turmoil of his own times, Milton first creates a Samson who must internalize the chaos and confusion of his national history as a precondition of wisdom. Secondly, like the writers and redactors of Judges, Milton seeks to discern the pattern that underlies the confusion of history in order to clarify the pattern for his reader. The biblical pattern consists of the cycle of apostasy which is the narrative formula of the Book of Judges. Milton combines the biblical pattern with a third model: the form of classical tragedy. Milton alludes to Aristotle's definition of tragedy in the preface to the poem. It is the "imitation of an action that is serious and complete and has sufficient size . . . exciting pity and fear, bringing about the catharsis of such emotions."[19] Aristotle's view of tragedy places the highest value on plot, or the clear and complete arrangement of episodes that produces the emotional and perceptual clarity of catharsis in its audience. Milton joins classical tragedy to biblical narrative to produce a clarity of perspective out of the psychological and political dissonance of history as it is refracted through Samson's experience. The alloy formed between these traditions transcends the simple invective of opposed discourses that surrounded the poem at the time of its writing.

The Book of Judges focuses on a cyclical pattern of apostasy and deliverance. The cycle intensifies a dialectic that generates much Old Testament narrative. Robert Alter summarizes these dialectical terms:

> The ancient Hebrew writers seek through the process of narrative realization to reveal the enactment of God's purposes in historical events. This enactment, however, is continuously

complicated by a perception of two, approximately parallel, dialectical tensions. One is a tension between the divine plan and the disorderly character of actual historical events, or, to translate this opposition into specifically biblical terms, between the divine promise and its ostensible failure to be fulfilled; the other is a tension between God's will, his providential guidance, and human freedom, the refractory nature of man. . . . the depth with which human nature is imagined in the Bible is a function of its being conceived as being caught in the powerful interplay of this double dialectic between design and disorder, providence and freedom.[20]

Samson Agonistes is perhaps Milton's most intense imagining of "refractory" human nature. Limited human perceptions circulate within an overarching providential design that is glimpsed only dimly, and often through the inadequate lens of political partisanship. Fragments of scripture comprise an aphoristic discourse analogous to the limits of human perception. The fragments resist an easy synthesis, yet are set against the circumspect clarity of Samson's final resolution to destroy the temple of his enemies. The tensions that impel our reading in aphoristic discourse are carried to the extreme as we debate the disjunction between strength and wisdom that opens the poem.

In his portrayal of Samson, Milton embellishes what is already disconcerting in the figure of the Judges narrative. At the same time, he invests solemnity and nobility in his troubled protagonist. We also find a psychological and political complexity in both Samson and Dalila that exceeds the reductive piety or simple villainy often portrayed in these figures by tradition. With all of these multivalent tensions in play, the poem now divides its readers. The poem's divisiveness manifests itself internally and psychologically in the tormented memory of its protagonist, and externally and politically in the opposition of Israelites and Philistines, with all that these terms might imply to both seventeenth- and twenty-first-century readers. The psychological and the political are linked because the hero understands that he is the embodiment of Israel's political expectations in both victory and defeat. His inward, psychological torment of self-recrimination is projected outwardly in the opposition of Israelite and Philistine and in the hierarchy of slaves and conquerors:

> Promise was that I
> Should *Israel* from *Philistian* yoke deliver;
> Ask for this great Deliverer now, and find him
> Eyeless in *Gaza* at the mill with slaves.
>
> (38–41)

The divisions in Samson's self-image are seen from conflicting vantage points in every episode of the poem. If the tensions and divisions that constitute the poem are resolved—and that they are resolved is questionable—they are first, as the Chorus suggests, "strain'd / Up to the height."[21] Some readers have resolved these "contrary blasts" by reading the episodes as necessary steps in the hero's regeneration as deliverer. Some few declare the hero to be a false, demonic messiah who has enslaved himself and others through his pride and frailty; others argue that the divided image of Samson, the deliverer and the slave, cannot be resolved at all.[22]

The juxtaposition of *Samson Agonistes* and *Paradise Regained* compounds the interpretive dilemma of Samson even further. The two poems were bound together in a single volume published in 1671. This feature of their material production intensifies the hermeneutic problems of division and resolution that inform *Samson Agonistes*. Situated within the political milieu of Restoration England, Milton's Jesus represents the nonconformist who preserves his revolutionary integrity in the face of a persecuting culture represented by Satan. Satan appears in Book 2, for example, in the guise of a Restoration courtier: "As one in City, or Court, or Palace bred" (2:300). Jesus is plainer in speech and dress. Samson also suffers in confrontation with a court culture—only the "vulgar" escape the catastrophe at the end—but the destruction of the Philistine temple, for many readers, is a futile gesture. It brings no genuine deliverance to Samson's followers; instead, it reinforces the cycle of violence that Jesus interrupts.

While focusing our attention on problems of interpretation, the joint publication should also highlight features common to both poems. Mary-Ann Radzinowicz has described *Paradise Regained* as a "hermeneutic combat": its central action is interpretive as Jesus and Satan contest the meaning and the method of reading scripture.[23] Satan degrades scripture by insisting on literal and material manifestations of Jesus' divine power, and by separating Jesus from his biblical precursors by enticing him toward nonbiblical models provided by Greek, Roman, and Parthian conquerors. Jesus consistently recovers the metaphoric and typological senses of scripture in order to bring different biblical types and figures into new and significant relationships. These relationships anticipate the methods he will use to teach and gather a new community through his public ministry. The meaning of Samson's destruction of the Philistine temple is unstable when placed beside the hermeneutic framework of *Paradise Regained*. Jesus names Job, Elijah, and Moses as his precursors, but not Samson. Nevertheless, the justification of Samson—indeed the main reason he receives attention in literature and theology up until Milton's time—is his typological association with Jesus.

Like *Paradise Regained*, *Samson Agonistes* is about reading the Bible. As Hugh MacCallum observes, the Bible in the world of this poem is an array of oral fragments of still-to-be-written scripture.[24] The tensions between prophecy and wisdom established in the fabric of biblical allusion in the poem, the modeling of characters' speeches on different biblical modes such as psalmody, prophecy, and wisdom, and the manner in which allusions extend their scopes of reference outward through the biblical canon from the local moment of Samson's final hours, combine to engage the "fit" reader in the tensions and paradoxes that inform the Bible. If Milton offered his readers a positive image of Samson for the sake of a defeated cause, he did so with a troubled typological complexity designed to disconcert the hermeneutic and political complacency endemic to traditional typological associations. If political movements are attached to the cycle of revolution, then poetry—especially poetry that makes the work of interpretation part of its central action—detaches its reader from that cycle through the achievement of critical perspective. Milton's *Samson Agonistes* achieves this critical perspective through a disconcerting complementarity, rather than a simple parody, with *Paradise Regained*. The poem gestures towards the hero of *Paradise Regained* at the impasse of martial heroism and charismatic leadership.

The fragmented Bible possessed by the characters in the poem is necessarily aphoristic. Aphoristic discourse is an aspect of the double scripture: its discontinuous, fragmented structure impels the reader to interpret and combine it into an internalized scriptural language. Scriptural fragments in *Samson Agonistes* take these hermeneutic conditions to an extreme. As the Chorus enters, recounting Samson's past exploits, Samson says: "I hear the sound of words, thir sense the air / Dissolves unjointed ere it reach my ear." This condition of verbal dissonance reflects the condition of scripture in the poem. Textual fragmentation, as an extreme instance of the discontinuity of aphoristic discourse, takes the concept of the internalized double scripture as its ultimate referent (Samson's blindness, or his complete dependence on the sense of hearing, reinforces these conditions). Psychological fragmentation, or the turmoil and suffering portrayed within Samson, makes the outward condition of defeat and subjection analogous to the fragmentation of scripture.

Like Jesus in *Paradise Regained*, Samson is positioned between the textual and material spheres, or between reading and acting in the world. Wisdom, not strength, is the pivotal link between reading and acting. Nathaniel Hardy distinguishes between wisdom that looks forward, or *pronoia*, and wisdom that looks backwards, or *metanoia*: "When the sinner with the prodigall cometh to himself, begins to be wise, reflects on his past life, and weepeth bitterly, this is *metanoia*, wisdomes after-wit, and having bathed himselfe in his teares, he walketh circumspectly that he be no more defiled, and this is *pronoia*, wisdomes forewit. Wisdome openeth the eyes to see the vilenesse of sinnes, and seeing she flyeth from it, as from a snare that would intangle her."[25] Jesus' wisdom is more *pronoia*; he anticipates the beginning of his public ministry. Samson demonstrates *metanoia* in the obsessive remembering of his past failures. The two aspects of wisdom are not, however, exclusive. Jesus gains a deeper sense of his messianic identity through the retrospective view of scriptural history and the Old Testament types who precede him. Samson undertakes a transition from the *metanoia* of self-recrimination to the *pronoia* of renewed purpose by passing through the structural events of recognition and reversal that define Milton's emplotment of the story. It is, of course, precisely the meaning of these events, and the significance of Samson's subsequent action, that divides readers. The reader must decide if wisdom, or the genuine connection between the textual and material spheres of action realized in Jesus, is evident in Samson's decision to go to the Philistine temple. I will argue that Milton's portrayal of Samson's fateful decision, even though his action lacks the definitive wisdom of Jesus in *Paradise Regained*, is still consistent with Milton's countering of Restoration discourses that cast Milton and others as enemies of providence and agents of mere chaos. It is, in other words, a part of Milton's idea of wisdom.

Samson interprets his failure and captivity through those fragments of scripture he possesses. These fragments include a knowledge of other judges, parts of the Mosaic law, the *fiat lux* of creation, and the "sayings of the wise." The Philistines represent the coercive forces Milton attacks in *Civil Power*: their command to Samson to perform at a riotous spectacle exercises outward force and ceremony over inner conscience and reading. Samson's violent response to these coercive forces on behalf of his defeated people is a disconcerting solution to the conflict between inner and outer forces. While the implications of this violence must be addressed, we should first recognize that the conflict between outer force and inner conscience, a conflict germane to Milton's political thinking, suggests that the poem is not only about the subjection of an individual and his people, but about the subjection of scripture itself. The textual and material spheres represent opposed directions in the poem. In the middle episodes, for example, the action of the poem is entirely verbal, although language is used to reflect on Samson's past exploits.[26] When Samson departs for the temple, he moves from the textual sphere of interpretive reflection to the material sphere of action. The reader, like Manoa and the Chorus, receives only a verbal record of Samson's violent death. The verbal record is consistent with Aristotle's precepts on drama: the Messenger's narrative is preferable to a sensational spectacle. More important, the Messenger's narrative recreates the priorities of scripture by grounding the audience in the continuing problems of interpretation. In all three of his major poems, Milton carefully ensures that his poetic endings are also interpretive beginnings for his readers. The "copious legend" into which the Chorus assimilates Samson exists, however, in tension with the persistent cycle of apostasy and deliverance in biblical narrative.

The Samson narrative in the Book of Judges reveals what von Rad calls a "pessimistic conception of the charismatic leader." "Behind the narrative," von Rad concludes, "lies the unspoken question, where is the one who serves his people as deliverer not merely on one occasion alone?" (1, 329). The pattern for this pessimistic vision of the narrative is the refrain that occurs between each of the Judges narratives. This refrain articulates the cycle of apostasy and deliverance that is repeated with some variations in the stories of each of the judges. The sequential quality of the Book of Judges, emphasizing an experiential pattern rather than a historical chronology, uses a narrative formula of apostasy and deliverance. Judges 3:7–9 generalizes the pattern: "And the children of Israel did evil in the sight of the Lord, and forgat the Lord their God. . . . Therefore the anger of the Lord was hot against Israel. . . . And when the children of Israel cried unto the Lord, the Lord raised up a deliverer to the children of Israel, who delivered them."

The cycle can be summarized according to its stages: apostasy (the children of Israel "did evil"); exile (the Lord "sold them"); petition ("the children of Israel cried unto the Lord"); deliverance (a judge is sent or "raised up" to "deliver" the people). Further apostasy ensues at the close of each narrative, and the cycle continues. The narrative formula is not simply repeated inflexibly; each repetition contains meaningful inflections and variations. A bold example is the early appearance of a woman judge, Deborah. Her courage and foresight distinguish her from the male figures she inspires, and her song extends the phase of deliverance in inspired speech.

The Samson narrative also contains a significant variation on the cyclical formula. The Samson narrative divides the narrative cycle in half. The phases of apostasy, exile, and the raising up of the judge occur at Samson's nativity. The phases of petition and deliverance do not occur until Samson's death: "And the children of Israel did evil again in the sight of the Lord; and the Lord delivered them into the hand of the Philistines forty years" (Jgs. 13:1). Samson's nativity narrative follows this first half of the cyclical formula, but we do not find any prayer of petition until the last moment of Samson's life: "And Samson called unto the Lord, and said, O Lord God, remember me, I pray thee, and strengthen me, I pray thee, only this once, O God, that I may be at once avenged of the Philistines for my two eyes" (Jgs. 16:28). Samson then brings down the temple, producing a chilling, final comment: "So the dead which he slew at his death were more than they which he slew in his life" (Jgs. 16:30). This verse may comment on failed leadership, but how does it relate to the division of the narrative formula with its deferral of prayer and de-

liverance to the close of the poem? Milton's treatment of Samson
suggests that he recognized these features of division and deferral in the narrative, and that this was a central premise in his
reading of the Judges narrative. Milton adapts this feature of
the Samson narrative in Judges to the structure of his poem,
which consists of nonnarrative intervals of dialogue poised between moments of significant action. This use of the nonnarrative interval emulates the concept of wisdom as holding action in
a state of potential. In *Samson Agonistes*, Milton further adapts
this feature of the Judges narrative to the distinctive structural
conventions of recognition and reversal. The unique variation on
the cycle of apostasy in Judges, and the structural moments of
recognition and reversal in tragic structure, combine to intensify
and interrogate the dialectic of divine and human wills that generates biblical narrative generally. As I will demonstrate, Milton
combines elements of biblical and tragic structure to address the
anxieties of his post-Restoration audience.

The deferral of the phase of petition to the end of Samson's life
makes the end the focal point in the narrative. For this reason,
Milton makes the "end" of the action in *Samson Agonistes* the
most emphatic motif in the poem:

> All is best, though we oft doubt,
> What th' unsearchable dispose
> Of highest wisdom brings about,
> And ever best found in the close.
>
> (1745–48)

Milton calls attention to endings, and hence to the reader's interpretive search for comprehensible endings, throughout the
poem. A close reading of the poem reveals that its Hebrew characters are intensely "end-conscious," and even "end-anxious."
The term "end" occurs fifteen times in the poem. It often signals
Samson's desire for the end of life:

> This only hope relieves me, that the strife
> With mee hath end.
>
> (460–61)

> His pardon I implore; but as for life,
> To what end should I seek it?
>
> (521–22)

and oft-invocated death
Hast'n the welcome end of all my pains.

(575–76)

These uses of the word "end" are also metapoetic because they explore the convergence of biblical and classical poetics. The Judges narrative defers the completion of its own narrative formula to the end of the Samson story; Aristotle considers the integrity of beginning, middle, and end as necessary to a tragic plot. Politics and poetics resonate in the reader's desire to find coherence in the midst of dissonance. Frank Kermode argues that the consonance of beginning, middle, and end is an anxiety for every generation of readers: "We achieve our secular concords of past and present and future, modifying the past and allowing for the future without falsifying our own moment of crisis. We need, and provide, fictions of concord."[27]

Milton understood that this search for coherence in the sphere of history characterized his audience after the Restoration. In citing David Pareus's designation of Revelation as the tragedy of Antichrist in the preface to *Samson Agonistes*, Milton intensifies the concerns of his readers in the context of political defeat. Revelation, as Collins observes, is the extreme case of polarization and resolution in the Bible: it produces an "unbearable tension" between "what was and what ought to have been." The tension is manifest in the opposition between symbols of God's rule and symbols of Satan's rule, between symbols of the authority and power of Christ and symbols of the authority and power of Caesar."[28] The contest "twixt God and *Dagon*" in *Samson Agonistes* is an instance of the conflict in Revelation. Collins calls this tension "cognitive dissonance, a state of mind that arises when there is great disparity between expectations and reality."[29] The cognitive dissonance effected by political defeat parallels the dissonance of language in Milton's poem. Whereas Adam is given the entire Bible in a coherent vision of the downfall of Antichrist in Revelation by Michael, Samson's "Bible" consists only of fragments, echoes, and cryptic allusions. Whereas the Son in Book 3 of *Paradise Lost* narrates the whole of redemptive history in its biblical canonical sequence, Samson's perspective is radically circumscribed in time. Samson cannot achieve the vision of the whole of scripture attained by Adam and the Son. The apocalyptic implications of the poem are similarly limited;

nevertheless, the reader can anticipate the Bible emerging from the turbulent history in which it is formed even as its copious biblical fragments form the scriptural texture of the poem.

The interval between Samson's prologue and his death consists of dialogues that remember Samson's random exploits. The narration of the past forms the middle of *Samson Agonistes* because language is all that remains for the defeated community of Israelites. They attempt to recombine the various fragments of Samson's life into a meaningful pattern, dwelling obsessively on the messianic prophecies of his nativity and his betrayal by Dalila. This middle of the poem suggests that Milton has adapted the divided cyclical narrative formula of the Samson narrative in Judges to his purpose. Part of this purpose is to adjust the proleptic features of biblical wisdom to tragedy. Edward Tayler describes the entire structure of *Samson Agonistes* as "proleptic": it relies "upon proleptic form, upon the anticipation of a known fulfillment,"[30] and its main thrust is "not from past to present but rather toward the future, toward the " 'Divine Prediction' that Samson 'Should *Israel* from *Philistian* yoke deliver.'"[31] Proleptic form registers in the first line of the poem—"A little onward lend thy guiding hand"—since this first, ambiguous line evokes the deferred prayer of petition for deliverance which concludes the Judges narrative and Milton's depiction of Samson's climactic moment. Milton, Tayler observes, "contrives to have the entire tragedy implicit in its opening line,"[32] yet the outcome of the drama must still unfold in the continuum of time. Proleptic form assimilates into the structure of the poem the themes of guidance and direction that are common in biblical wisdom literature.

Proleptic form implies a view of the beginning and ending of the poem *sub specie aeternitatis*. Unlike *Paradise Lost* and *Paradise Regained*, however, there are no heavenly councils in *Samson Agonistes* to confirm a transcendent perspective. The poem is preoccupied with the limits of fallible human perception. The Chorus offers provisional attempts at critical perspective by identifying Samson's antagonistic visitors. But its judgments are ironic because of the limitations of its perspective. Milton was naturally skeptical of similar judgments made by preachers who claimed to see and know with some finality the plain and self-evident hand of providence in the Restoration. The wisdom of providence exceeds the contending perspectives

that constitute both the textual and material spheres of human
knowing. *Samson Agonistes* is a poem that emphasizes contending perspectives. As in the Book of Judges, however, God is
silent.

"HONIED WORDS": THE PERSPECTIVE OF DALILA

Of all the characters who engage in dialogue with Samson in
the middle episodes of the poem, it is Dalila who shows the
deepest understanding of polarized perspectives and oppositional reading. Dalila holds a mirror up to Samson by portraying herself as the deliverer of the Philistines. She does this by
constructing a feminine countertypology of national heroines
from the resources of Samson's own identity: the Book of
Judges. Her bold claim to the status of deliverer occurs only
after Samson rejects her more tender advances with threats of
physical violence. Dalila is the only character, with the exception of Samson himself, who can speak out of the experience of
crossing political and religious borders because of her marriage
to Samson. She also speaks across the perspectives of private
and public, domestic and political spheres of action. Although
she is reduced to simple villainy in many treatments of the
story, Milton deepens and complicates both her experience and
perspective, making her a remarkable embodiment of the conflicts he sought to recreate in his major poems. The larger
structure of the poem appears to foreclose on her credibility and
her claims. She presumably perishes with the Philistines in the
Temple of Dagon. Her perspective, however, provides another
metapoetic comment on the larger structure that subsumes her
perspective. Through Dalila, Milton comments on the moments
of reversal and recognition that bring about the ending of the
poem. As I will argue, her claims are integral to Milton's revaluation of the classical convention of recognition or *anagnorisis*
in the context of biblical typology, which is the basis for Dalila's
claim to be a counterdeliverer. Recognition, which Aristotle defines as "a change from ignorance to knowledge—resulting in
love or hate—by those marked out for good fortune or bad fortune," is a central criterion of tragic structure. The structural
coincidence of reversal and recognition distinguishes Aristotle's
idea of the complex plot. In *Samson Agonistes,* recognition and

reversal coincide when Samson experiences the "rousing motions" that reverse his prior intentions and lead him to proceed to the Philistine temple.

Whether or not providence is the implied source of Samson's "rousing motions" is a contentious issue in criticism. Certainty vanishes in the poem's ambiguities, but Milton still appoints the Chorus to interpret and validate Samson's illumination from a tentative and limited human vantage point. The Chorus searches out "th'unsearchable" by *judging* the authenticity of Samson's "rousing motions" at the close of the poem. Prior to Samson's climactic recognition, the Chorus also judges the moments of recognition that occur in each of the middle episodes and that define their separate structures. The recognition of Harapha as a hollow boaster is an example of one such moment, and the judgment the Chorus passes upon him comes with hindsight. How do these smaller moments of recognition comment on the larger structure of the poem? We should first consider the judgment the Chorus passes on Dalila. While the Chorus recognizes Samson's virtue after he destroys the temple, it earlier refuses to recognize Dalila's claim to heroic stature made in her moment of self-recognition. This moment occurs when Dalila compares herself to Jael and, implicitly, to Deborah, two heroines from the early period of the Judges, the latter endowed with wisdom and prophetic authority. The typology that connects Dalila to Jael and Deborah is a necessary focus for the relation between wisdom and recognition in *Samson Agonistes*.[33]

"Honied words" alludes to Proverbs. The phrase signals the Chorus's rejection of Dalila's identification with Jael and Deborah. The phrase occurs in the Choral speech which marks the departure of Dalila and the arrival of Harapha. As Dalila makes her exit, the Chorus tells Samson to

> Look now for no enchanting voice, nor fear
> The bait of honied words; a rougher tongue
> Draws hitherward.
>
> (1065–67)

The "rougher tongue" belongs to the giant Harapha, who is imagined in Samson's visually descriptive challenge as a heavily-armed ancestor of Goliath. Why, then, does the Chorus identify him by his "rougher tongue"? One reason is that *Samson*

Agonistes, like *Paradise Regained,* consists of dialogue in which words are the weapons of a spiritual warfare. Speech is perhaps most intensely experienced in the condition of blindness. A more central reason is the priority that biblical wisdom literature places on the power of speech. *Samson Agonistes* emulates and interprets biblical injunctions concerning the moral gravity of the spoken word, and the power of language to injure or to heal, to edify or destroy, to frame riddles or to break vows. It is in this context especially that Harapha's "rougher tongue" succeeds Dalila's "honied words."

Honey is frequently the Bible's metaphor for its own laws, precepts, poems, and narratives. Consider Psalm 19:9–10:

> The fear of the Lord is clean, enduring forever: the
> judgments of the Lord are true and righteous altogether.
> More to be desired are they than gold, yea than much fine
> gold: sweeter also than honey and the honeycomb.

Bunyan uses honey in this sense when he speaks of the "drop of that honey" from the lion's carcass.[34] The negative sense of honey in the phrase "honied words" constructs a tension with this positive sense of the honey of the scriptural word. We can observe the significance of "honied words" primarily in the typological frameworks of the Book of Judges and Proverbs with some consideration of important elements in the New Testament. In the typology of Judges, the allusion links Dalila directly to Deborah. In Proverbs, the allusion evokes the dichotomous personifications of wisdom, a woman of understanding, and folly, a strange, foreign, and seductive woman. Typology is a necessary focus because it is essential to Milton's poetic strategies and because Dalila's comparison of herself to Deborah amounts to the construction of a typology: her "honied words" connect her to Deborah through the etymological meaning of the name Deborah: "the honey bee."[35] *Samson Agonistes* works out a pattern of history, on a scale necessarily more limited than that of *Paradise Lost*, by emphasizing typology, a mode of interpretation based on a view of history. Samson and Dalila seek the evidence of that pattern, and their location within it, by debating the wisdom of their actions in time. Their perspectives and readings are radically opposed and equally counterhistorical in their resistance to the labels and designations history will apply to them.

The Chorus's exhortation to Samson to fear no more "the bait of honied words" reads like a proverb: the elders are telling Samson what he should do. The immediate source of "honied words" is surely Proverbs 5:3.

> for the lips of a strange woman drop as a honeycomb, and her mouth is smoother than oil.

This portrait of the so-called foreign or stranger woman of Proverbs, the temptress whose presence contrasts with the virtuous woman of wisdom, gives priority to her words, not her looks. The same priority is evident in Milton's treatment of Dalila. True, the Chorus does dwell on her spectacular entrance, but their description of her is largely a composite of biblical allusions, especially to the destruction of the ships of Tarshish in Psalm 48. When she exits, it is her words they remember: her "honied words." Whatever threat Dalila poses consists in the arguments she constructs and the narratives she creates more than in whatever visual erotic appeal her presence provokes in Samson's memory.

The priority of the verbal over the visual in the case of Proverbs 5:1–3 is emphasized by James Williams: "The theme of language is so pervasive in older wisdom, as represented in Proverbs, that it may be the key to comprehending the image of the 'stranger woman' who appears as a seductive lure to the man trying to negotiate his way through life's hazards. . . . her weapons are not so much her beauty or sexually seductive wiles as her manner of using language."[36] How does Dalila use language? Let us assume that "honied words" refers specifically to her comparison of herself to Jael and Deborah, given the etymology of Deborah's name. Here Dalila uses language to interpret her own position in the poem. Dalila is perhaps most threatening to Samson in her bold but persuasive and compelling comparison of herself to Jael, who assassinated Sisera, the leader of an invading army (Jgs. 4), and to Deborah, who inspired the armies of Israel in the face of invasion and who celebrated Jael's deed in her famous song (Jgs. 5). This, then, is Dalila's interpretation, and it appropriates that which Samson and the Israelites most prize: the narratives of their salvation history. As a Judge in Israel, Samson is the supposed successor to Deborah, but he lacks wisdom equal to his strength until he claims valid inspiration at the climax. Dalila defies the "wise fathers" who surround and control her by claiming a valid comparison between herself and Jael and Deborah. The Chorus, siding naturally with Samson, is left to conserve its own judgments concerning the validity of both claims. Succession and comparison are typological: they establish order and continuity in history. By allowing his characters to seek justification in the field of typology, Milton tests the very nature of typological thought.

When the Chorus tells Samson to fear no more "the bait of honied words," they indicate in part that the situation is changing, and a new situation requires a new proverb. As we have already noted, the phrase "honied words" classifies Dalila in terms of the dichotomous personification of the feminine that informs the text of Proverbs. One part of the dichotomy is the personification of wisdom as a woman of honor and integrity; the second part involves the figure of the stranger or foreign woman whose acquaintance brings folly and disaster. It is one thing to identify the source of the allusion, profiting, like the Chorus, from the *anagnorisis* of hindsight. What also matters are the consequences and implications of the act of classification, which is the event of naming or *recognizing* Dalila as the foreign woman of Proverbs by the Chorus, and potentially by literary critics.

Generally speaking, the classifying or naming of a particular character or individual provides a means of neutralizing the threat which that character poses to a particular group. Samson, who appears to have been neutralized as a military threat to the Philistines, feels the sting of words—"Am I not sung and proverb'd for a Fool / In every street" (203–4)—and the sting of sight: "Perhaps my enemies . . . come to stare / At my affliction" (112–13). The relevant biblical illustration is found in the Epistle to the Hebrews :

> But call to remembrance the former days, in which, after ye were *illuminated*, ye endured a great fight of afflictions;
> Partly, whilst ye were made a *gazingstock* both by reproaches and afflictions; and partly, whilst ye became companions of them that were so used. (10:32–33, emphasis mine).

Two kinds of recognition are distinguished in this passage: the spiritual and the corporeal. The ensuing chapter, Hebrews 11, enshrines Samson as a hero of faith after defining faith as the object of spiritual recognition, "the evidence of things not seen."

Like Samson, Dalila is subjected to the judgmental gaze of others. Her defense, interpreted as defection from the law of marriage by Samson, is, in her own view, revolutionary. It takes the form of a comparison of herself to the heroines of Israel as she compares the narrative of Jael and Sisera to her own experience. The comparison begins, interestingly, with a proverb:

> Fame if not double-fac't is double-mouth'd,
> And with contrary blast proclaims most deeds;
> On both his wings, one black, the other white,
> Bears greatest names in his wild aery flight.

> (971–74)

Her maxim on fame argues that history is purely a matter of how one looks at it. She then elaborates the particulars of her "contrary blast" from the generalities of her proverb:[37]

> My name perhaps among the Circumcis'd
> In *Dan*, in *Judah*, and the bordering Tribes,
> To all posterity may stand defam'd,
> With malediction mention'd, and the blot
> Of falsehood most unconjugal traduc't.
> But in my country where I most desire,
> In *Ekron, Gaza, Asdod,* and in *Gath*
> I shall be nam'd among the famousest
> Of Women, sung at solemn festivals,
> Living and dead recorded, who to save
> Her country from a fierce destroyer, chose
> Above the faith of wedlock bands, my tomb
> With odors visited and annual flowers.
> Not less renown'd than in Mount *Ephraim,*
> *Jael,* who with inhospitable guile
> Smote *Sisera* sleeping through the Temples nail'd.
> Nor shall I count it heinous to enjoy
> The public marks of honor and reward
> Conferr'd upon me, for the piety
> Which to my country I was judg'd to have shown.

> (975–94)

Blots and marks pertain to writing. The black and white wings of fame suggest the black and white of ink and paper. Dalila concedes that she will be considered a blot or stigma in the written records of Israel, even as writing itself is a stigma upon a blank page.[38] In the still-to-be-written records of her own country, however, the public marks of honor are still possible. The page is still clean. By comparing herself to Jael, Dalila appropriates, if only temporarily, the narrative in which Samson has been trying to find his place: a narrative of national deliverance. The Chorus's reference to Dalila's "honied words" attempts to repudiate her comparison with Jael, and seeks to neutralize her claim by identifying her with a different, less honorable aspect of the feminine within their own traditions.

The allusion appears to mediate our understanding of the middle episode of *Samson Agonistes* by inviting us to read the text of Judges, the source of the dramatic action, in terms of the text of Proverbs, the source of the allusion. Proverbs are often uttered by characters immersed and implicated in the very circumstances they seek to understand. It is wise to search for understanding but folly to presume one possesses it totally. Samson learns this distinction; so too does the Chorus over the course of the poem. In order to account thoroughly for the function of wisdom allusions in *Samson Agonistes*, we must evaluate the fallibility of the Chorus. Let us therefore consider a second, misogynistic edict delivered by the Chorus:

> Favor'd of Heav'n who finds
> One virtuous, rarely found,
> That in domestic good combines:
> Happy that house! his way to peace is smooth:
> But virtue which breaks through all opposition,
> And all temptation can remove,
> Most shines and most is acceptable above.
>   Therefore God's universal Law
> Gave to the man despotic power
> Over his female in due awe,
> Nor from that right to part an hour,
> Smile she or lour:
> So shall he least confusion draw
> On his whole life, not sway'd
> By female usurpation, nor dismay'd.
>
> (1046–60)

This edict follows the traditional formula of wisdom by offering advice in a specific, experiential context. In this case the context is marriage. The statement concerning "God's universal Law" is offered with the force of a general, timeless truth. This is not Milton's endorsement of patriarchal power; it is the Chorus's provisional interpretation of the law in a tragic, and therefore limited, context. Indeed, the tragic element is made more acute by the evocation of Proverbs 31:10–31, the portrait of the woman of worth, which precedes the maxim of "despotic power," and which establishes the dichotomous personification of the feminine completed by the phrase "honied words" which appears just seven lines later. There can be no timeless quality to this edict because the events which the Chorus interprets have not yet reached their conclusion. In fact, the rigidity of the Chorus's law is about to be destabilized by the motions of grace. A hint of this irony is conveyed even in the structure of the Chorus's statement since the verb "Gave" and its object "power" connote grace and law respectively.

We can regard the generalizations of the Chorus within the circulation of antifeminist proverbs in Renaissance tracts and commonplace books without imputing their simple misogyny directly to Milton. Many commentators on Proverbs 31 could not praise the woman of worth without invoking her contrasting type. Peter Muffett remarks, she "speaketh not of toyes or of trifles, but of faith, repentance, of the feare of God, of such other duties and points of religion."[39] Wilcocks observes that "shee speaketh wisely, and frameth her selfe to speake not of toies and vaine things, as women commonly use to doe, but of grave matters, as of wisdome and vertue."[40] Lists of misogynistic proverbs, sometimes numbered to enhance their rigid sense of authority, appear in Robert Cawdray's *Treasurie*, Thomas Draxe's *Bibliotheca Scholastica Instructissima or Treasurie of ancient Adagies, and sententious Proverbes, selected out of the English, Greeke, Latine, French, Italian, and Spanish* (1633), and the anonymous *A Dialogue Conteyning the Number of the Effectual Proverbes in the English Tongue* (1566). Although these proverbs are primarily folkloric or "homely," biblical support is invoked. "As a vessell, the weaker it is, the more it is to be favored and spared, if wee will have it to continue: Even so a Woman, because of her infirmities, is much to bee borne withall. 1. Pet. 3:7."[41] Draxe shifts to Latin to enhance his authority: "*Foeminae sunt fraudulentae.*"[42]

In addition to discouraging critical response, the typographical presentation of a list implies that an entire cultural consensus lies behind it. As the repositories of antifeminist discourse, these lists reduce human complexity and experience to the rudiments of stereotypical perception. Hamlet's exclamation "Frailty, thy name is woman" is among the best-known examples of the spontaneous deployment of this crude, cultural apparatus in a complex domestic and emotional crisis. An example of the same deployment in Renaissance painting occurs in Andreas Mategna's painting of Samson and Dalila (1430). The canvas shows Dalila shearing off Samson's locks as he slumbers with his head in her lap. Behind Dalila, carved in the bark of a tree, are the Latin words: *"Foemina Diabolus Tribus Assibus Est Malius Peior"* [a bad woman is worth threepence less than the devil]. If, as the Chorus in *Samson Agonistes* suggests, the sayings of the wise were many, then so were the sayings of the misogynists. The *Patrikon Doron*, a version of King James' *Basilikon Doron* in verse quatrains, assigns blame to Dalila, Eve, and all other "syrens" in one quatrain:

> Frustrate, by wisdom, the Bane-boding Charms
> (As did Ulysses) of a Syren-tongue:
> From thence it was stout Sampson took his harmes;
> From thence it is our first of mischief sprung.[43]

Aphoristic discourse impels the mind to seek connections through reading and interpretation. The antifeminist catalogs, even though they consist of discrete and discontinuous sayings, do the opposite by inhibiting critical response. The difference is the difference between precept and cliché. The precepts of biblical wisdom imply a larger architectonic quality, as Milton shows in *Areopagitica* by linking a sequence of aphorisms in continuous prose with a larger, architectonic structure. Biblical wisdom also implies a poetic "deep structure," to use Haskin's term, that directs us to recognize wisdom as an expansive creative and critical agency in the reader's mind. The cliché, in contrast, is never expansive or enlarging. The misogynistic catalogs, even if they assume a cultural consensus, impel reduction and simplification. If the Chorus in *Samson Agonistes* at times adheres to this impulse, the poem as a whole unsettles and complicates it.

Instead of directly attributing the Chorus's misogyny to Milton, readers should consider how Milton characterizes the Chorus in terms of the social motivation of wisdom. In the case of *Samson Agonistes*, the proverbs delivered by the Chorus represent attempts to bring the dissonant facts of Samson's career, and particularly his experience with Dalila, into some form of interpretive coherence. The interpretive process characterizes the Chorus as fallible. The use of proverbs by the Chorus in the wake of Samson's exchange with Dalila reflects their anxieties for continuity and interpretation, two anxieties which are, perhaps, ultimately inseparable. According to Frye, if prophecy is the individualizing of the revolutionary impulse in biblical history, then wisdom is the individualizing of the law. Ideally, this means allowing the morality of the law to govern and inform our thoughts, actions, and perceptions. Samson's career falls short of the ideals of the revolutionary role that was prophesied for him, while many of the proverbs of the Chorus, particularly its assertion of despotic male authority, fall short of the ideal of the law. What we discover in those choral proverbs that presume, in their rhetorical nature as generalized truths, to transcend the temporal movement of the drama, is the verbal counterpart, in the sphere of the law, of Samson's failed efforts as a revolutionary in the sphere of prophecy: both *presume* a degree of divine authority that they perhaps have not been granted. In the final act, the Semichorus assumes an authority that seeks to validate the inward illumination that causes Samson, after the recognition of the "rousing motions," and with caution rather than reckless presumption, to proceed to the temple.

When the Chorus labels Dalila as the foreign woman of Proverbs, they react against her claim to have fulfilled for the Philistines the very offices to which Samson was appointed for Israel: deliverer, prophet, and giver of wisdom. Deborah was all of these things, and Dalila emulates Deborah by predicting the sweetness of her own future reputation. Deborah was a popular first name in the seventeenth century; Milton gave the name to his third and perhaps favorite daughter.[44] Again, the name means "honeybee," and the notion that the biblical Deborah was a speaker of "honied words" is played upon by a number of Renaissance poets and theologians, including Thomas Heywood:

> The name Deborah, in the originall, implyeth a word, or a Bee; neither was her name any way averse to her nature, for as she was mellifluous in her tongue, when she either pronounced the sacred oracles of God, or sat upon any judicatory causes, amongst his people: so she had also a sting at all times, upon any just occasion to wound and be avenged on his enemies the Canaanites, who then most barbarously and cruelly oppressed his owne chosen nation.[45]

The sixteenth-century theologian Peter Martyr also speaks of Deborah as fulfilling the meaning of her name:

> And if we should look upon the Etimology of her name, we shall thinke that her orations were verye sweete. For Deborah with the Hebrues is a bee, which beast we know is a diligent artificer in makyng of hony.[46]

For both writers, the exception of Deborah as woman judge is made to reinforce the rule of a male-dominated hierarchy of the sexes. For Heywood, the judgeship of Deborah is a necessary scourge to male pride; for Martyr it is evidence that God's power "is not bounde unto noble men and strong men, but he can easilye use the weake and feable ones."[47]

Milton presents a wise and spiritually warfaring Lady in *Comus*, but disparages the historical figure of the woman warrior in his treatment of Boadicea in the *History of Britain*. He dismisses antique historians who suppose that "with the Britans it was usual for Woemen to be thir Leaders" (*CPW* 5:79). In *Samson Agonistes*, the propriety of roles in relation to gender corresponds to the distinction between public and private responsibilities. Both Jael and Dalila take action in private, domestic settings, offending against the laws of hospitality and matrimony for the sake of public or national interests. Samson sets up a double standard in his condemnation of Dalila: public and private interests were joined in his proposed first marriage to the Woman of Timna, since the marriage was supposed to have provided some means or "occasion" to advance the public cause of Israel's deliverance, though it is hard to see how. We can say, at least, that the condition of double standards and the necessity of divided loyalties justify Milton's choice of the tragic form. Perhaps Milton saw in Judges, with its sense of historical crisis, its questioning of charismatic leadership, and its close interconnection of sexual and political violence, the disturbed and disorderly reflection of the biblical culture in which he lived and wrote.

Samson is established as a type of Christ when he is named a hero of faith in Hebrews 11:32. The same verse, incidentally, omits Deborah in favor of Barak, the doubt-ridden Hebrew general who turned to Deborah for inspiration. In the local context of the Book of Judges, Samson can be linked typologically to

Deborah through the honey he gathered from the body of the
lion he killed on his way to Timna, as well as through the riddle
he invented afterwards—"Out of the eater came forth meat, and
out of the strong came forth sweetness" (Jgs. 14:14). The riddle
is a device of wisdom literature. Milton's Samson poses a riddle
when he asks, "What is strength without a double share / Of
wisdom?" Within Judges, the link between honey (Samson's lion)
and the honeybee (Deborah) serves to contrast the wise prophet-
ess from the errant, aimless, practical joker the biblical Samson
so often is. The difference between Deborah's success and
Samson's failures implies a gradual falling away from the ideals
of the divine summons or *charisma* of judgeship. The Book of
Judges therefore gives us, as Gerhard von Rad argues, a pessimistic view of charismatic political leadership.[48] In the larger
context of Christian typological exegesis, however, we find that
Samson's failures do not necessarily threaten his status as a
type. Samson, observes William Gould in *Moses Unveiled* (1658),
"assayed his strength first on a Lion, who assaulted him in the
way, when he was going to seek his wife, out of which a little
thereafter he took forth honey. . . . So did Christ manifest his
matchless strength, first on Satan, who tempted him in the
wilderness. . . ."[49] Gould's treatment of the difference or "disparity" between Samson and Christ places no blame on Samson for
his downfall: "Samson lost his former strength when he was betrayed, and was apprehended, 'cause he could not be able to
resist; but so lost not Christ Jesus his powerful strength when
he was betrayed."[50] Milton's Samson, in contrast, must "acknowl-
edge and confess" his responsibility. The dialectic of similarity
and difference in typological relations is a crucial element in the
encounter between Samson and Dalila. Perhaps what embitters
Samson most is his sense of similarity to Dalila when she claims
the office of deliverer while reminding him of his "effeminate"
weakness.

Dalila's claims to be the deliverer comparable to Jael and Deborah illustrate what Mieke Bal terms "counter coherence" in her
reading of Judges. For Bal, literary representation is an integral
part of the record of history. If the record is constituted in the interests of certain versions of political coherence, then its status
as representation makes it both "a meaningful act of cultural expression as well as an instrument of political and social repression."[51] What Bal terms "counter-coherence," really a strategy of

reading, makes it possible to "glimpse a possible alternative main line that changes the entire status of the book as document."[52] One feature of this alternative is the positive comparison of Dalila and Jael, a comparison that opens the relations between gender and political violence to new scrutiny. For DiSalvo, the equation of Dalila and Jael in *Samson Agonistes* becomes, as it does for Bal in Judges, an "alternative reconstruction of the text."[53] For Bal, the story of Dalila, which has been traditionally used to illustrate "an 'eternal' truth: women are treacherous, especially in love," can be reversed. She argues that since "the identity of men depends heavily on their control over women as sexual beings, this reversal of power is what threatens them most."[54]

Dalila's claims present an example of counter-coherence as an alternative or reversed reading of Judges. Her reading reflects the situation of the Bible in Milton's cultural milieu, as opposed voices and contending perspectives draw from common biblical texts to claim their truths. Counter-coherence is a marked feature of the entire Book of Judges. From the appearance of Deborah onward, exceptional women appear to illustrate the deficiencies of the male judges. The cutting of Samson's hair is symbolically connected to Jael's actions because Jael also applies a sharp object, a tent peg, to the head of Sisera: "Then Jael Heber's wife took a nail of the tent, and took a hammer in her hand, and went softly unto him, and smote the nail into his temples, and fastened it into the ground: for he was fast asleep and weary. So he died" (Jgs. 4:21). Abimelech, whose name means "my father is king," also dies from a head wound inflicted by a woman: "And Abimelech came unto the tower, and fought against it, and went hard unto the door of the tower to burn it with fire. And a certain woman cast a piece of a millstone upon Abimelech's head, and all to brake his skull." (Jgs. 9:52–53). The millstone is a symbolic parallel with the pillars that fall upon Samson from above when he destroys the Temple of Dagon, and the fiery battle parallels the strong association of Samson with fire. The story of Jephthah and his daughter involves a rash rather than a broken vow, and so resonates with the hubris of Samson and with the theme of sacrifice and slaughter. In her resignation to her fate, Jephthah's daughter in turn invites comparison with the nameless concubine who is horribly raped and cut into twelve pieces, at the end of the Book of Judges (Jgs. 19).

The event leads to civil war in Israel. The narrator remarks coldly on the presumption of the Israelites in a closing statement: "In those days there was no king in Israel, and every man did that which was right in his own eyes" (Jgs. 21:25).

The Bible presents many exceptional women who act wisely and influentially within the constraints of the domestic sphere and a patriarchal culture. We have seen that Milton represents the devotion and loyalty of Ruth in Eve at the conclusion of *Paradise Lost*, suggesting not only a renewed and reconciled marriage, but also the strength and fortitude needed to cope in the postlapsarian world. Milton also emphasizes Mary's protection of the infant Jesus from Herod's deranged violence in *Paradise Regained*. Milton's Dalila offers Samson a kind of maternal protection that would deliver him from the mill. Her offer awakens his rage in part because it recalls to his mind the maternal image of Samson sleeping in her lap when the Philistines set upon him, an image that also parallels the sleeping Sisera, whose sleep is induced by warm milk. Even more, it recalls to Samson his own appointed destiny as the deliverer of Israel, a destiny he has not only failed but also relinquished to Dalila. His threat to tear Dalila limb from limb must evoke the murder of the nameless concubine in Judges 19. The temporary deliverance of the Philistines by Dalila may construct a profoundly ironic self-image for Samson and the Israelites in the final movements of the Samson story.

Are heroines extolled for their actions in Judges, or merely used as ironic counterpoints to the failures of men? In order to assess Milton's interpretation of Judges and gender, we should recall his consistent attention to political icons and the human propensity for political idolatry. Iconoclasm, whether it is the destruction of the groves of Baal by Gideon or the Temple of Dagon by Samson, is a strong theme throughout Judges. Even political assassinations are iconoclastic: Eglon, the Moabite king killed by Ehud, is iconic in the regal splendor that is ridiculed by the narrator; Sisera is iconic in the formidable military splendor that is routed by Deborah and Barak. At the same time, the judges lapse into idolatry, as Gideon does at the close of his narrative by collecting spoils of gold after battle and building an "ephod" which "became a snare unto Gideon, and to his house." (Jgs. 8:27). The judges are much like the people they lead when they mingle with the "strange gods" they should resist. Like

Eglon and Sisera, the judges can also become icons themselves. Milton is particularly aware of this possibility in his treatment of Samson. When Milton's Samson recalls that he walked like a "demi-god" he confesses to a kind of Greek hubris, but also sees that he has idolized himself in the assumption of his divine charisma. Idolatry and icon-making are dangerous not simply because they represent defections to other gods, but because, in Milton's terms, they represent that stasis of conformity that degrades scripture. Iconoclasm is turned against the judges themselves by exceptional women figures. Women in Judges are iconoclastic of masculine self-idolization. The text is increasingly skeptical of what Milton terms the "presumption" of divine agency in the impulses of its heroes. The shattering of presumption, which is Samson's hubris, like the shattering of military charisma that flawed the interregnum and the monarchical mystique that flawed the Restoration, are preconditions to the "new acquist / Of true experience" (1755–56).

Both *Paradise Regained* and *Samson Agonistes* focus on the relationship between knowledge of self and knowledge of God. The reciprocity of these two kinds of knowledge was both a political and a poetic premise for Milton, especially when self-knowledge is a function of political idolatry. A locus for this knowledge is Psalm 135:

> The idols of the heathen are silver and gold, the work of men's hands.
> They have mouths, but they speak not; eyes have they, but they see not;
> They have ears, but they hear not; neither is there any breath in their mouths.
> *They that make them are like unto them*: so is every one that trusteth in them.
>   (Ps. 135:15–18, emphasis mine)

Monarchy, to Milton, is a reciprocal idolatry between the monarch and the people. Scripture is amenable to idolatry when it is used passively and uncritically to support such projections. Jesus in *Paradise Regained* resists such projections, and reclaims the vitality of scripture in consequence. Samson succumbs to self-idolization in his hubris, and to the idolization of scripture in his presumptions concerning the promising oracles of his nativity. Samson's suffering in the middle episodes of the poem entails an effort of reading scripture in the fragmented echoes of psalms and narratives that he and the Chorus possess. If the image of self and God changes through a redemptive pattern of suffering, it changes from the stasis of idolatrous reflection to the activity of disciplined liberty. The change registers as both motion and recognition through Milton's revaluation of the classical convention of *anagnorisis*.

The contending perspectives of Samson and Dalila make the poem both a faithful adaptation of the Book of Judges and a disturbing reflection of Milton's biblical culture. How, in turn, are these perspectives aligned with the conventions of tragedy? *Samson Agonistes* is a tragic poem modeled on the greatest classical examples as well as the critical precepts of Aristotle. As such, its central *anagnorisis* or moment of recognition defines, to a large extent, the structure of the entire poem. Dalila's identification with Jael and Samson's "rousing motions" are structurally parallel: both consist of moments of recognition followed by departures. What distinguishes the two recognitions is that Samson's recognition defines the overall structure of Milton's representation of the Judges narrative. Dalila's does not.[55]

Samson's "rousing motions" provide the structural hinge of a tragic poem. These motions signal Samson's return to the sphere of history from which he has been exiled and determine the outcome of the poem. Dalila's identification with Jael is lyrical: it is a rhapsodic flight that resides within a larger poem without really defining or determining its overall structure. Both recognitions are prophetic. Dalila predicts she will acquire the "marks of public honour"; Samson says, "This day shall be remarkable in my life," that is, re-*mark*-ed, re-written, re-interpreted, re-deemed. The sense of the "remarkable" becomes a nexus of literary form and the interpretation of history. The structure of the poem does subordinate Dalila's recognition to Samson's; this subordination does not, however, easily reassert the normative male history disrupted by extraordinary female treachery which Samson narrates in the middle episodes. The exploits Samson recounts are, for the most part, purposeless and disconnected. His impulsive actions and reckless license parody the discipline of liberty. Dalila's "honied words" become an iconoclastic attack on the confusion of license and liberty in Samson's thinking. As *Paradise Regained* demonstrates, authentically counterhistorical actions emerge from the consonance of human and divine wills. This concept of action is, when connected to Milton's ethic of patience, an aspect of genuine liberty.

Proverbs 8:30 says that God made the world by wisdom, and that wisdom played before the throne of God before the world was made: "I was daily his delight, rejoicing always before him." *Samson Agonistes* presents a demonic parody of the playfulness of wisdom when Samson is invited to play and sport before the Philistine lords in their temple. In the same manner, the soldiers who mock Christ during his passion enact a cruel sport in the presence of a royal figure. Both actions represent demonic analogies of divine creation since they transpire in the fallen world. At the same time, for both Samson in the temple and Christ in his passion, there is the sense in which submission to human authority coincides perfectly with obedience to the divine will. The authenticity of the "rousing motions" that direct Samson to the temple remains, of course, a contentious issue in Milton criticism. What is impressive about the climax of *Samson Agonistes*, however, is the manner in which outward circumstance, particularly in the summons of the Officer, and free, inward promptings, or the "rousing motions," converge into a unity of purpose and occasion. In spite of this, the condition of divisive uncertainty is maintained in the Messenger's description of Samson's final moment: "he stood, as one who pray'd / Or some great matter in his mind revolv'd." The emphasis on image or similitude in the observation rather than on the confirmation of Samson's inner condition, admittedly retains the minimal possibility of disjunction between Samson's will and God's. It is precisely in this respect that Dalila bears a fleeting resemblance to Samson, for while her comparison of herself to Jael is rejected out of hand by the reactionary Chorus, it persists as a tangible possibility from her perspective, as well, perhaps, as from the perspective of many readers. Dalila's comparison of herself to Jael is perhaps an important corollary of Samson's position at the climax: it is either an imposture or a possibility, two alternatives which the poem never entirely relinquishes.

The differences and similarities between Samson's actions and Dalila's, and the perspectives from which they are viewed and judged, are part of the debate on authority and liberty that is developed throughout the poem and that governs its climax. Part of this debate is conveyed in the symbol of the temple. The Temple of Dagon is a site of material display in the poem. The

Bible presents the temple as a symbol of the human form created in God's image in Christ's passion: "Destroy this temple,
and in three days I will raise it up" (John 2:19). The temple also
symbolizes wisdom in the seven-pillared temple of Proverbs
9:1–5. In the invocation to *Paradise Lost*, Milton invokes the
Spirit that prefers "Before all Temples th' upright heart and
pure" (1:18). He identifies temple ritual with inwardness, and
the conscientious expression of the Word of God. Throughout his
writings, Milton examines assaults upon this inner temple by
external forces of authority. In *Civil Power*, we recall, Milton
argues that God works only from within, drawing people "by the
inward perswasive motions of his spirit and by his ministers;
not by the outward compulsions of a magistrate or his officers
(*CM* 6:27). This is an important gloss on the "rousing motions"
Samson finds within himself. He is, Milton suggests, "persuaded
inwardly that this was from God" ("The Argument"). Dalila, in
contrast, is continually pressured by voices outside of her—"the
Priest / Was not behind, but ever at my ear" (857–58). She was
finally persuaded, she concedes, by

> that grounded maxim
> So rife and celebrated in the mouths
> Of wisest men, that to the public good
> Private respects must yield.
>
> (865–68)

Samson's moment of insight defines the overall structure of
the poem by providing its *perepeteia* or reversal as well as its
anagnorisis or recognition. As the passage from *Civil Power*
suggests, reversal in Milton invariably focuses on authority, including the kind of authority Dalila confronts. Reversal of authority in *Samson Agonistes* is signaled when Samson resumes
the discourse of wisdom and proceeds to instruct his elders. His
speech is suddenly rich in sayings and aphorisms: "Commands
are no constraints" (1372), "Masters' commands come with a
power resistless" (1404), "So mutable are all the ways of men"
(1407), "Lords are Lordliest in thir wine" (1418). This point of
reversal in *Samson Agonistes* offers the proverb as prophecy:
the formula of hindsight presents the prospect of a suddenly
open future; the enormous divisions between law and grace,
wisdom and prophecy, past and future, divisions which are, as

the Chorus observes "strain'd / Up to the height, whether to hold or break," are finally to be calmed and spent (1348–49).[56]

The scattering of aphorisms in Samson's final speeches offers perspective on the structure of biblical tragedy as Milton conceived it. Aphoristic discourse is, by nature, broken, disjoined, and divided. So too are the episodes of *Samson Agonistes* disjoined from the moment of reversal and recognition. Illumination need not be the predictable culmination of a causal sequence. As Achsah Guibbory has remarked, Milton's view of time emphasizes "newness" and the "break with the past."[57] Milton adapts the divisions or breaks in the narrative formula of Judges to his view of time: the phases of petition and deliverance are deferred to "the close." He also signals the break with the past in Samson's three refusals to attend the festival. The three refusals to attend the festival that precede the reversal are numerically significant. They establish a symmetry with Samson's three rejections of Dalila's entreaties prior to his downfall. In this respect the structure of the reversal symbolically undoes the damage of his downfall by seeking to affirm rather than compromise his relationship with God. Three is also the number of the middle episodes in the drama, which suggests that the reversal provides another illustration of Milton's treatment of time. Samuel Johnson insisted that nothing in the middle episodes hastens or delays the catastrophe.[58] By the same token, nothing in the three refusals anticipates or causes the final consent; like the structure of the entire poem, Samson's final consent breaks with the past and turns to the future. This reading would perhaps not satisfy Dr. Johnson or Aristotle; nevertheless, it demonstrates the way in which Milton amalgamates biblical narrative and tragic conventions in order to emphasize the need to break with the past.

The break with the past occurs on psychological, social, and political levels. It does not follow, however, that Milton recommends the violent narratives of the Book of Judges as models for outward action. His consideration of these narratives, as they are recounted in the middle episodes of his interpretation of Samson, is nearly exhaustive. The obsessive reiteration of these narratives in Samson's consciousness reinforces their tragically repetitive rather than transforming effect. At the same time, the sequential pattern of providential actions that the poem conveys in its overall structure, especially in the breaking with a tragic past and the linking of significant moments, corroborates von Rad's thesis concerning the distinctive historical consciousness of ancient Israel: "history can only exist as the times in which God performed his acts and gave his guidance."[59] The relationship between Samson's refusals and his consent, especially as it unfolds the canonical relationship between law and gospel, introduces a logic of hope which defeats a logic of despair in Milton's readers. The destruction of the Temple of Dagon attacks a political culture of material display with an intensity equal and opposite to the violent spectacles of punishment and retribution that accompanied the celebratory pomp of the Restoration. But the attack is poetic, and its intensity is a function of language, specifically the primacy of the biblical language Milton offers his readers as a medium of purposeful transformation. Therein lies the therapeutic effect of tragedy for Milton's post-Restoration readers.

By identifying recognition, or the passage from ignorance to knowledge, with wisdom, as the discernment of divine intent, Milton adapts the structure of the poem to his argument by indicating a central premise in his interpretation of the Judges narrative: providential history consists of those moments in which God acts. In terms of Milton's general thesis of "Christian liberty," the form of this history is only recognizable when license and presumption are distinguished from liberty and patience in the mind of the reader. The distinction is apparent in the motions of divine grace; the structure of *Samson Agonistes* gives priority to Samson's experience of these motions. If Milton presents the image of a "faithful champion," it is by means of a "faithful" interpretation of the Book of Judges. Such an interpretation retains the conflicts of the times it represents; above all, it maintains the different, contrasting perspectives it recreates. By considering the contrasting perspective Dalila presents when she compares herself to Jael and Deborah, Milton clearly recognizes the possibility of alternative perspectives even as he proceeds with his own. His complex portrait of Dalila thereby occupies a space between the contrary blasts of Restoration political discourse with its presumed typologies and its penchant for demonizing opponents. Hers is the voice of counterorder that persists as a condition of the scriptural society Milton imagines, and of his own counterhistorical voice.

4

"The Promis'd Kingdom": Wisdom and Revelation in *Paradise Regained*

> From the Scripture, I believed, and do believe Your Majesty
> to be that David which God promised to raise . . . Therefore I
> concluded that Your Majesty was not to come in and reign
> personally, until You came to the Age that David began to
> reign in, and that is 30.
>
> —Arise Evans,
> *To The Most High and Mighty Prince Charles the II*, (1660)

"THIS PRECEPT OF CHRIST": SCRIPTURE AND POLITICAL THEORY

IN HIS REJECTION OF SATAN'S PRESENTATION OF ATHENIAN WISDOM IN
Paradise Regained, Jesus declares the supremacy of the Bible as
political theory. In scripture, he asserts:

> is plainest taught, and easiest learnt,
> What makes a Nation happy, and keeps it so,
> What ruins Kingdoms, and lays Cities flat;
> These only, with our Law, best form a King.
>
> (4: 361–64)

This claim might have seemed a commonplace in the biblical
culture of seventeenth-century England. If so, it was a commonplace for people who radically disagreed and even fought vio-
lently over its implications. Opponents and supporters of the
Restoration found the Bible equally congenial and supportive.
Christopher Hill remarks that the Bible was not the equivalent
of a revolutionary manifesto comparable to the manifestos of
later European revolutions in part because opposed parties and

separate sects found constant support in it.[1] Milton's prose writings do use biblical precepts to advance specific political options; *The Readie and Easie Way*, for example, is built around Matthew 20:25–26: "Ye know that the princes of the Gentiles exercise dominion over them, and they that are great exercise authority upon them. But it shall not be so among you: but whosoever will be great among you, let him be your minister." This precept functions in an argument that Royalist—and equally biblical—discourse would find abhorrent.

The Jesus of *Paradise Regained* makes claims for scripture that are focused, radical, and even original. For there is a difference between using the Bible to register contrary allegiances and mutual contempt on the one hand and using it to offer coherent political theories and imagine political emancipation on the other. Although *Paradise Regained* is a poem and not a political treatise, the claims it makes for scripture reiterate Milton's response to the Restoration. The Restoration clearly tested Milton's confidence in the social dynamic he envisioned in 1644: the general conflict of voices idealized in *Areopagitica* had not effected the progressive emancipation promised at the core of Milton's understanding of the Bible. In *The Readie and Easie Way* he writes of the people as "an inconsiderate multitude " who are "madd upon" the return of monarchy (*CM* 6:134). In *Paradise Regained*, Jesus characterizes the people as

> a herd confus'd,
> A miscellaneous rabble, who extol
> Things vulgar, and well weigh'd scarce worth the praise.
> (3:49–51)

In *A Holy Commonwealth,* published in 1659, and having the distinction of being burned by the Oxford University Convocation along with Milton's writings in 1683, Richard Baxter placed no confidence in the ability of the "people" to share in sovereignty: "Multitudes in England, and more in Wales, Cornwall, Ireland, the Highlands, are scarce able to talk reason about common things! And are these fit to have the Sovereign Power to Rule the Commonwealth?"[2] Although Milton may have shared Baxter's harsh view of the larger "Multitudes," his Jesus directs his disgust more toward Satan as the author of images that confuse and enthrall the people. Taken in context, Jesus' apparent scorn for the people responds to Satan's invitation to establish himself as a political idol in the line of Alexander the Great, Cyrus, Scipio, Pompey, and Julius Caesar "whom now all the world admires" (3:39). Satan invites Jesus to become an idol of divine majesty; political idolatry, Jesus replies, confuses and degrades a nation. The ideals of *Areopagitica*, with its vision of an empowered reading public, are not entirely forsaken in Jesus' harsh characterization of the people in *Paradise Regained*: the poem itself enacts a war of truth and reading between Jesus and Satan, and reaffirms this activity as the fit alternative to the political stagnation of idolatry which, in seeking to assimilate the messiah in a line of military and political idols, mirrors the nation as a "muddy pool of conformity."

The Readie and Easie Way, in contrast, is limited as political theory: it laments the haste in which it is conceived and revised, and is pessimistic in its expectations for forestalling the Restoration. If the treatise is tentative as political theory, it is more confident as social typology: it conceives of its rulers as formed by the same spirit that writes scripture inwardly: "the pattern of the Kingdom's laws, both spiritual and natural, is being cleared in the hearts of believers by the Spirit, and it is their duty to strive for a commonwealth modelled, though imperfectly, on it."[3] The alternative to such striving is the conformity of monarchy; to conform for Milton is to succumb to temptation.

The Readie and Easie Way develops the concept of political temptation that functions in *Paradise Regained*. The aphoristic key to the entire treatise is the "precept of Christ" to the sons of Zebedee: "Ye know that the princes of the Gentiles exercise dominion over them, and they that are great exercise authority upon them. But it shall not be so among you: but whosoever will be great among you, let him be your minister" (Matt. 20:25–26). The treatise in turn links this precept to the Israelites' plea for a king in 1 Samuel 8, a passage used as a touchstone by Milton and by Thomas Hobbes and James Harrington. Taken together, the two biblical passages present a pattern of political conformity. Throughout *Paradise Regained*, temptation consists in the offer to conform to worldly models of power and to substitute Satan's worldly wisdom for scripture. *The Readie and Easie Way* predicates political wisdom on scriptural precepts, refusing to replace their priority in conscience with the external authority of an idol. Whatever the limitations of the treatise, it is the crucible from which *Paradise Regained* would emerge. The poem presents an elementary configuration of the solitary, dissenting hero confronting an enthralled and enthralling world; the figure reinstates Milton's confidence in the English people to become their own wise counselors, and in the potential of scripture to be a manifesto of liberty.

Scripture remained, however, amenable to contending perspectives. Royalists embraced scripture as the formative principle in the making of a good prince. In Milton's view, it was perhaps easier for people to project their own potential onto a monarchical idol than to develop their own potential. Freedom is always the harder discipline in Milton's argument. With this in mind, Milton concerns *Paradise Regained* with the tradition of the education of a prince, the subject of many books of conduct and courtesy, in order to set his prince apart from that tradition. Milton's Jesus envisions an endless kingdom that is neither otherworldly nor of this world; instead, it opposes the formative myths that confuse spiritual and earthly kingdoms and neutralize the conflict of spiritual and material vision.

That scripture should have a central role in political education was readily acknowledged from all perspectives. As early as 1515, Erasmus had emphasized the example of Solomon and made biblical wisdom the first prescribed reading for a young prince: "But if any should desire to make use of my plan, as soon as the elements of language have been taught, he should set forth the Proverbs of Solomon, Ecclesiasticus, and the Book of Wisdom, not with the idea that the boy may be tormented with the four senses (sensus) of the theologian by a vaunting interpreter, but that he may fitly show in a few words whatever pertains to the functions of a good prince."[4] Solomon's wisdom is identified as the primary text for the "art of ruling": "You are the son of a king, yourself a future king you will hear what the wisest king of all teaches his own son, whom he is preparing to be his successor. Later take the Gospels."[5] After scripture, Erasmus recommends the *Apothegmata* of Plutarch, Aristotle's *Politics*, and selections from Seneca, Cicero, and Plato. The entire curriculum is predicated on the Bible. The Bible is therefore an education in reading. Erasmus directs the prince from what Milton's Jesus calls the "luggage of war" to the arts of peace; hence, the prince should reflect critically on the treatment of war in the Old Testament and not emulate it thoughtlessly or literally: "Let him learn that the battles and the butcheries of the Hebrews, and their barbarity toward their enemies, are to be interpreted allegorically; otherwise it would be most disastrous to read them."[6] In a comparable manner, Jesus consistently confounds Satan's temptations in *Paradise Regained* by elevating Satan's offer of a literal imitation of military action into a metaphor for spiritual conflict.

In the *Basilikon Doron*, James I follows Erasmus by counseling his son Henry, Prince of Wales, to follow the way of wisdom: "remember also, that by the right knowledge and feare of God (which is the beginning of wisedome, as Salomon saith) ye shall know all the things necessarie for the discharge of your duetie, both as a Christian, and as a King; seeing in him, as in a mirrour, the course of all earthly things, whereof hee is the spring and onely moover."[7] The *Eikon Basilike* perpetuates this paternal model by addressing its penultimate chapter to the Prince of Wales, who would become Charles II.[8] In a speech given to the Star Chamber, James invoked the models of biblical wisdom: "And therefore all good Kings in their government, must imitate God and his Christ, in being just and righteous; David and Salomon, in being godly and wise: To be wise, is understood, able to discerne, able to judge others. . . ."[9] Impelled in part by his role as head of the church, James integrates his authority with biblical types:

> Give thy judgements to the king, O God, and Thy righteousness to the Kings Sonne. These be the first words of one of the Psalmes of the Kingly Prophet David, whereof the literall sense runnes upon him, and his sonne Salomon, and the mysticall sense upon God and Christ his eternall Sonne: but *they are both so woven together*, as some parts are, and can onely bee properly applied unto God and Christ, and other parts unto David and Salomon, as this verse, Give thy Judgments to the King, O God, and thy Righteousnesse to the Kings Sonne, cannot be properly spoken of any, but of David and his sonne; . . . both senses, as well literall as mysticall, serve to Kings for imitation, and especially to Christian Kings: for Kings sit in the Throne of God, and they themselves are called Gods.[10]

The interweaving of the biblical types and attributes of kingship lays claim to divine authority: "Kings are properly Judges, and Judgment properly belongs to them from God: for Kings sit in the throne of God, and thence all Judgment is derived. . . . As kings borrow their power from God, so judges from Kings: And as Kings are to accompt to God, so judges unto God and Kings; and both Kings and judges by imitation, have two qualities from God and his Christ, and two qualities from David and his Salomon: Judgment and Righteousnesse, from God and Christ: Godlinesse and Wisedome from David and Salomon. . . ."[11]

In the 1650s we find authors, including Milton, translating, editing, and publishing the maxims of political advice of earlier authors. The *Basilikon Doron* is one example. Henry Delaune converted the treatise into verse quatrains and published it under the title *Patrikon Doron or A Legacy to His Sons, Being a Miscellany of Precepts; Theological, Moral, Political, Oeconomical, Digested Into Seven Centuries of Quadrins*. The second edition appeared in 1657, perhaps striking a chord with the Royalist cause at that time. In 1659, William Prynne published *Thomas Campanella, an Italian Friar and Second Machiavel, His Advice to the King of Spain for Attaining the Universal Monarchy of the World*. The tract was a reissue of Edward Chilmead's *A Discourse Touching the Spanish Monarchy*, a translation of Campanella published in 1654 just prior to Chilmead's death. The purpose of Prynne's volume is cautionary: Campanella viewed sectarianism within national borders as a prelude to the advent of a universal Catholic theocracy. The tract begins with an "Admonitorie Preface" by William Prynne, the prolific pamphleteer who had lost his ears for offending the queen years earlier, but was now, in 1659, a strong advocate of the Restoration. In treating Campanella as a cautionary example, Prynne warns that discord within the English body politic would only play into the hands of other European powers. England had already incurred "that fatal doom which Christ himself hath predicted to every Kingdome and City in our present condition, Mat. 12.25. every Kingdome divided against it self, is brought to desolation, and every City or House divided against itself shall not stand. Which Campanella laying for his ground, made it his master-piece to set down stratagems to divide us and other Kingdoms and Nations against and between themselves . . . so the Spaniard and Pope might without much difficulty seise upon them while in that condition, which imminent danger and approaching ruine, we have no probable means left to prevent, but by a speedy cordial Christian union between our lawful King long exiled Head and members."[12] Christ's cautionary precept is placed in the balance against Campanella's utopian prophecies.

Milton's publication of the *Cabinet Council* in 1658 takes these republications as part of its context and political timing. In the preface he nonchalantly remarks that the manuscript was given to him by a friend and rediscovered by chance amongst some of his old papers. He therefore resolved to publish it. These remarks suggest that the republication was politically innocuous, but it is more likely that Milton sensed an occasion. This was the year of Cromwell's death, and a political crisis was approaching. The treatise is not Milton's answer to this crisis; that answer was the *Readie and Easie Way*. The book is, however, both in timing and genre, part of a wider discourse of advice on the "Art of Empire, and Mysteries of State" at a crucial historic moment. The treatise begins with conventional distinctions between monarchy and tyranny, and includes certain Machiavellian ideas: "The Art Military is of all other qualities most necessary for Princes"; "The Last, yet not the least of power, consisteth in Fortune; whereof daily experience may be seen; for the success of all humane actions seems rather to proceed from fortune than vertue."[13] As the treatise unfolds, however, elements that would occupy Milton in *Paradise Regained* emerge. There is, for example, a strong emphasis on providence as a mitigating force against human guile. The best defense against treason, Raleigh suggests, is "destiny, which may truly be called the will of God; in whose only power it resteth to protect and defend good princes."[14]

Destiny is a term in Raleigh's consideration of the causes of civil war, a topic Milton was surely conscious of as he looked back to the wars of the 1640s and forward to the world of Restoration. A key cause of civil war, Raleigh thought, is "excesse, riot, and dissolute life; for nothing breedeth Civil Fury so soon as over great happiness; also pompous apparell, banquetting and prodigall spending consumeth riches, and plenty is turned into poverty; for by these means are men brought into desperation."[15] The passage both recalls and anticipates court luxury and extravagance under monarchy; Milton recreates Raleigh's precept in the image of the king as a "demi-god" with a luxuriant entourage in *The Readie and Easie Way*. It also anticipates Satan's appearance as a youthful courtier in the second temptation in *Paradise Regained*. Raleigh calls sedition a cause of civil war, but sedition is sometimes a reaction to oppression, fear, or poverty.[16] Above all, "sedition cometh of tyranny, insolency, or mutinous disposition of certain captains, Cavaliers, or Ringleaders of the people."[17] Tyranny, in consequence, is a "certain violent Government, exceeding the Laws of God and nature. The difference between Kings and Tyrants is this; the one employeth arms in defence of Peace, the other useth them to terrifie those of whom his cruelty hath deserved hate."[18] These maxims recall some of the rhetoric leading to the trial of Charles I, whose adversaries called him a "man of blood" and a maker of war upon his own people. Raleigh's reflections on the fate of tyrants allowed Milton to remind the English people of the tyranny of monarchy, and to warn them against any relapse. Tyrants "for the most part are deposed or slain; for as Kings live long and deliver their Dominions to their children, and Posterity: so Tyrants being hated and feared of all men, cannot continue in their estate."[19] The Satan of *Paradise Regained* fulfills some of the roles identified in the *Cabinet Council*, even when these roles are incompatible. He is a would-be counselor to a new king, an archetypal tyrant of existing earthly kingdoms, and an agent of political and religious persecution. Raleigh poignantly recommends the central tenet of Miltonic heroism as the remedy for tyranny: "To conclude, we may say that the best remedy against Tyranny, is Patience."[20]

Raleigh is careful to distinguish a good king from a tyrant. Milton would agree that the distinction is legitimate. Milton's point, however, is that the distinction is not within the control of the English people. Whether a monarch is good or not is entirely a matter of chance, and requires submission rather than choice on the part of subjects. These conditions become the central argument of *The Readie and Easie Way*, published in a second, revised edition in April, 1660. Its central point of political theory is Matthew 20:25–26, that "precept of Christ." This precept is framed, however, by Milton's reading of 1 Samuel 8, in which Samuel warns Israel of the "manner of the king that shall reign over them" (1 Sam. 8:8). Displeased that the Israelites have asked for "a king to judge us like all the nations" (1 Sam. 8:5), Samuel warns that a king will take their lands and children for his own purposes:

And ye shall cry out in that day because of your king which ye shall have chosen you; and the Lord will not hear you in that day. Nevertheless the people refused to obey the voice of Samuel; and they said, Nay; but we will have a king over us; That we also may be like all the nations; and that our king may judge us, and go out before us, and fight our battles. And Samuel heard all the words of the people, and he rehearsed them in the ears of the Lord. And the Lord said to Samuel, Hearken unto their voice, and make them a king. (1 Sam. 8:18–22).

Milton's antimonarchical reading of this passage was unequivocal; predictably, the passage generated readings equally congenial to monarchy. King James, not surprisingly, offers one such reading. In *The Trew Law of Free Monarchy*, James addresses this text in support of monarchy. "First," James argues, "God commandeth Samuel to doe two things: the one, to grant the people their suit in giving them a king; the other, to forewarne them, what some kings will doe unto them, that they may not thereafter in their grudging and murmuring say, when they shal feele the snares here forespoken; We would never have had a king of God, in case when we craved him, hee had let us know how we would have been used by him, as now we find but overlate. . . ."[21] Samuel holds the people to their word rather than the king who remains, in James' view, above the law. James denies that a binding contract is formed between a king and the people at a coronation, but prudently suggests that kings could act as if there were: "Not that I deny the old definition of a King, and of a law; which makes the king to bee a speaking law, and the Law a dumbe king. . . . For albeit trew that I have at length prooved, that the King is above the law, as both the author and giver of strength thereto; yet a good king will not onely delight to rule his subjects by the lawe, but even will conforme himselfe in his owne actions thereunto. . . ."[22] "As to this contract alledged made at the coronation of a King, although I deny any such contract to bee made then, especially containing such a clause irritant as they alledge; yet I confesse, that a king at his coronation, or at the entry to his kingdome, willingly promiseth to his people, to discharge honorably and trewly the office given him by God over them. . . ."[23] Here James reaches a central question of seventeenth-century political theory, without imagining that the hypothetical situations he considers, including rebellions and trials, would overtake and destroy his heir.

England's trauma from the civil wars to the Restoration and beyond make stability a priority in political theory. Biblical texts such as 1 Samuel 8 inevitably occur in the work of theorists who explore the relationship between divine sovereignty, ecclesiastical responsibility, and scriptural authority in a pervasively biblical culture. Hobbes's solution offered a theory of voluntary obedience, whereby the political subject transfers his political will to the lawful sovereign in the interests of political stability. Hobbes's scriptural reflections on sovereignty and authority appear in the context of a "particular consideration of the Kingdome of God"[24] and also of its opposite, the "Kingdome of Darknesse," two considerations that comprise the final phase of *Leviathan*. Hobbes recognizes God as the original sovereign of ancient Israel. He is "King of all the Earth by his Power: but of his chosen people, he is King by Covenant."[25] Specific figures in the history of God's chosen people experience his sovereignty by direct command, beginning with Adam: "From the very Creation, God not only reigned over all men *naturally* by his might; but also had *peculiar* Subjects, whom he commanded by a Voice, as one man speaketh to another. In which manner he *reigned* over Adam, and gave him commandement to abstaine from the tree of cognizance of Good and Evill."[26]

The presence of God's voice as a medium of authority plays a crucial role in Hobbes's use of scripture. Adam, Abraham, and Moses have a unique prophetic authority from God as mediators and interpreters of his word. No other person in the societies they governed possessed this authority: "they to whom God hath not spoken immediately, are to receive the positive commandements of God, from their Soveraign; as the family and seed of Abraham did from Abraham their Father, and Lord, and Civill Soveraign. And consequently in every Common-wealth, they who have no supernaturall Revelation to the contrary, ought to obey the laws of their own Soveraign, in the externall acts and profession of Religion."[27] Hobbes's argument does not inculcate a form of thought control: "inward thought" does not "fall under obligation."[28] The subjection of the will, however, is crucial to the political stability gained through obedience: "by the Captivity of our Understanding, is not meant a Submission of the Intellectual faculty, to the Opinion of any other man, but of the Will to Obedience, where obedience is due."[29] Hobbes is concerned to neutralize individual claims to divine authority through the private interpretation of scripture, or through the fallible experience of dreams and visions: "God almighty can speak to a man, by Dreams, Visions, Voice, and Inspiration; yet he obliges no man to beleeve he hath so done to him that pretends it; who (being a man) may erre, and (which is more) may lie."[30] Hobbes responds to the apparent social disintegration that occasioned *Areopagitica*, but where Milton imagines that all the Lord's people might become prophets, Hobbes insists that only the lawful sovereign can make prophecy into policy.

For Hobbes, the "Civill Soveraign is the Supreme Pastor, to whose charge the whole flock of his Subjects is committed, and consequently that it is by his authority, that all other Pastors are made."[31] This complete investment of civil and ecclesiastical authority in the sovereign is a version of Erastianism, or the primacy of state authority, in this case the monarch, over the church. The sovereign of *Leviathan* delegates ecclesiastical power to the clergy. The clergy maintains this power *jure civilli* and not, like the sovereign, *jure divino*. Among other ecclesiastical prerogatives, the civil sovereign is the supreme interpreter of scripture for his subjects. While this prerogative suggests a divine authority comparable to that of Adam, Abraham, or Moses, it is so only by analogy and not as fact. Hobbes's sovereign is not a divine oracle but a power to whom the people voluntarily transfer their obedience. Hobbes's suspicion of direct divine authority extends even to the sovereign. If the people submit to the authority of the supreme interpreter, they do so rationally and willfully, and not in a state of religious delusion induced by political mystique.

Richard Tuck has argued that Hobbes's Erastian views promote religious toleration. This promotion occurs because the sovereign maintains at most a "minimal Christianity," consisting of the central doctrine that Jesus is the Christ.[32] The sovereign need not impose upon subjects in every nuance of theology. Thus, it follows "that the sovereign would have no right to impose doctrines on its citizens unless he sincerely believed that doing so would preserve them; and, Hobbes implied, it was extremely unlikely that such circumstances would arise."[33] Doctrinal minimalism may limit the occasions upon which the imposition of sovereign authority is necessary. For Milton, however, the measure of liberty consists less in occasions than in conditions. Liberty does not exist under conditions that can negate it even if the occasion to demonstrate this fact never arose. If the sovereign holds the power of supreme interpreter then the people are not free, even if the sovereign never exercised his interpretive supremacy. Milton's hostility to Erastian arguments is forcefully articulated in *Civil Power*, where he argues against the imposition of any state prerogative in matters of religion.

A central aspect of Milton's opposition to Hobbes consists in their differing definitions of the kingdom of God, and in the differing historical continuums in which they locate that kingdom. The kingdom of God for Hobbes is emphatically real and literal, never figurative or metaphorical: "The Kingdome therefore of God, is a reall, not a metaphoricall Kingdome; and so taken, not onely in the Old Testament, but the New; when we say, *For thine is the Kingdome, the Power, and Glory,* it is to be understood of God's Kingdome, by force of our Covenant, not by the Right of Gods Power; for such a kingdome God alwaies hath; so that it were superfluous to say in our prayer, *Thy Kingdom come,* unlesse it be meant of the Restauration of that Kingdome of God by Christ."[34] The kingdom can only be restored at the end of time through Christ's real and literal second coming; it is an error, Hobbes argues, to see the kingdom as beginning with Christ's historic resurrection: "if the Kingdome of God began . . . at the Resurrection; what reason is there for Christians ever since the Resurrection to say in their prayers, *Let Thy Kingdome Come?*"[35] The reiteration of a literal reading of the Lord's Prayer is further evidence of Hobbes's association of metaphorical reading with false prophetic authority. As Victoria Kahn observes, because Hobbes "associated spiritual covenants with the false prophet's metaphorical interpretation of Scripture, he prosecuted his argument in large measure through an ostentatiously literal-minded interpretation of biblical texts."[36] 1 Samuel 8 therefore plays into Hobbes's hands by positing a historic termination of the direct sovereignty of God. The kingdom of God "by revolt of the Israelites had been interrupted in the election of Saul."[37] Prior to this revolt, "it is evident, that God himself was then their King."[38] The succession of rulers from this event until the end of time is amenable to Hobbes's theory of civil sovereignty.

A further implication of Hobbes's consistent literalism occurs in the dimension of history. If the kingdom is literal, and if it can only appear at Christ's second coming, then no manifestation of the kingdom is possible in the continuum of history until that event. Hobbes's eschatology effectively empties history of significance. As Pocock suggests, Hobbes abandons "diachronic for philosophical thinking" in order to "erect a system of authority on rational certainty."[39] The suppression of sectarian enthusiasm and false claims to authority comes at the cost of meaningful development in the sphere of history. Political stability is synchronic and spatialized, not diachronic and progressive. Milton counters this kind of thinking in *The Readie and Easie Way* by radically situating England in the context of a prophetic Jeremiad that laments the nation's determined backsliding. More broadly, *Civil Power* extends *Areopagitica* by arguing that the most basic ideals of the Reformation, including the relationship between scripture, reading, and individual conscience, are dynamic forces in contemporary history and in the public sphere.

The sites of Jesus' resistance to Satan in *Paradise Regained* delineate a clear opposition to Hobbes's theories, bearing out David Quint's remark that " 'Hobbes' could be the name for that which all the various political strategies of *Paradise Regained* converge to resist."[40] As many critics have observed, Jesus consistently recovers a metaphorical reading of scripture from Satan's persistent literalism, beginning with his designation of bread as the word of God rather than the lifeless object Satan holds before him. Jesus will not turn stones into bread, but he proclaims the kingdom as a metaphoric "stone that shall to pieces dash / All Monarchies besides throughout the world" (4:149–50). The kingdom is also a metaphoric tree "Spreading and overshadowing all the Earth" in its subversive, irrepressible growth (4:148). While these metaphors appear at first to defer the kingdom to the future in a manner that might suit Hobbes, their power and potential always reside in the present moment. *Paradise Regained* is thus a poem with an intense sense of history as Jesus emerges in the charged climate of *kairos,* or significant time, proclaiming, not the Hobbesian vacancy of history, but the temporal identity of a present kingdom as it is actualized in the small, dialogic, scriptural societies and communities that preserve its potential.

Like Hobbes, James Harrington's political theories respond to perceived political disorder. His republican theories are not

formed from an antimonarchist position. He had, in fact, served
Charles I, and his theories transmute his anguish at the king's
death. As Pocock points out, "there is a sense in which the fall of
monarchy made men republicans, rather than ideological republicanism acting as a cause of its fall."[41] If Hobbes abandons diachronic historical thinking for the stability of a synchronized
contractual obedience, Harrington gives a stable and synchronized model republic a noticeable millenarian resonance. 1
Samuel 8:8 remains a place at which Israel deposed God as its
"civil magistrate."[42] The kingdom of God can be recovered, however, when the natural wisdom of prudence and reason, even
from nonscriptural sources, is harmonized with the precepts of
scripture: "we may observe a little farther how the heathen
politicians have written, not only out of nature, but as it were
out of Scripture: as in the commonwealth of Israel, God is said to
have been king, so the commonwealth where law is king is said
by Aristotle to be the kingdom of God. And where, by the lusts or
passions of men, a power is set above that of the law, deriving
from reason which is the dictate of God, God in that sense is rejected or deposed that he should not reign over them, as he was
in Israel."[43] A commonwealth ruled by a rotating body of wise
rulers exercising virtues that manifest the divine image might
achieve a self-replicating stability, if not immortality. As Pocock
observes, the "reign of an immortal republic might come closer
to being itself a millennial kingdom than the civil authority of a
mortal god ever could. In Harrington's political universe men
might become as gods; in Hobbes's never, unless by person-
ation."[44] Harrington strikes a clear millenarian chord that
Hobbes would disavow: "Now if you add unto the propagation of
civil liberty, what is so natural unto this commonwealth that it
cannot be omitted, the propagation of liberty of conscience, this
empire, this patronage of the world, is the kingdom of Christ.
For as the kingdom of God the Father was a commonwealth, so
shall be the kingdom of God the Son; *the people shall be willing
in the day of his power.*"[45]

Milton preferred a permanent rather than rotating body of
wise leaders as being more detached from the wheel of fortune.
And he would dissent from Harrington's call for an endowed ministry through tithing that would align the national church with
the national conscience. Milton and Harrington are, however,
united more by their common adversaries than their theoretical

differences. Milton's *The Readie and Easie Way* is not the massive volume of political theory produced by Hobbes or Harrington. It has, however, a profound sense of an immediate historical moment, and a determination to respond to that moment in a prophetic voice that uses scriptural metaphor as its vehicle. The tract seeks to sustain the "children of reviving libertie" as a potential community after the failure of all systems, theoretical and actual. What *Paradise Regained* takes from *The Readie and Easie Way*, in order to envision as a poem what the treatise could provoke the English people to fulfill, is at the core of my argument: the text is the poetic type, not the systemic theory, of the holy community, and its typological counterpart is in every reader's mind.

The embattled immediacy of the treatise serves, however, as the crucible of the later poem. Beneath its hurried and untenable political theorizing lie deep reflections on the nature of conformity and resistance, temptation and self-realization, that could be meditated at length in *Paradise Regained*. Milton's awareness of Hobbes, Harrington, and other voices impelling him to predicate political theory on the basis of scripture is discernible in *The Readie and Easie Way*. Like Jesus in the desert, Milton confronted ideas "instilld of late by som deceivers, and nourishd from bad principles and fals apprehensions among too many of the people" (*CM* 6:111), and heard the "insultings of our newly animated common enemies crept lately our of thir holes, thir hell, I might say, by the language of thir infernal pamphlets, the spue of every drunkard, every ribald" (*CM* 6:139). One such prominent deceiver was Matthew Wren, whose *Monarchy Asserted* (1659) made a sustained attack on Harrington's *Oceana* without any recourse to scriptural arguments. Wren cites proverbs to validate monarchy and to make Harrington eccentric: "For though God has declared universally That by Him Kings reign, yet in reference to the People of Israel He was pleased to own a more particular Concernment, and did by an express Declaration of his Will to and by Moses, both at first enact their Lawes and Modell their Government, and reserve to himself the Result of their most Important Affaires."[46] He refuses scriptural arguments lest error escalate into impiety, reserving, in a move that perhaps suggests Hobbes's view of authority, scriptural interpretation for the clergy.[47]

Harrington and Milton found a second, common enemy in "G.S.," who rehearsed divine-right theory to please Charles II. Addressing Milton directly, he asserts: "It is a poor Sophisme that you use, Sir, that God gave Israel a King in wrath, and imputed it a sin to them that they asked one, if it be certain, that God had before blessed Abraham with the promise of Kings to come out of his loyns, and the Government of the seed of Jacob, was to be by a Scepter, and this to spring out of Judah, and the King of Kings (God for ever blessed) was to be cloathed with humane flesh, from one that lineally descended of King David, and his Grandfathers to be a continual succession of Kings."[48] Israel's fault is not in asking for a monarch, but in asking to be like other nations, and for failing to affirm the sovereignty of God. Christ springs from the "Kingly stock of the house of Judah, Two of whom, David and Salomon, were immediate Types of him, and Prophets divinely inspired. Certainly, Mr. Milton, this will argue something for Kingship, or Kingly Government."[49] George Starkey, though not equal to Harrington or Milton in argument, later enjoyed ridiculing Harrington's *Commonwealth of Oceana* and other republican proposals while viewing the pageant of Charles's entry into London:

> What newes from th' *Ocean,* I fain would know?
> How doth the *Rota* turn? my pretty Boyes,
> What hopes *Republicans* in such a show?
> Certainly these are *Babylonish* toyes.[50]

Milton's treatment of Harrington is respectful but divergent in places that show the common goal of political theorists either to protect or deliver England from the vagaries of Fortune's wheel. It is the visionary patience of Jesus in *Paradise Regained* that best demonstrates the emancipation from Fortune's wheel, but the appeal for emancipation comes first in *The Readie and Easie Way*. Milton addresses the tract to a people poised to "fall back or rather to creep back so poorly as it seems the multitude would to thir once abjur'd and detested thraldom of Kingship, to be our selves the slanderers of our own just and religious deeds" (*CM* 6:117). Milton uses the gospel metaphor of the tower builder (Luke 14:28–30) to characterize the state of the nation:

And what will they at best say of us and of the whole *English* name, but scoffingly as of that foolish builder, mentiond by our

Saviour, who began to build a tower, and was not able to finish it. Where is this goodly tower of a Commonwealth, which the English boasted they would build to overshaddow kings, and be another *Rome* in the west? The foundation indeed they laid gallantly; but fell into wors confusion, not of tongues, but of factions, then those at the tower of *Babel;* and have left no memorial of thir work behinde them remaining, but in the common laughter of *Europ.* (*CM* 6:117–18)

Milton grounds the precedence of commonwealth over monarchy in the words of Christ with a partial reference to 1 Samuel 8. A free commonwealth is

planely commended, or rather enjoind by our Saviour himself, to all Christians, not without remarkable disallowance, and the brand of *gentilism* upon kingship. God in much displeasure gave a king to the *Israelites,* and imputed it a sin to them that they sought one: but *Christ* apparently forbids his disciples to admitt of any such heathenish government: *the kings of the gentiles,* saith he, exercise lordship over them; and they that *exercise authoritie upon them, are call'd benefactors: but ye shall not be so; but he that is greatest among you, let him be as the younger; and he that is chief, as he that serveth.* (*CM* 6:119)

Christ speaks in reproof of Zebedee's sons, who asked to be exalted in the kingdom of heaven. But the reproof extends to the whole of civil government, with a free commonwealth coming nearest to Christ's precept. The leaders of a commonwealth are also its servants: they are not "elevated above their brethren" and "walk the streets as other men" (*CM* 6:120). A king, in contrast, violates Christ's precept: he must "be ador'd like a Demigod, with a dissolute and haughtie court about him" (*CM* 6:120). He sets "a pompous face upon the superficial actings of State, to pageant himself up and down in progress among the perpetual bowings and cringings of an abject people, on either side deifying and adoring him for nothing don that can deserve it" (*CM* 6:121). Milton turns to Proverbs for further admonition: "we need depend on none but God and our own counsels, our own active vertue and industrie; *Go to the Ant, thou sluggard,* saith Solomon; *consider her waies, and be wise; which having no prince, ruler, or lord, provides her meat in the summer, and gathers her food in the harvest.* Which evidently shews us, that they who think the nation undon without a king, though they look grave or haughtie, have not so much true spirit and understanding in them as a pismire" (*CM* 6:122).

Milton implicitly follows the argument of 1 Samuel 8 by citing monarchy as an abdication of the liberties and responsibilities that would be more diligently exercised in a commonwealth. He presents a terrible image of the groveling thralldom enjoined in Hobbes's argument of conscientious subjection while scorning the blasphemous pageantry that affects Godhead entailed in divine-right theory. Above all, he warns that monarchy is a derivative and imitative condition: "the kingdom of Christ our common King and Lord, is hid to this world, and such gentilish imitation forbid in express words by himself to all his disciples" (*CM* 6:124). "Gentilizing" becomes a term denoting the imitative impulses of the Israelites and the English; it manifests a lack of faith, an unwillingness to heed the scriptures, and a condition of apostasy.

> This is not my conjecture, but drawn from God's known denouncement against the gentilizing *Israelites;* who though they were governd in a Commonwealth of God's own ordaining, he only thir king, they his peculiar people, yet affecting rather to resemble heathen, but pretending the misgovernment of *Samuel's* sons, no more a reason to dislike thir Commonwealth, then the violence of Eli's sons was imputable to that priesthood or religion, clamourd for a king. They had thir longing; but with this testimonie of God's wrath; *ye shall cry out in that day because of your king whom ye shall have chosen, and the Lord will not hear you in that day.* (*CM* 6:137–38)

Milton agrees with Harrington's proposal for a governing council of wise rulers in place of a monarch, but recommends that rotation be avoided "as having too much affinitie with the wheel of fortune" (*CM* 6:127–28). His central political foundation, however, remains the text of scripture as it is internalized in each reader's conscience, diverging from Harrington's postulate that a "national religion," endowed by tithing in a manner Milton could not accept, would amount to a "national conscience." Milton reiterates the core ideas of *Civil Power* on this point: "That this is best pleasing to God, and that the whole Protestant Church allows no supream judge or rule in maters of religion, but the scriptures, and these to be interpreted by the scriptures themselves, which necessarily inferrs liberty of conscience"

(*CM* 6:141–42). And liberty of individual conscience, rather than the synchronization of Harrington's national and religious consciences, is most assured in a free commonwealth.

"Studious Musing": The Further Education of a King

The common ground between *The Readie and Easie Way* and *Paradise Regained* concerns the position of scripture in political theory. This position can be identified in the following ways. First, scripture for Milton is the central text upon which political theory is based. Models and authorities from secular and classical authorities can be incorporated around the central text, but the precepts of Christ on servanthood and the view of Israel's desire for a king in 1 Samuel remain central. This is crucial to Milton's idea of temptation: First, Satan is determined to replace, not supplement, the Bible with nonbiblical texts and precepts. Second, as we will discover in Jesus' response to the Athenian temptation, scripture is designated as the inspired original of "what makes a Nation happy," while other models are perceived as derivative, imitative, or "gentilish." Imitation is another aspect of Milton's concept of temptation: Satan exhorts Jesus to imitate or conform to, not criticize or subvert, the worldly or nonbiblical models of citizenship, conduct, and political wisdom. Third, Jesus' posture of detached but perceptive criticism exemplifies the ideal shared by political theorists of emancipating the subject and the nation from fortune's wheel. Satan seeks to assimilate Jesus' messianic energy and vision into worldly models of power, and to attach his mission to fortune's wheel. Finally, in addressing the covenant between Israel and God as a basis for alternative forms of scripturally-authorized government, Milton dramatizes, not the systemic model that exercised Harrington, but the internalization of law and all other scriptural texts by the individual conscience in the act of reading and interpreting. The internalization of the law is wisdom. Wisdom in turn provides the basis for new and alternative communities based on reading. These communities are illustrated in the relationship between Jesus and Mary.

Wisdom as the internalization of scripture is apparent in the incorporation of distinct phases of biblical revelation in specific episodes in the poem. As an epic poem, *Paradise Regained* seeks the same encyclopedic range as *Paradise Lost*, even if this range is limited in the shorter, brief epic. Political theory is a crucial component of this range because Jesus must redefine the office of king. The poem explores the forms of education provided for future kings in scripture and in the fallen world. The tradition of the "triple equation" that gives structure to the three temptations allows Jesus to define the offices of prophet, king, and priest in terms of his visionary kingdom. Of the three, it is the office of king that Milton greatly expands upon in the second temptation. The first temptation to turn stones into bread affirms the priority of the Word of God at the beginning of the poem: it instructs the reader in the nature of temptations by appropriating the symbolism of the Eucharist, particularly in Jesus' refusal to perform a work of objective transformation, into the sphere of language and reading defined in *Areopagitica*. The third temptation on the pinnacle of the temple is a dramatic climax at the end of the poem: it prefigures the crucifixion as the historical action that consolidates the community of believers Jesus summons. In canonical terms, the first temptation evokes the typological phases of revolution and prophecy in its sharp rebuke of Satan, while the third evokes both gospel and apocalypse in its visionary imagery.

The second temptation occupies the phases of law and wisdom. It consists of a protracted interval of dialogue that anticipates future action while maintaining that action as potential. Satan, in contrast, asks Jesus to actualize his messianic potential immediately in spectacular but politically repetitive modes of action. As a contest between the divine wisdom of Jesus and the worldly wisdom of Satan, the second temptation illustrates Milton's concept of wisdom both as the internalization of the law at the threshold of a public ministry that will extend the canon of scripture itself, and as the discerning application of the inner scripture to specific life situations. The association of wisdom with the office of king is more than a simple typological connection between Jesus and Solomon; it entails a textual and critical synergy between the precepts of wisdom in Proverbs and Ecclesiastes and the yet to be articulated precepts in the Gospels. This synergy occurs in the mind of each reader.

Satan's "politic maxims," and the scriptural wisdom Jesus uses to counter these maxims, locate the second temptation within a debate on the best training for a political leader, illustrated by

Erasmus and King James I, and the best model for a stable political state, illustrated by Hobbes and Harrington. The wisdom of Athens has a legitimate place in this debate; Jesus must reject it in the form Satan offers it in order to maintain the priority of scripture in his ethical formation. Satan offers Jesus a panoply of ancient wisdom, including the ideas of Plato, Aristotle, and Socrates, along with the philosophy of the stoics, the epicureans, and the cynics. These varieties are contained within an academy that is a type of *hortus conclusus*:

> See there the Olive Grove of *Academe*,
> Plato's retirement, where the *Attic* Bird
> Trills her thick-warbl'd notes the summer long;
> There flow'ry hill *Hymettus* with the sound
> Of Bees; industrious murmur oft invites
> To studious musing.
>
> (4:244–49)

The academy is a parody of Eden. As a site of contemplation, it is replete with the arts and sciences endowed in the potential of the original paradise. Satan wants to neutralize the threat Jesus presents to his worldly kingdom, and so he offers an innocuous substitute for the paradise Jesus will regain.

The Athenian temptation recreates an old tension in Christianity. Finding the proper relationship between Athens and Jerusalem, or between Greek philosophy and biblical revelation, occupied the early church. Elements of Jesus' rejection of Athens occur in various patristic sources. For Lactantius, the eloquence of philosophy was empty: "They were able to speak well as erudite men, but they were in no way able to speak truly, since they had not learned truth from Him who is its source."[51] Justin Martyr argued that Greek philosophy was derivative, plagiarized, and "ill-imitated": "Moses is more ancient than all the Greek authors. Everything the philosophers and poets said about the immortality of the soul, or retribution after death, or speculation on celestial matters, or other similar doctrines, they took from the Prophets as the source of information, and from them they have been able to understand and explain these matters. Thus, the seeds of truth seem to be among all men, but that they did not grasp their exact meaning is evident from the fact that they contradict themselves."[52] Clement of Alexandria saw Greek wisdom as a preparation for the Gospel: "philosophy too was a direct gift of God to the Greeks before the Lord extended his appeal to the Greeks. For philosophy was to the Greek world what the Law was to the Hebrews, a tutor escorting them to Christ."[53] Tertullian rejects Athens in order to condemn "human wisdom which pretends to know the truth, whilst it only corrupts it, and is itself divided into its own manifold heresies, by the variety of its mutually repugnant sects. What indeed has Athens to do with Jerusalem? What concord is there between the Academy and the Church?"[54] Augustine moderated this view by arguing that there is a right use for philosophy: "if those who are called philosophers, and especially the Platonists, have said aught that is true and in harmony with our faith, we are not only not to shrink from it, but to claim it for our own use from those who have unlawful possession of it"[55]

Milton's contemporaries inherited the debate over the sources of wisdom in a culture of division and dissent. John Bunyan dismissed nonscriptural learning as unnecessary in *The Doctrine of Law and Grace Unfolded*: "If thou do finde this book empty of Fantastical expressions, and without light, vain, whimsical Scholar-like terms, thou must understand, it is because I never went to School to Aristotle or Plato, but was brought up in my fathers house, in a very mean condition, among a company of poor Country-men."[56] Bunyan's attitude emulates the confrontations between the unlearned disciples of Jesus and the educated Pharisees in the Gospels. Bunyan sees the credibility of his writing in the aphoristic texture that emulates the teachings of Jesus: "if thou do finde a parcel of plain, yet sound, true, home-sayings, attribute that to the Lord Jesus, his gifts and abilities, which he hath bestowed upon such a poor creature as I am, and have been." The disavowal of Plato and Aristotle places greater emphasis on the authority of the scripture and of grace. As Michael Mullett notes, Bunyan's attitude can be situated amongst Levellers, Diggers, and Quakers who challenged the need for academic training for ministry.[57] Milton's Jesus dismisses classical learning as tersely as Bunyan. He also amply demonstrates that he possesses an abundance of learning. Milton is clearly not legitimating ignorance in the cause of faith; rather, he is seeking the right relation of learning to Jesus' ultimate purpose. Milton's Jesus is also not interested in the doctrinal speculation outlined by Justin Martyr; he politicizes the debate by defining history as his sphere of action. His posture of apparent rejection, made necessary by Satan's use of wisdom, anticipates an eventual inclusion and, from the Christian perspective, redemption of classical wisdom beyond the immediate context of temptation.

A less radical response perceives gradations of wisdom between the divine and demonic levels. Nathaniel Hardy treated the opposition of the two forms of wisdom in two sermons published jointly as *Wisdomes Character and Counterfeit* (1656). Hardy proposes a threefold division that distinguishes carnal wisdom from the useful aspects of natural wisdom: "Carnall wisdome is the cunning, which is in the children of this world, whereby they are wise to doe evill"; "Naturall is that sagacity which more or lesse is in every rationall creature, to discerne of naturall things, and manage secular affaires"; "Sacred is the wisdom either of Science, or of operation, the former is that whereby the minde is savingly enlightned, to discerne the things of God, and the mysteries of Salvation, *sapientia quasi sapida scientia*, a savoury, and cordiall knowledge of supernaturall objects, doth well deserve the name of Wisdome: The latter is that whereby a man is enabled to fixe a right end of all his actions, and to make choyce of the fit meanes conducing to that end, this is called by the Latines *Prudentia*, and though the other be not excluded, yet doubtlesse this is principally intended in this Scripture."[58] Hardy enlarges the scope of natural wisdom without compromising the dependence of true wisdom on divine grace: "Mans spirit is able to understand much, but to the understanding of Divine things, there must be an inspiration of the Almighty. The truth is, whereas humane is attained *Deo aspirante*, God assisting, this Divine wisdome is onely to be obtained *Deo inspirante*, God inspiring with an especiall grace."[59] Hardy isolates the purely carnal or hostile forms of wisdom in his second sermon, *Wisdomes Counterfeit: or Herodian Policy*, where demonic cunning is figured in the stratagems of the king who sought to murder the infant Christ.

Charles Herle also divides the forms of natural wisdom in *Wisdom's Tripos* (1670), a collection of three treatises covering worldly policy, moral prudence, and Christian wisdom. Herle's work examines the "vanity of the First," the "Usefulness of the Second," and the "Excellency of the Third."[60] Worldly policy is equated with aspects of the three temptations Christ faced in the wilderness:

The End of Worldly Policy, is Worldly Happiness, or the enjoyment of what the world affords: now the Apostle tells us, *All that is in the world, 'tis the lust of the flesh, the lust of the eye, and the pride of life*. The Devil began with these in that first temptation in Paradise, and that in this very order. . . .[61]

Moral Prudence is natural wisdom that supports the higher Christian wisdom, making it the "Handmaid to Divinity": "it must be considered, that the Science is Practical; and Truth is here rather a Guide, than an End."[62] The highest Christian wisdom "makes man Denizon of the upper, Regent of the lower world, Correspondent of both."[63] Its end is "Reconciliation, and Communion; Attonement with God, and enjoyment of him."[64] It succeeds, moreover, by making the wisdom "of flesh, world, and devil" serviceable to a higher purpose, as Jesus does in *Paradise Regained*.

Milton's Jesus shows little interest in intermediate natural wisdom; instead, he polarizes demonic and divine wisdom. He does so because *Paradise Regained* is, on one level, a study in religious persecution: Satan pressures Jesus to conform to the satanic or worldly norms of religious and political behavior. Satan's pressure requires a radical response. The temptation of Athenian learning serves the theme of religious persecution because Satan uses it to divert Jesus from a life of meaningful action in the world into a life of contemplation, or else to base his actions in the world on Greek philosophy rather than on the scriptures.

> Be famous then
> By wisdom; as thy Empire must extend,
> So let thy mind o'er all the world,
> In knowledge, all things in it comprehend.
> All knowledge is not couch't in *Moses'* Law,
> The *Pentateuch* or what the Prophets wrote;
> The *Gentiles* also know, and write, and teach
> To admiration, led by Nature's light.
>
> (4:221–28)

Jesus is alert to the implications of the temptation, for he identifies Socrates, who suffered death for his convictions, as the wisest of the Greeks. Yet he rejects Athenian wisdom as a delusion:

Who therefore seeks in these
True Wisdom, finds her not, or by delusion
Far worse, her false resemblance only meets,
An empty cloud.

(4:318–21)

As Douglas Bush has remarked, "it is painful indeed to watch Milton turn and rend some main roots of his being, but we must try to understand him."[65] Jesus' rejection of the classics is, in fact, a function of the dramatic situation Milton creates in this poem. Athenian wisdom must be rejected in this context because it is offered as the demonic wisdom Hardy equates with cunning. It serves Satan's attempt to neutralize the threat Jesus poses by quarantining him in an Athenian Eden outside of history as history is redefined by the Incarnation. By reasserting the primacy of scriptural revelation, Jesus provides a point of orientation that allows for a supportive rather than antagonistic relationship between classical and Christian wisdom. Jesus rejects classical wisdom as a commodity to be exchanged for, rather than related to, biblical revelation. The classics are

unworthy to compare
With *Sion's* songs, to all true tastes excelling,
Where God is prais'd aright, and Godlike men,
The Holiest of Holies, and his Saints;
Such are from God inspir'd not such from thee.

(4:346–50)

The poetic context of the rejection of Athenian wisdom offers one solution to the critical problems surrounding the episode. We need, however, to look beyond these solutions to the more positive claims Jesus makes for biblical wisdom. Education, and particularly the education of a future king or sovereign—a true "Righteous Ruler," to appropriate Spencer's theme—is a central thematic concern in *Paradise Regained* which, as a species of epic, is committed to an inclusive survey of topics and ideas. A ruler's education must be as encyclopedic as the epic form itself, and Jesus argues that this comprehensive education is available in scripture alone. Satan seeks to *exchange* classical for biblical wisdom, and so to isolate Jesus' revolutionary vision from the sphere of history; Jesus insists that the classics can only complement scriptural revelation when the unique historical and temporal vision presented in the Bible is kept in perspective.

The prose treatises were written with the urgent hope that the course of events could still be altered; the major poems, written with the Restoration well-established, instill the thesis of liberty in the indefinite future and in successive generations of readers. Milton therefore emphasizes growth towards social maturity and political wisdom. The processive dimension, envisioned in the extension of biblical typology after the Fall, also complements the educative function of the epic and tragic forms as the growth and reformation of individual consciousness in Adam's final vision, in Jesus' temptations, and in Samson's analysis of his past, present different aspects of regeneration in the body politic. If the basis of Jesus' warfare against Satan is wisdom, the basis of the new community he envisions is his relationship with Mary.

The growth and development of audience is vital to Milton's political vision. But the fallen world tends to present a more synchronized status quo. Satan wants to block change in the fallen world, and therefore offers Jesus models of action that are imitative. Jesus' critical discernment negotiates the "metanoia" of the fallen world with the "pronoia" the forward-moving, narrative framework of providential history. Ecclesiastes is a model for the detached, critical perspective Jesus cultivates in his survey of the fallen world in *Paradise Regained*. Ecclesiastes 1:4 assesses the pattern of recurrence in fallen, earthly existence: "one generation passeth away, and another generation cometh: but the earth abideth for ever." Thomas Granger comments on these recurring patterns:

> All things whatsoever a man can particularize, are the same, that have beene; the same I say, *Specie,* in kind or nature, not *numero,* the very selfe-same without individuall or circumstantiall difference. Here then is wisdome to discerne the times and seasons, and to apply afterthings rightly to the former, or rather to behold things past that are present; but that is hidden from most mens eyes, and it is given to few to behold that which they heare, and reade of, though it never be so plainely acted before their eyes; yea, and he is even now acting it himself.[66]

Milton again politicizes Ecclesiastes' response to the earth "that abideth forever." He must recognize that the models of

political action and military heroism offered by Satan are old, re-
current, and derivative. The temptations allow Jesus to recognize
the recurring form of the fallen world before proceeding to present the visionary counterorder of the Gospels. Jesus intuitively
recognizes Satan as an ancient adversary in spite of Satan's dissembling appearances: "Why dost thou then to me suggest dis-
trust, / Knowing who I am, as I know who thou art?" (1:35–56).
Jesus counters Satan's concealment of his sameness under forms
of mutation with Jesus' own constancy. Jesus uses typology to
recall Satan's past defeats at the hands of prophetic figures.

> In the Mount
> *Moses* was forty days, nor eat nor drank,
> And forty days Eliah without food
> Wandr'd this barren waste; the same I now.
>
> (1:351–54)

Typology is also the construction of a national and political
memory for Jesus, and is thus indispensable to the formation of
the "children of reviving liberty" after the restoration. Typology
is also integral to the scriptural formation of his messianic character. Ecclesiastes is an important source for the character of
Jesus in *Paradise Regained*. The text represents a clear, critical
survey of the fallen world at the threshold of Jesus' public ministry. Since the temptation of Athens elaborates the office of
monarch as Jesus fulfills it, Milton argues that Jesus' education
must mobilize his intellect in an iconoclastic mode that avoids
the replication of the norms of the fallen world. Milton's use of
Ecclesiastes in *Paradise Regained* shows that he saw the critical
perspective of wisdom in Ecclesiastes as the proper prelude to
the visionary perspective of wisdom in the Gospels, and the rejection of Satan as the proper prelude to the gathering of a renovated community. It is to this community that we now turn.

"Fit Audience": Mary and the New Community

Paradise Regained contrasts the maternal wisdom of Mary,
the mother of Jesus, who remembers and contemplates her "sayings," with the cynical, worldly wisdom of Satan who provokes
Jesus with "politic maxims."[67] Milton's Dalila is a figure stigma-
tized by the letter of masculine vilification, yet Milton succeeds

in investing her with a psychological and political complexity needed to achieve both credibility and durability in the system of contending perspectives that comprises the poem. Milton's Mary is equally written upon or impressed by tradition, although here, until the Protestant dethronement of Mary after the Reformation, it is the tradition of veneration rather than vilification that is problematic. Milton portrays Dalila as marked or written upon by the pen of history, and Mary as receiving and containing the Word of God which she inwardly contemplates in patient silence. If Dalila acquires a series of cruel and derogatory labels in posterity, then Mary also acquires labels in the form of titles in the posterity of Church doctrine. Mary's titles include Mother of God, Word Bearer, and Queen of Heaven.[68] Luther felt it was proper that "men have crowded all her glory into a single word, calling her Mother of God."[69] Milton did not endorse these titles or traditions, although he maintained the doctrine of the virgin birth of Christ because it is recorded in scripture. The veneration of Mary in Catholic tradition made her equivalent to the elevated hypostasis of divine *sophia*; Milton, however, prefers the human typologies of feminine wisdom in his depiction of the second Eve. Dayton Haskin has shown how Milton uses the metaphoric potential of word-bearing for a community of believers to locate Mary on the shared ground of human reading and interpretation. Mary is a nurturer and teacher of Jesus in her capacity "as an interpreter who could reassemble scriptural texts into a personal synthesis."[70] Her situation is analogous to the situation Milton assumes of his readers: she is located in the midst of the temporal process that converts historical events into scriptural texts, yet she has the patience to resist interpretive closure in order to remain attentive to the further work of providence. As I will argue, Mary is a site in the poem for the synthesis of the typological phases of revelation with emphasis on the Old Testament; her synthesis implies, ultimately, the formation of the larger community which Jesus must gather and preserve even as he confronts and excludes Satan.

A crucial connection between the historical and textual grounds of community is ritual. Ritual connects the individual to the larger community even as the collective memory of the larger community is formed, and consistently articulates the community's sense of its own origins and destiny in the course of time. Moments of ritual evoked in the poem include the presentation of the infant Jesus at the temple, the baptism, and the Eucharist. The discovery of Jesus reading in the temple at the age of twelve even evokes a "bar-mitzvah," as Jesus assumes responsibility for his reading of scriptures under the law. Satan conducts forms of demonic ritual in the three temptations by seeking to indoctrinate Jesus into the fallen order with its time-worn conventions of political and heroic action and its collective memory of conquest and subjugation. The temptations follow Jesus' baptism by John, a ritual that extends the amalgamation of Jesus' individual and national identities initiated with the annunciation and confirmed in Simeon's *nunc dimitis* at the temple.

The refusal of the first temptation of turning stones into bread implies the eventual institution of the Eucharist as a community rite, even though the nature of that rite is revalued by Milton's Protestant theology; the refusal of the third temptation—set on the pinnacle of the temple—locates Jesus at the spatial center of ritual in Israel, while also setting the inner sanctum of conscience, the temple of "th' upright heart and pure," above the material spatial center with which it is, for that instant, aligned. The second and most lengthy temptation focuses on education, especially the education required in a future ruler. Milton follows the order of temptations found in Luke rather than Matthew in order to bring the poem to a more dramatic climax at the temple. Luke's order also allows Milton to analyze the world in its parts in a manner comparable to the survey of the mundane world in Ecclesiastes, with its sense that there is nothing new under the sun. The diachronic ritual of education incorporated into the synchronic analysis of the world allows Milton to consider maturity, which can only be deepened with the course of time, as a quality of the fit ruler. This implies that society itself has the capacity to mature out of the "perpetual childhood of prescription" described in *Areopagitica*. Restoration was, in Milton's view, not simply a bad political choice but a regression to immaturity.

Mary is perhaps the central instrument of Jesus' maturity in *Paradise Regained*, even when signs of his maturity lead to conflict between mother and son. She reveals for us the more positive relationships between ritual, education, and Old Testament law. Milton's treatment of the presentation at the temple clearly illustrates Mary's role as a site for the synthesis of the different phases of scriptural revelation. In her role as a teacher, she shows a clear awareness of the public and private aspects of Jesus' destiny. "By matchless Deeds express thy matchless Sire" she exhorts her son (1:233). This is the language of kingship, and it focuses on the threshold between private and public life. In teaching Jesus to search the scriptures for his identity, she fulfills Erasmus's core precept of grounding the education of the future ruler in scripture.

Torah, the central textual foundation of Jesus' education, is perhaps better translated as "essential teaching" rather than "law." James Sanders notes that the word "is derived from a Semitic root which means to cast or throw."[71] The image of God casting the foundations of the world at creation plays upon the root of *Torah* (Job 38:6–7). Greek translations of the Old and New Testaments continue to play upon the sense of *Torah* as "casting" in their use of the Greek verb *balein*, to cast.[72] Sanders observes this wordplay in Matthew 7:6: "Do not cast your pearls before swine." Using the resonance between casting and creating conveyed in *Torah*, this saying exhorts its listeners not to be self-destructive. Self-destruction is the core of the third temptation in *Paradise Regained*. Jesus is tempted to *cast* himself down from the pinnacle of the temple.[73] His refusal enacts the definition of wisdom as the internalization of the law in a moment of self-possession. Hence, he acknowledges the Torah as the creative foundation of self and society in *Paradise Regained*.[74]

Torah is a source of shared identity and community. As Frye suggests, it plays a "leading role in defining a society, in giving it a shared possession of knowledge, or what is assumed to be knowledge, peculiar to it."[75] Jason Rosenblatt's exposition of Milton's view of Torah and law also recovers for us the essential Hebraic identification of law and love, an identification that makes the law a binding spiritual force between people both before and after the Fall. Indeed, the continuing purpose of the law before and after the Fall allows Milton to "reconcile belief in an original state of perfection with belief in an evolutionary deity whose successive dispensations (natural law, Mosaic law, gospel) manifest divine benevolence ever more clearly and fully."[76] Typology is an exemplary image of community in its presentation of an array of just persons, and signals the progress towards Christian revelation in the postlapsarian world as enigmatically prophesied in the *protevangelium*; the Edenic books of *Paradise Lost* are, as Rosenblatt argues, non-typological in their depiction of synchronized order and perfection, yet the original "torah" of Paradise—to "be fruitful and multiply"—also persists in the postlapsarian world in the spiritual sense of forming and expanding a community of "fit readers" in each successive generation. Milton's major poems fulfill this prelapsarian command.

As a phase of revelation that emphasizes the individual's inward possession of Torah, wisdom is conveyed through discontinuous proverbs that provide successive generations of readers with educative and experimental precepts. The written Gospels present the life of Jesus in a sequence of discontinuous episodes or "pericopes" often constructed around a central lesson or saying. Meaning literally to "cut around," the pericope as episode is analogous to the discontinuity of aphoristic wisdom. Indeed, it is perhaps the natural literary structure for the portrayal of an inspired teacher of wisdom whose acts and sayings were at first disseminated through the early Christian community before being written down. Some of the perceived "coldness" of *Paradise Regained* may be due to the curt, self-contained quality of the sayings Jesus uses to dismiss Satan. But, as I have argued, the notion of a "coldness" in Jesus' character distracts us from the specific impulses in the canon of scripture that Milton seeks to embody in Jesus in *Paradise Regained*. Jesus' sayings are powerful centers of critical energy in the poem, and his elaboration of his own sayings releases an iconoclastic energy. Satan is the image-maker rather than the image-breaker: he encourages Jesus to accept conventional models of power, knowledge, and action. Jesus instead demonstrates the revolt of reason against these conventional models, and Satan becomes the target of his iconoclastic energy.

Jesus' rejection of Satan emulates the inspired and discerning wisdom of scripture, while Satan's arguments express forms of worldly wisdom associated with habit and cunning. The contemplative and intellectual potential of Jesus' sayings are clearly not for Satan's benefit; the sayings project the community implied in Jesus' teachings. Phases of scriptural revelation can project forms of community. If Torah is essential to the formation and definition of a scriptural society, then *kerygma*, or the rhetoric of proclamation associated with the Gospels, develops

the sense of community in its audience.[77] The metaphoric relations and connections Jesus discovers in reclaiming scriptural
passages from the isolated literalism Satan imposes upon them
are both literary and social in their dimensions. Torah and
kerygma become an integrated language of social concern in
Jesus' development. This language defines and develops a holy
community and scriptural society. The language of metaphor
that Jesus recovers in his resistance to Satan's literal readings
effects not only a hermeneutic transformation but a potential
social transformation as well.

The community Jesus gathers beyond his rejection of Satan is
implied in Milton's concept of the fit reader. Such a community
must maintain a dynamic of critical dissent within itself in
order to be vital. Frye uses the term "concern" to designate the
social dimension of community formation in scripture and "freedom" to designate the importance of individual dissent. The tension between concern and freedom in biblical wisdom is thus
both literary and social in its dimensions. Concern is the conser-
vation and continuity of a community based, as in the giving of
the law at Sinai, upon the rejection of what is idolatrous and
unimaginative; freedom functions not only as the legitimate
voice of dissent, but also as the tolerance and acceptance of what
is different and unconventional yet vital and enriching to the
community that accepts it. If social concern alone were pervasive the result would be the mindless conformity Milton condemns in *Areopagitica*; if freedom prevailed in isolation there
could be no consummate vision of a nation of prophets envisioned in *Areopagitica*, for such a vision is social in its scope. A
mature society desires, seeks, and discovers a self-critical, toler-
ant, and dynamic equilibrium between concern and freedom.
Areopagitica is an early modern articulation of this dynamic.
Indeed, the vision of a nation "rousing herself like a strong man
after sleep" clearly illustrates Milton's attention to the parameters of freedom and concern, for it is a vision that identifies a
nation as an individual. More than twenty-five years later,
Milton embodied the potential of the English nation in Jesus,
the individual hero of *Paradise Regained*.

The broad social tension between concern and freedom is
analogous to the critical tension between order and counterorder
in the canon of biblical wisdom literature. If the aphoristic
wisdom of order affirms society and tradition, the wisdom of

counterorder issues productive, critical challenges to that order.[78] Jesus unites the elements of order and counterorder in his teachings. He is the ordering principle in the divine plan of redemption; he appears in the world as an individual challenging human complacency as well as authority. He opposes the fallen order of Satan by rejecting Satan's concerns; he preserves and educates his own community by positively interpreting its concerns. This latter community is represented in the poem by John the Baptist, Simeon, Anna, the Disciples, and Mary. It is Mary, however, who most fully articulates the vision of order as social concern.

That Mary and Satan represent two different orders is apparent in the parallels between them. Both watch over Jesus from his infancy, Mary as a caring mother and teacher, Satan as a loitering eavesdropper and spy. Mary and Satan both ponder and interpret the "meaning" of Jesus in terms of his real nature, his purpose, and his ultimate destiny. Both "bear" Jesus to the temple, one in loving observance of ritual, the other in force and violence. Both experience rejection by Jesus, though for vastly different reasons. Jesus' disappearance in the desert after his baptism instills a deeply-troubled sense of abandonment in the disciples as well as in Mary. For Mary, however, the event triggers the memory of an earlier disappearance related in Luke 2:46–50:

> And it came to pass, that after three days they found him in the temple, sitting in the midst of the doctors, both hearing them, and asking them questions. And all that heard him were astonished at his understanding and answers. And when they saw him, they were amazed: and his mother said unto him, Son, why hast thou thus dealt with us? behold, thy father and I have sought thee sorrowing. And he said unto them, How is it that ye sought me? wist ye not that I must be about my father's business? And they understood not the *saying* which he spake unto them. (emphasis mine)

In *Paradise Regained*, Mary recalls:

> when twelve years he scarce had seen,
> I lost him, but so found, as well I saw
> He could not lose himself; but went about
> His Father's business; what he meant I mus'd,
> Since understand; much more his absence now
> Thus long to some great purpose he obscures.

But I to wait with patience am inur'd;
My heart hath been a storehouse long of things
And sayings laid up, portending strange events.
(2:96–104)

The patience that waits for further knowledge is part of the virtue that seals the community. As the central, ethical principle in Milton's major poems, patience is perhaps the most basic, communal knowledge these poems impart. Jesus understands this principle when, alone and hungry in the desert, he submits to an uncertain future with this saying: "what concerns my knowledge God reveals" (1:293).

Mary's introduction of the term "sayings" as a generic term draws attention not only to the important role of wisdom in the poem but its prominence in Renaissance commonplace books or "treasuries." Giovanni Diodati compared Proverbs to "a *Cabinet* filled with rich, and orient pearles and Jewels, not tyed or linked together in any chain, or connection, but scattered here and there without *Method*." [79] Dayton Haskin remarks that Milton looked upon Mary's heart as "a writer's commonplace book," or a metaphoric provision or "storehouse" of sayings. Haskin further notes the New Testament comparison of the kingdom of heaven to a treasure chest: "Therefore every scribe who has been trained for the kingdom of heaven is like a householder who brings out of his treasure what is old and what is new" (Matt. 13:52). [80] A central symbol of aphoristic wisdom in *Paradise Regained* is the temple, which spatially orients Mary's memories through her encounter with Simeon and Anna, and provides the setting for the climax of the poem. Diodati further combines temple and treasury in his description of the structure of the Old Testament Book of Proverbs: "We may therefore compare this Book to a *stately House*, built, not on a continued, contiguous foundation, but on severall distinct, polished Pillars, as *Wisdome* built her house here, *Chap*. 9.1." [81] Wisdom also gains a special character in the domestic setting. In the seventeenth century the instilling of piety through reading was intensified in household settings, as parents read the scriptures to their children and schooled them in interpretation almost daily. [82] The spiritual economy of the household setting clearly influences Milton's depiction of the relationship between Mary and Jesus. Two seventeenth-century books of instruction reveal the gendered division of labor within this economy.

Richard Brathwaite recommends private education for the kingdom of heaven to young women in *The English Gentlewoman* (1631). Calling a woman's rhetoric "a moving silence," he recommends seclusion from temptation as the best venue for meditation: "make then your Chamber your private Theatre, wherein you may act some devout scene to Gods honour. Be still from the world, but stirring towards God. Meditation, let it be your key to open the Morning, your locke to close the Evening."[83] The public sphere is for the exceptional few, like Deborah: "Now for Publike Employments, I know all are not borne to be Deborahs, to beare virile spirits in feminine bodies. Yet, in chusing the better part, you may fit and accommodate your persons to publike affaires, well sorting and suting with your ranke and quality."[84] Anna, whom Mary and Joseph meet at the steps of the temple, is exemplary: "Devout mention is made of zealous Anna, who made recourse to the temple, offring her incessant prayers, a viall of sweet odours, that she might conceive a sonne: of whom, to her succeeding memory, the Scripture recordeth, that after her teares so devoutly shed, her prayers so sincerely offred, her religious vowes so faithfully performed, her countenance was no more altered; Piety begot in her divine love, faith in Gods promise made her beleeve, and zeale to Gods house caused her to persevere: thus sighing she sought, seeking she obtained, and obtaining she retained a gratefull memory of what she received."[85] Milton's "prophetic Anna," focused plainly, like Mary, on the vocation of political prophecy, outweighs Brathwaite's lengthy depiction of an emotive saint.

In *The Mothers Legacie to her unborne Childe* (1624), Elizabeth Jocelin opens her treasury of maternal wisdom for both sons and daughters, although she acknowledges that only a son may enter into the public sphere of ministry. She prays that a son might "bee an inheritour of the Kingdome of Heaven. To which end I humbly beseech Almighty God thou maiest bend all thy actions, and (if it bee his blessed will) give thee so plentiful a measure of his grace, that thou maist serve him as his Minister, if he make thee a man."[86] She hopes for a balance of learning and wisdom in a daughter, though if "she have all this in her, she will hardly make a poor mans wife."[87] In both cases, however, the mother's teaching should fit the child against the dangers of temptation, just as Mary helps to prepare Jesus for temptation in *Paradise Regained*: "The devils malice is as easily perceived, for even now he lies lurking ready to catch every good motion from thy heart, suggesting things more delightfull to thy fancy, and perswading thee to deferre thy service of God though but for a little while."[88] Hence her teaching is modeled on the opening admonition of Ecclesiastes: "The first charge I give thee, I learned of Solomon, Eccle. 12:1, remember thy Creator in the daies of thy youth. It is an excellent beginning, and a fit lesson for a childe. Looke with what the Vessell is first seasoned, it retaines the taste: and if thou beginnest to remember to serve God when thou art young, before the world, the flesh, and the devill take hold on thee, God will love thee, and send his holy Spirit to take possession of thee, who shall resist those enemies, & not suffer them to hurt thee"; "To move thy heart to remember thy Creator betimes, meditate upon the benefits thou continually receivest: First, how hee hath created thee when thou wert nothing, redeemed thee being worse than nought, and now of meere grace he hath given thee his holy Spirit, sanctifying thee to an eternall Kingdome."[89]

Milton's Mary, whose prophetic Magnificat merges, like its precursor, the Song of Deborah, the private and public spheres, is a mother who has bequeathed a spiritual legacy of reading, teaching, and remembering to her son. The currency of her spiritual treasure is her "sayings," a term that calls our attention first to the biblical aphorisms of wisdom or *meshalim*, and second to Mary's Magnificat, the hymn of praise she sings in response to the Annunciation (Luke 1:46–55). Mary-Ann Radzinowicz suggests that Mary's recollection of the Magnificat in *Paradise Regained* combines the dichotomous modes of praise and lament because it is a "joyful past moment recalled sadly in an anxious present."[90] Mary's sayings therefore comprise a nexus between the past and the future, retrospection and anticipation, as she anticipates the manifestation of Jesus' wisdom in his teachings and the fulfillment of her own prophecy. Her sayings imply a power of discernment which makes experience recognizable in light of a prior instruction. By looking back upon biblical wisdom as well as forward to the revolutionary fulfillment of messianic prophecies, her sayings also bring together the ideas of order and counterorder, concern and freedom, in a manner that typifies Milton's search for their ultimate unity.

As James Williams suggests, "Wisdom thinking in the Old Testament focuses on divine order, and this order is mediated in human existence through the proper use of language."[91] Proverbs also demands interpretive skill in its readers. This skill characterizes the close relationship between Mary and Jesus in *Paradise Regained*. The interpretive conversation between Mary and Jesus, which is featured in the memories of both characters because they are separated in the action of the poem, helps to illustrate the position of the reader in the poem. In particular, this interpretive conversation illustrates the dynamic relationship between the wise sayings of Jesus and the narrative in which they are contained. Jesus' soliloquy in Book 1 provides an intimate parallel to Mary's soliloquy in Book 2 because it tells of Jesus' childhood, including the episode of his disappearance in the temple. The soliloquy emphasizes the problem of translating knowledge into action, a central issue in Renaissance ideas of wisdom:

> When I was yet a child, no childish play
> To me was pleasing, all my mind was set
> Serious to learn and know, and thence to do
> What might be public good.
>
> (1:201–4)

Jesus remembers Mary as an observer and teacher of great insight:

> These growing thoughts my Mother soon perceiving
> By words at times cast forth, inly rejoic'd
> And said to me apart: High are thy thoughts
> O Son, but nourish them and let them soar
> To what height sacred virtue and true worth
> Can raise them, though above example high;
> By matchless Deeds express thy matchless Sire.
>
> (1:227–33)

There are two aspects of Jesus' self-knowledge suggested in the language of this soliloquy. The first is maturity, as the sense of continuous, "growing thoughts" anticipating the climactic fruition of "matchless Deeds." The second is teaching, as the scattering of "words at times cast forth" like the sowing of seeds. As MacCallum remarks, the "grains of truth are scattered in the field of time, and Milton emphasizes that each is taught in due place and season."[92] The scattered word is absorbed and recollected at crucial moments in the narrative, as Mary demonstrates in her soliloquy by pondering her son's difficult and various sayings. The process of internalization and recollection with a view to the imaginative possession of the text is the kind of reading experience Milton expects from his readers in *Paradise Regained*. Milton portrays this kind of experience in the figure of Mary.

The power of interpretation emphasized in biblical wisdom implies a concomitant power over one's own life direction and experience. Milton, let us remember, incorporates the notion of *mashal* as sovereignty in his definition of wisdom as a virtue: we must "govern all our actions by its rule" (*CPW* 6:647). The entire theory is enacted in the climactic temptation in *Paradise Regained*. Satan invites Jesus "if not to stand" then to hurl himself down from the pinnacle of the temple. Jesus responds with a saying from Deuteronomy:

> Also it is written,
> Tempt not the Lord thy God; he said, and stood.
> (4:560–61)

As these words are uttered, Jesus stands firmly on the pinnacle of the temple while Satan falls "smitten with amazement" (4:562). The sequence of verbs in the climactic statement, which proceeds from writing to saying to standing ("it is *written*," "he *said*," "and *stood*," emphasis mine) precisely illustrates Milton's concept of the internalized "double scripture." Wisdom becomes the "individualizing of law" (the law of Deuteronomy 6:16, in this instance) as it applies "to specific and variable situations."[93] Jesus fulfills the first meaning of *mashal* by ruling over his situation decisively. He fulfills the second meaning of *mashal* by making visible his relationship and similitude to God the Father.[94] The progression from writing to speaking to standing *incarnates* the very words Jesus cites, and this connects him more strongly to Mary by characterizing the textual and interpretive basis of his relationship with her. This implicit connection to Mary affirms the textual grounds of community in the poem. Satan invites Jesus to undertake the pseudorevolutionary move of breaking with this community, as Satan did in *Paradise Lost* by tempting God. Breaking with Satan is the more authentically revolutionary action for Milton because Satan controls the political order of the fallen world. The coincidence of communication (as the communitarian connection with Mary) and revolution (as the final break with Satan) in Jesus' victorious act of standing locates and realizes the ultimate unity of order and counterorder. Order is conserved in Jesus' use of the Torah to defeat Satan; counterorder is voiced in Jesus' rejection of temptation. This union of orders adds a new dimension to the event of *anagnorisis* or recognition which occurs at the climax on the pinnacle.[95]

Milton enhances Mary's role as mother and teacher of her son through the parallels between Jesus' soliloquy in Book 1 and in Mary's soliloquy in Book 2. Mary's soliloquy in Book 2 is further juxtaposed to a demonic council in which Belial advises Satan to "Set women in [Jesus'] eye" (2:154). While Belial's suggestion emphasizes sexual temptation, it contemplates women

> more like to Goddesses
> Than Mortal Creatures, graceful and discreet,
> Expert in amorous Arts, enchanting tongues
> Persuasive, Virgin majesty with mild
> And sweet allay'd, yet terrible to approach.
>
> (2:156–60)

The juxtaposition of this temptation with Mary's soliloquy may implicitly convey Milton's criticism of the cultic veneration of Mary, especially as it may have influenced courtly love. The same criticism runs through *Paradise Lost*; Adam's fall, for example, is foreshadowed in his homage to Eve:

> All higher knowledge in her presence falls
> Degraded, Wisdom in discourse with her
> Loses discount'nanc't, and like folly shows.
>
> (8:551–53)

Raphael sternly rebukes Adam for this speech. Satan's rejection of Belial's suggestion in *Paradise Regained* echoes Raphael's rebuke of Adam, although with Satan's perverse motivation and logic. The sense of "ethereal, unearthly" distance in Belial's view of women provides a focused contrast for the human proximity and intimacy Milton achieves in his portrait of Mary.

The typological relationship between Mary and Eve, especially as it encompasses the figure of feminine wisdom in Proverbs, is an important consideration in Milton's treatment of Mary. Justin Martyr presented Mary as a "second" Eve in the patristic era: "For Eve, being a virgin and uncorrupt, conceived the word spoken of the serpent, and brought forth disobedience and death. But Mary the Virgin, receiving faith and grace" gave birth to him "by whom God destroys both the serpent and those angels and men that became like it."[96] Bishop Joseph Hall reaffirmed this typology in his *Contemplations:* "It was fit our Reparation should answer our Fall. An evill Angel was the first Motioner of the one to Eve, a Virgin, then espoused to Adam, in the Garden of Eden: A good Angel is the first Reporter of the other to Mary, a Virgin, espoused to Joseph."[97] Milton abandons the virginity of Eve by insisting on the sanctifying and edifying nature of sex before the Fall. In *Paradise Lost* he develops the typology of Mary as a second Eve, using allusions to the Nativity narrative in Luke. When Raphael greets Eve in Book 5, we read:

> [upon Eve] the Angel *Hail*
> Bestow'd, the holy salutation us'd
> Long after to blest *Mary*, second *Eve*.
>   Hail Mother of Mankind, whose fruitful Womb
> Shall fill the World more numerous with thy Sons
> Than with these various fruits the Trees of God
> Have heap'd this Table.
>
> (5:385–91)

And at the close of *Paradise Lost*, after her dream of a redeemer, Eve issues her own, brief Magnificat:

> though all by mee is lost,
> Such favor I unworthy am voutsaf't,
> By mee the Promis'd Seed shall all restore.
>
> (12:621–23)

Mary's "sayings" in *Paradise Regained* can be identified with the Magnificat because they portend "strange events." The Magnificat speaks of scattering "the proud in the imagination of their hearts" and putting "down the mighty from their thrones." In *Paradise Regained*, in comparison, Jesus likens his "throne" to a "stone that shall to pieces dash / All Monarchies besides throughout the world" (4:149–50). This image deliberately reverses Royalist discourse, which saw kings as cornerstones. Clement Ellis called Charles I a "stone indeed . . . so truly precious in himselfe, and for those many signall excellencies, which never shone brighter to the eye of the Christian world (as such true starres and Diamonds use to do) in the darkest night of his persecution."[98] Supporters of the commonwealth are thus destroyers of God's foundation: "A good King is indeed a most precious stone, the most solid foundation of the Church's peace and the People's happynes: remove this stone, and the whole house comes down upon your head."[99] Jesus' prediction of the destruction of earthly monarchies, being an extension of Mary's Magnificat, simultaneously builds up the new community symbolized by Jesus and Mary. In 1649, Milton cited the Magnificat as evidence that God builds up the community consisting of "the True Church and Saints of God" by subverting earthly tyranny: "And wherfore did his Mother the Virgin *Mary* give such praise to God in her profetic song, that he had now by the comming of Christ *Cutt down Dynasta's or proud Monarchs from the throne. . . .* Surely it is not for nothing that tyrants by a kind of natural instinct both hate and feare none more then the true Church and Saints of God, as those most dangerous enemies and subverters of Monarchy, though indeed of tyranny" (*CM* 5:23–24). Milton evokes the Magnificat throughout *Paradise Regained* to connect Jesus' concerned preservation of the community represented by Mary with his revolutionary rejection of Satan.

Mary and Satan thus illustrate the contrast between spiritual and natural perception (1 Cor. 2:14–15). Luther remarks that "magnifies" means "to make great, to exalt, to esteem on highly, as having the power, the knowledge and the desire to perform many great and good things. . . . [God] is magnified in our knowledge and experience when we greatly esteem Him and highly regard Him."[100] In contrast to this kind of inner, spiritual magnification, Milton frequently characterizes Satan in terms of outward, optical distortion, through his ability to change his appearance, or through the simile of an optic lens (4:40). Typological metaphors associated with Mary develop this contrast in other ways.[101] The most comprehensive is Mary's title as Bearer of the Word, a title conferred upon her at the Council of Ephesus in A.D. 431.[102] Mary "bears" the Word by conceiving it, as well as in the physical act of holding Christ, witnessed in various paintings of the Madonna and Child or the Presentation at the Temple, or in statues such as Michelangelo's *Pietà*. Mary's office as word-bearer, in Milton's depiction of her, is extraordinary but ultimately not exceptional. As Dayton Haskin has shown us,

Milton's Mary anticipates the "activity of other bearers of the Word, that is, of both the evangelists like Luke and latter-day poets like Milton himself."[103] Thus, in the invocation to *Paradise Regained*, the poet-narrator asks his muse to "bear" his "prompted Song" with "prosperous wing full summ'd" (1:12–14). Psalm 91:12, the text Satan paraphrases in the final temptation (4:551–59), reads: "[The Angels] shall bear thee up in *their* hands, lest thou dash thy foot against a stone." For his own part, Satan parodies word-bearing by forcibly carrying Jesus to the pinnacle of the temple: "he caught him up, and without wing / Of *Hippogrif* bore through the Air sublime" (4:541–42). Milton's use of demonic parody illustrates how the reader is called upon to divide the divine from the demonic by relating different, often discontinuous points comprised of narrative events, poetic images, and instructive sayings. Mary's soliloquy is a paradigm of this kind of reading because it pursues the connections between these literary elements. Ultimately, this interpretive process of division and relation illustrates how Jesus subsumes his primary conflict with Satan in his gathering of a community of readers.

At the end of her soliloquy in Book 2, Mary reaches the limits of interpretation for the time being: "But I to wait with patience am inur'd" (2:103). Her soliloquy is uttered in the space between wisdom and knowledge. This space defines, perhaps, her real sense of separation from her son. Her "sayings" provide the potential to encounter and interpret new events and situations. She is prepared to know more at the appropriate time, and, in fact, her dialogue with her son is resumed at the close of the poem. Her waiting is clearly the sum of wisdom, even when her knowledge is incomplete. The limit of her interpretation is reached when the normal order of authority established in wisdom literature, an order in which parents teach children, is reversed. With this in mind, Mary remembers the twelve-year-old Jesus who, after eluding his parents, was discovered in the temple interpreting the law to his elders. Satan also recalls this episode, having "witnessed" it in his usual way. Satan remarks that Jesus was "discovered" to be "Teaching, not taught" (4:220). Discovery is recognition; the reversal of teaching authority implies freedom; teaching itself implies concern. The episode becomes another example of how Mary's soliloquy provides a compressed model for the interpretation of the poem as a whole, especially as its adaptation of reversal and recognition, two important features of our literary experience, engage with the concepts of freedom and concern.

The episode of the young Jesus' disappearance and discovery is a memory held in common by Mary and Satan; it therefore demonstrates how the community which Jesus conserves, and which is represented by Mary, is envisioned in his rejection of Satan. The disappearance of the twelve-year-old Christ is an episode that clearly parallels the disappearance of the adult Christ in the desert. Milton emulates the narrative strategy of his biblical sources. The Gospels present the life of Christ, not as a continuous biography, but in pericopes, which are discontinuous sequences of episodes; moreover, Gospel pericopes frame the teaching of a specific precept or parable. In *Paradise Regained,* discontinuous, aphoristic "sayings" present a rhetorical counterpart to the discontinuous narrative pericopes recreated in the poem. The proverb or saying, as Williams observes, is the "literary expression of a type of consciousness whose quest for order is modified by acceptance of experience as multifaceted and unsystematizable."[104] Discontinuity both invites and resists an interpretive synthesis. The synthesis is pondered, pursued, and then patiently relinquished in Mary's soliloquy.

A definitive synthesis would require a complete knowledge of Jesus' entire ministry, with its climax in his death and resurrection and his eventual return to earth, a return which many seventeenth-century sects treated with a naive literalism. Mary's knowledge is clearly less complete than the reader's in this respect. Milton, however, perceives his reader as located in medias res, or within a stretch of history that can at best be perceived in terms of its revealed origin and its promised end. Accordingly, Milton takes Mary's situation as typical: he uses her to seek the connection between Jesus' ultimate destiny, as it is conditioned by his trial in the desert, and his origins, as they are remembered in Mary's soliloquy. The Presentation in the Temple, which Milton summarizes through Jesus (1:255–58) and through Mary (1:86–92), illustrates this connection. Jesus' ultimate destiny, the crucifixion, fulfills the disconcerting prophecy made by Simeon when the infant Christ is presented at the temple: that through Mary's "very Soul / A sword shall pierce" (2:90–91). The themes are also related in terms of the act of standing which is decisive at the climax of *Paradise Regained.* Simeon and Anna interpret Jesus' presence in the temple "to all that present stood" (1:258); at the crucifixion, Mary stands at the foot of the cross.

At the temple, Mary encounters "Just *Simeon* and Prophetic *Anna*" (1:255), who together form a microcosm of the community Jesus will redeem. Part of what defines them as such are the adjectives Milton appends to their names. "Just" and "Prophetic" imply law and prophecy. Law and prophecy in turn provide the general, biblical categories of concern and freedom which must be integrated in human community. The tension between the "Just" and the "Prophetic" is, as always, first directed towards a single individual, Mary, who discovers that to internalize the tension, to ponder it, and to express it meaningfully in community is the work of a lifetime. The connections read in and through Milton's depiction of the Presentation at the Temple illustrate the interpretive patterning in Mary's soliloquy: her interpretations continually seek the relatedness of events.

The microcosmic community suggested in Mary's encounter with Simeon and Anna would appeal to Milton because it is based in scripture. The formation of community requires acts of ritual, rites of passage, and public acts of ceremony and social affirmation. The presentation is one such ritual. The Restoration was replete with such rituals and rites of passage: the day of public thanksgiving on 28 June 1660 was only one of many examples. The desecration of Cromwell's body and the bodies of the regicides at Tyburn was another. The formation of the alternative community or "endless kingdom" envisioned by Milton includes ritual. The baptism at the beginning of *Paradise Regained* is one such ritual, and the three temptations in the desert mark a rite of passage from Jesus' private to public life. Reading itself is the foundational rite of passage for the renovated society. Alberto Manguel makes this salient point in his *History of Reading*: "In every literate society, learning to read is something of an initiation, a ritualized passage out of a state of dependency and rudimentary communication. The child learning to read is admitted into the communal memory by way of books, and thereby becomes acquainted with a common past which he or she renews, to a greater or lesser degree, in every reading."[105]

Milton's Mary is particularly attentive to the rituals of reading. Dayton Haskin has shown us that the word Luke uses to characterize Mary's reading—*symballousa*—suggested "to Milton a series of roles for Mary. Literally, *sym* 'with' and *ballein* 'throw' (the root of our English word symbol), suggest a particularly active and creative role. The word hints that she 'combined' what she saw and heard and remembered in her heart into the coherent collection of narratives Luke later recorded."[106] The verb to throw also evokes the root sense of Torah, and hence the ritualistic initiation of Jesus into the skills of reading under his mother's tutelage. As Manguel notes, in medieval painting and sculpture there "are numerous representations of Mary holding a book in front of the child Jesus, and of Anne teaching Mary, but neither Christ nor His Mother was depicted as learning to write or actually writing; it was the notion of Christ reading the Old Testament that was considered essential to make the continuity of the Scriptures explicit."[107] Milton follows the example Luke offers by connecting the initiation into reading effected by Mary in Jesus' youth to the climactic moment on the pinnacle of the temple. Satan asks Jesus to cast himself off the pinnacle. Luke's verb again is *bale*, to throw or cast. Satan seeks to initiate Jesus into the kingdoms of the world. Jesus prevails in a feat of reading that throws or casts his situation together with the larger framework of the Torah. He reclaims the sense of Torah in the same creative sense Luke implies in his depiction of Mary as a reader. Satan's use of the verb *bale* is literal, murderous, and destructive. The idea of Torah as both the initiation into reading and the foundation of a new community is at the center of Milton's vision of the "endless kingdom" promised in Mary's Magnificat and in Jesus' refusal of the kingdoms of the world.

Afterword: Society and Its Readers

MILTON DID NOT EXPECT THE MATERIAL OR LITERAL MANIFESTATION OF the endless kingdom, for both the interregnum and Restoration showed that much of what is materially apparent is also repressive. It is Satan in *Paradise Regained* who tempts Jesus to degrade the visionary potential of scripture into material demonstration, and to dissipate its renovating spirit into political habit. Milton's purpose was to preserve scriptural vision for future generations by exercising the critical eye of reason and by empowering reason's critical voice. Milton's response to the defeat of his own political expectations was to shift England's naive messianic fervor, a fervor promoted from both pulpit and press, to a hermeneutic and literary apocalypse of critical reading. His emphasis on moments of *anagnorisis* or recognition in all three of his major poems demonstrates this shift as he encouraged it in his readers. The *anagnorisis* at the end of *Paradise Lost*, for example, is the recognition of the "paradise within thee, happier far." This inner paradise was Milton's typological metaphor for the Bible as a viable space of critical reflection that Adam and Eve carry forward into the wilderness of the world with its succession of tyrannical kingdoms. This space is transformed from the metaphor of the garden into the metaphor of the endless kingdom in *Paradise Regained*. Jesus is a type of king, and his vision of a kingdom without end, refined in the experience of temptation, elaborates Mary's Magnificat in its critical survey of worldly kingdoms. Samson does not achieve the extensive clarity of these typological metaphors in his condition of servitude and exile. Samson's conscience, as a troubled model of Milton's concept of the double scripture whereby the text of scripture is possessed inwardly as it is written by the Spirit on

185

the heart of each reader, is nevertheless energized by the same scriptural fragments that cohere in the vision of an endless kingdom in *Paradise Regained*. Samson illustrates a confrontation with self that is a necessary part of a redemptive pattern; his moment of recognition situates him locally in the converging and intersecting patterns of the contending, antagonistic perspectives that constituted Milton's biblical culture. Samson therefore takes his place in the overall expression of a scriptural society in a combined reading of Milton's three major poems.

Adam and Eve succumb to idolatry in their falls and recover from idolatry as they prepare to leave Eden. Jesus consistently refuses the idols Satan presents to him. In his former pride, Samson succumbs to and recovers from the self-idolizing tendencies of those who presume their perspective comprehends God's perspective. Idolatry for Milton is a mutual projection between people and structures of authority, and is characterized by passive reflection. Psalm 135:18 states, "They that make them are like unto them," meaning that those who make idols are like idols. The distinction is germane to Milton's sense of the potential of scripture both to emancipate and be emancipated in reading. The scriptural society is illustrated at its best in the interpretive conversations between Adam and Eve and between Jesus and Mary more than in the tragic isolation of Samson. Such conversations treat scripture as the medium of emancipation rather than repression. The interpretive conversations portrayed in the major poems model the rudiments of the scriptural society because they present a counterhistorical mode of criticism that challenges the kingdoms of the world. Milton's poems open a space of critical reflection that develops between a religious radicalism that can founder in fanatical literalism on the one hand and a repressive political authoritarianism consolidated in an iconic literalism on the other. That textual space is Milton's scriptural society. Milton's vision of that society fulfills the function of the epic as a national poem by encouraging a counterhistorical mode of reading.

We live in a time when questions of justice and emancipation continue to generate opposed perspectives through the interpretation of scripture. That the Bible is found on both sides of various social and political questions is the persistent paradox of its social and political condition. As I have tried to demonstrate, Milton is an exceptionally keen observer of this condition in our cultural history. Psalm 135:18 may approximate Milton's political frustrations, but the emancipation of reader and text is also reciprocal. In the framework of biblical typological relationships that both unite and complicate Milton's major poems, the implied, and perhaps ultimate, typological relationship is that between the reader and the text. As Northrop Frye has said, "every text is a type of its own reading. Its antitype starts in the reader's mind, where it is not a simple reception but the unfolding of a long and complex dialectical process."[1] The dialectical process involves the reader's exploration and integration of different phases of biblical revelation. The critical interaction between the phases of typological revelation that comprise scripture can occur because the text of the Bible truly is the type of its own reading: the text as a counterhistorical medium of emancipation mirrors every fit reader. Milton's major poems both illustrate and create this typological relationship between reader and scriptural text, using even the smallest proverb to explore the dimensions of authority, experience, and vision. Society is always a third term in this relationship, for society is the type not merely of those who exist in it, but of those who, like Milton, attempt to read it, and who find in the attempt the potential of a new and transformed society.

Notes

FOREWORD

The opening epigraph is from *The Complete Poetry and Prose of William Blake*, ed. David Erdman (New York: Anchor, 1982), 524.

1. The image of Milton as a withdrawn poet after the Restoration is refuted by Sharon Achinstein, *Milton and the Revolutionary Reader* (Princeton: Princeton University Press, 1994) and David Norbrook, *Writing the English Republic* (Cambridge: Cambridge University Press, 1999), among others. Achinstein sees Milton as actively constructing a revolutionary audience in his major poems by reiterating "the period's intense conflicts," 25. Norbrook argues that the "closer we bring *Paradise Lost* to its original context . . . the harder it becomes to square a blandly apolitical or defeatist reading of the epic with its author's values," 433.

CHAPTER 1. THE RIGHTEOUS RULER

The opening epigraph is from the *Speech of July 4, 1653, Cromwell*, ed. Maurice Ashley (Englewood Cliffs, N.J.: Prentice-Hall, 1969), 16.

1. John Spencer, *The Righteous Ruler, A Sermon Preached at St. Maries in Cambridge, June 28, 1660* (Cambridge, 1660), title page.

2. Ibid., "Epistle to the Reader," Sig. A3v.

3. William Riley Parker, *Milton: A Biography*, 2 vols. (Oxford: Clarendon Press, 1968), 1:567–76. See also Neil Keeble, " 'Till one greater man / Restore us . . .': Restoration Images in Milton and Bunyan," *Bunyan Studies* 6 (1995–96): 6–33, 7–8.

4. Clement Ellis, *A Sermon Preached on the 29th of May 1661, The Day of his Majestie's Birth and Happy Restauration After a Long Exile, To His Crown and Kingdome* (Oxford, 1661), 25. Ellis was commanded by his patron, the Marquis of Newcastle, to preach the sermon on its first anniversary, the king's thirty-first birthday, 29 May 1661. Ellis published the sermon shortly afterwards.

5. George Starkey, "Dedicatory Epistle," *Dignity of Kingship Justified* (London, 1660), Sig. A4r–A4v.

6. William Riley Parker makes a persuasive case for Starkey. See introduction to *The Dignity of Kingship Justified* by G.S., reproduced in Facsimile from the Edition of 1660 with an introduction by William R. Parker (New York: Columbia, 1942). The tract is signed "G.S.," and is variously attributed to Gilbert Sheldon, the future archbishop of Canterbury, George Searle, an M.P., and George Starkey, physician, poet, and pamphleteer. Masson speculated that G.S. might be Gilbert Sheldon, but [William Riley] Parker's argument [for George Starkey], based on Starkey's style, opinions, and other publications, is ultimately persuasive. Parker remarks that "If 'G.S.' was ever rewarded for his pains, there seems to be no record. Perhaps his book was recognized as a piece of temporizing. Perhaps it was but little read. Certainly there were enough copies of the first and only edition still unsold in 1661 to justify their re-issue with a new and more timely title page." The new issue replaced Milton's name with the more sweeping "Monarchy triumphing over Traiterous Republicans." See Parker, vi–viii.

7. George Starkey, *Royal and Other Innocent Bloud Crying Aloud to Heaven For Due Vengeance*, (London, 1660), 15, 18.

8. Ibid., 6–7.

9. Ellis, *Happy Restauration*, 37.

10. Ibid., 25–26. Of the biblical analogy between kings and fathers supposed by Robert Filmer and others, Joan Bennett writes: "In place of social contracts, developing at some point after the Fall, the following course of events was held to have occurred: Adam's right to lordship descended from him to the next Father/Kings, the patriarchs. After the Flood, divine right reverted to Noah, who divided his kingdom among his three sons, who became the Father/Kings of new kingdoms." Salmasius, Bennett notes, also charged the English with "parricide" as well as regicide (*Defensio Regia*, 1649). Joan Bennett, *Reviving Liberty: Radical Christian Humanism in Milton's Great Poems* (Cambridge, Mass.: Harvard, 1989), 25.

11. Ellis, *Happy Restauration*, 24–25.

12. George Morley, *A Sermon Preached at the Magnificent Coronation of the Most High and Mighty King Charles the IId* (London, 1661), Sig. A3r.

13. Ibid., Sig. A3r.

14. Ibid., Sig. A2r.

15. Ibid., 16.

16. John Ogilby, *The Relation of His Majestie's Entertainment Passing through the City of London, To His Coronation* (London, 1661), 4.

17. Morley, *Magnificent Coronation*, 16, 17, 21.

18. Ibid., 33.

19. Ellis, *Happy Restauration*, 24.

20. Morley, *Magnificent Coronation*, 28.

21. Symon Patrick, *A Sermon Preached before the King and Queen at White-hall, April 16, 1690, Being the Fast-Day, by Symon, Lord Bishop of Chichester* (London, 1690), 27.

22. Edward Phillips, "The Life of Milton," *John Milton: The Complete Poems and Major Prose*, ed. Merritt Y. Hughes (Indianapolis: Bobbs-Merrill, 1984), 1035.

23. Matthew Griffith, *The fear of God and the King, Press'd in a Sermon, Preach'd at Mercers Chappell, on the 25th of March, 1660* (London, 1660), Sig. A3r, Sig. A3v.

24. Parker, *Milton: A Biography*, 1:551–52.

25. Griffith, *God and the King*, Sig. A1r.

26. Ibid., Sig. A1v.

27. Ibid., 86.

28. Ibid., Sig. A2v.

29. Ibid., Sig. A2r.

30. Ibid., Sig. A2v.

31. Ibid., Sig. A3r.

32. Ibid., 53.

33. Ibid., 53.

34. Ibid., 60.

35. Ibid., 61.

36. Christopher Hill, *The English Bible and the Seventeenth-Century Revolution* (London: Penguin, 1993), 5.

37. Ibid., 5, 6.

38. Ibid., 377, 378.

39. Griffith, *God and the King*, 107–8, 94, 79.

40. Northrop Frye, *The Great Code* (Toronto: Academic Press, 1982), 233.

41. Stephen R. Honeygosky has demonstrated Milton's consistent application of the term conscience: "In *The Reason of Church Government* Milton calls conscience God's 'Secretary' (I: 822), that is, 'one entrusted with the secrets or commands of God.' Milton's age understood conscience 'as a God-given sense that knew the right intuitively; hence it is privy to God's commands and secrets' (CPW 1:822 n. 159)." Individual conscience is, as Honeygosky argues, an "ultimate guide on earth." See *Milton's House of God: The Invisible and Visible Church* (Columbia: University of Missouri Press, 1993), 140.

42. Hill, *The English Bible*, 7.

43. Spencer, *The Righteous Ruler*, 3.

44. Northrop Frye, *The Double Vision: Language and Meaning in Religion* (Toronto: University of Toronto Press, 1991), 13.

45. Ibid., 14.

46. Thomas Luxon, *Literal Figures: Puritan Allegory and the Reformation Crisis in Representation* (Chicago: University of Chicago Press, 1995), 5.

47. Janel Mueller has demonstrated how Milton recovers the root meaning of heresy (from the Greek "hairesis") as choice in *Civil Power*. See "Milton on Heresy," in *Milton and Heresy*, ed. Stephen Dobranski and John Rumrich (Cambridge: Cambridge University Press, 1998), 21–38.

48. James Harrington, *The Commonwealth of Oceana*, in *The Political Works of James Harrington*, ed. J. G. A. Pocock (London: Cambridge University Press, 1977), 185.

49. Harrington was also critical of Milton's *Means to Remove Hirelings* in his *Aphorisms Political* (London, 1659). Aphorism XXIX: "To hold that

hirelings (as they are termed by some), or an endowed ministry, ought to be removed out of the church is inconsistent with a commonwealth." *Political Works*, 765.

50. Edward Stillingfleet, *A Sermon Preached before the King, March 13, 1666* (London, 1667), 1–2.

51. Morley, *Magnificent Coronation*, 2, 2, 2.

52. Ibid., 3.

53. Joseph Hall, "Dedicatory Epistle," *Salomon's Divine Arts* (London, 1609), Sig. A2r.

54. Ibid., Sig. A2v.

55. Edward Browne, *Rules for Kings* (London, 1642), 3–6, 2.

56. William Pemble, *Salomons Recantation and Repentance: or, the Book of Ecclesiastes Briefly and Fully Explained* (London, 1627), 101–2.

57. Thomas Granger, *A Familiar Exposition or Commentarie on Ecclesiastes. Wherein the worlds vanity, and the true felicity are plainely deciphered* (London, 1621), 203. Granger was born in 1578. A scholarly, erudite minister with Calvinist views, he published eleven sermons and commentaries between 1616 and 1622, including treatises on grammar and logic. He emphasized his call to the ministry of the word by identifying himself on his title pages as "A Preacher of God's Word." His commentary on Ecclesiastes is rich in its articulation of the traditions and ideas related to this biblical text.

58. Thomas Fuller, *The Marvellous Wisdom and Quaint Conceits of Dr. Thomas Fuller, D.D.* (London: Pickering and Chatto, 1893), 149–50.

59. Symon Patrick, *A Paraphrase Upon the Books of Ecclesiastes and the Song of Solomon* (London, 1685), 216–17.

60. Carole Fontaine, "Proverbs: Introduction," *Harper's Bible Commentary*, ed. James L. Mays et al. (San Francisco: Harper's, 1988), 496.

61. Ibid., 496.

62. Robert Allen, "Epistle to the Reader," *Concordances* (London, 1612), Sig. B2r.

63. Carole Fontaine, *Traditional Sayings in the Old Testament* (Sheffield: Almond, 1982), 81. Fontaine examines proverbs in terms of context and situation. Proverb performance, in her theory, consists of the "architectural formula" which I have called the contrastive or antithetical structure, the "image," or poetic analogy or metaphor that informs the proverb, and the "message," which is the sense or meaning of the proverb in paraphrase.

64. Edward Reynolds, *Annotations on the Book of Ecclesiastes* (London, 1669), 1–2.

65. Ibid., 8.

66. Frye, *The Great Code*, 123.

67. James G. Williams, *Women Recounted* (Sheffield: Almond Press, 1982), 21.

68. Nathaniel Hardy discusses the numerical symmetries between wisdom and the Beatitudes: "The number of these effects is by some reduced to seven, and so they oppose them to the seven deadly sins, compare them to the seven Pillars which wisdome heweth to build the house where she vouchsafeth to dwell. By others the number is inlarged to eight, and so they observe a fit correspondency in them to the eight beatitudes, four of which, (to wit) purity,

peace, meeknesse, mercy, are here expresly mentioned, and the rest may easily be parallel'd, as if all the qualifications fitting for blessednesse, were so many maids of honour attending on this Queen of Wisdome." *Wisdomes Character and Counterfeit* (London, 1656), 8.

69. James G. Williams, *Those Who Pondered Proverbs* (Sheffield: Almond Press, 1981), 70.

70. Robert Cawdray, "The Epistle Dedicatorie," *A Treasurie or Store-house of Similies* (London, 1600), Sig. A3v–A4r.

71. Ibid., Sig. A4v.

72. Robert Alter, *Art of Biblical Poetry* (New York: Basic Books, 1985), 169.

73. Peter Muffett calls proverbs "the verie keys of knowledge, and rules of all righteousnesse." *A Commentarie on the Booke of the Proverbes of Salomon* (London, 1592), dedicatory epistle, Sig. A2v.

74. Dod and Cleaver, *A Plaine and Familiar Exposition of the Thirteenth and Fourteenth Chapters of the Proverbs of Salomon* (1608), 36.

75. Charles Herle, *Wisdom's Tripos Or Rather its Inscrition, Detur Sapienti, in Three Treatises*, (London, 1670), 300–7.

76. Ibid., 66.

77. Ibid., 307.

78. Williams, *Those Who Pondered Proverbs*, 39.

79. Frye, *The Great Code*, 121.

80. James I, King of England, *Basilikon Doron*, *The Workes of the Most High and Mightie Prince, James* (London, 1616), 150.

81. George Herbert, *George Herbert: The Complete English Works*, ed. Ann Pasternak Slater (London: Everyman, 1995), 56.

82. Jane Melbourne, "Biblical Intertextuality in *Samson Agonistes*," *Studies in English Literature* 36 (1996): 113–14.

83. Frye, *The Great Code*, 106.

84. Ibid., 121.

85. Dod and Cleaver, *A Plaine and Familiar Exposition*, 4.

86. Frank Kermode, *The Sense of an Ending: Studies in the Theory of Fiction* (London: Oxford University Press, 1966), 9.

87. Keeble, "Restoration Images," 23.

88. Anthonie Sadler, *Mercy in a Miracle, Shewing, The Deliverance, and the Duty, of The King, and the People. A Sermon Preached at Mitcham in Surry, June 28, 1660, In a Solemne Congratulation for the Restoration of his Majesty to his Royal Throne* (London 1660), 16, 17.

89. Ellis, *Happy Restauration*, 15.

90. Ibid., 18–19.

91. Keeble, "Restoration Images," 25.

92. George Starkey, *Britan's Triumph for Her Imparallel'd Deliverance, And her Joyfull Celebrating the Proclamation of Her Most Gracious, Incomparable King Charles the Second* (London, 1660), st. 57.

93. See Joseph Wittreich, *Visionary Poetics: Milton's Tradition and His Legacy* (San Marino: Huntington Library, 1979); William Kerrigan, *The Prophetic Milton* (Charlottesville: University of Virginia Press, 1974).

94. Frye, *The Great Code*, "Typology II," 105–38.

95. Dayton Haskin, *Milton's Burden of Interpretation* (Philadelphia: University of Pennsylvania Press, 1994), 85.

96. Ibid., 85.

97. Bennett, *Reviving Liberty*, 157–60.

98. Ibid., 202.

99. See, for example, Laura Lunger Knoppers, *Historicizing Milton: Spectacle, Power and Poetry in Restoration England* (Athens, Ga.: University of Georgia Press, 1994), 10, and Norbrook, *Writing the English Republic*, 433.

100. Frye, *Double Vision*, 16.

CHAPTER 2. "HAPPIER LIFE"

The opening epigraph is from Patrick, *A Sermon Preached*, 27.

1. In the *Christian Doctrine*, Milton argues that the Tree of Knowledge "was not a sacrament, as is commonly thought, for sacraments are meant to be used, not abstained from; but it was a kind of pledge or memorial of obedience" (*CPW* 6:352). See also John Shawcross, "Milton and Covenant: The Christian View of Old Testament Theology," in *Milton and Scriptural Tradition*, ed. Leland Ryken (Columbia: University of Missouri Press, 1984), 166.

2. "Chance or fortune that falls to anyone; luck, lot" (*OED*).

3. Granger, *A Familiar Exposition*, 2–3.

4. Patrick, *A Paraphrase*, viii.

5. Theodore Beza, *Ecclesiastes, or the Preacher* (Cambridge, 1589), title page.

6. Knoppers, *Historicizing Milton*, 1.

7. Spencer, *The Righteous Ruler*, 1. Spencer glosses this passage with Eccles. 8:17.

8. Ibid., 2.

9. Ibid., 3.

10. Ibid., 3.

11. Ibid., 29.

12. Ibid., 16.

13. Ibid., 5.

14. Ibid., 15–16.

15. Patrick, *A Sermon Preached*, 27.

16. Beza, *Ecclesiastes, or the Preacher*, Sig. A7r.

17. John Heydon's *The Idea of the Law Charactered* (1660), qtd. by Parker in his preface to *The Dignity of Kingship Justified*, xvii.

18. Starkey, *Britan's Triumph*, st. 57, 15.

19. Spencer, *The Righteous Ruler*, 1.

20. Herle, *Wisdom's Tripos*, 190.

21. Ibid., 195.

22. Ibid., 198–99.

23. William Ramesay, *A Short Discourse of the Eclipse of the Sunne, On Monday, March 29, 1652* (London, 1652).

24. Nicholas Culpepper, *Catastrophe Magnatum* (London, 1652), 35, 69.

25. Lawrence Price, *The Shepherds Prognostication* (London, 1653), Sig. A4v.

26. Spencer, *The Righteous Ruler*, 43.

27. John Gauden, *Eikon Basilike* (London, 1649), 64. Emphasis mine.

28. As Neil Keeble observes, "since the sun was a traditional symbol of divine royalty it may implicitly, as the licenser realized, associate evil with kings and Satan with Charles I." See *The Literary Culture of Nonconformity in Later Seventeenth-Century England* (Athens: University of Georgia Press, 1987), 119.

29. See Thomas A. Copeland's "Raphael, The Angelic Virtue," *Milton Quarterly* 24 (1990): 117–28, 118.

30. Richard Hooker, *The Laws of Ecclesiastical Polity*, ed. Arthur Stephen McGrade (Cambridge: 1989), 28.

31. William McKane, *Proverbs: A New Approach* (Philadelphia: Westminster, 1970), 24.

32. David Loewenstein offers the fullest analysis of this subject in "Treason against God and State: Blasphemy in Milton's Culture and *Paradise Lost*," in *Milton and Heresy*, ed. Stephen Dobranski and John Rumrich (Cambridge: Cambridge University Press, 1998), 176–98. My purpose here is to suggest how the Nayler case compounds Milton's response to the implicit blasphemy he saw in the Restoration.

33. Starkey, "Dedicatory Epistle," *The Dignity of Kingship*, Sig. A4v.

34. John Brinsley, *An Antidote Against the Poysonous Weeds of Heretical Blasphemies* (London, 1650). Brinsley defines blasphemy as "any wrong, injurie, indignity offered to the good name, credit, reputation of another, whether of God or of Man," 4.

35. John Brayne, *A Treatise of the High Rebellion of Man against God in Blasphemy* (London, 1653), title page.

36. John Dryden, "Absalom and Achitophel," 1.:584, *Selected Poetry and Prose of John Dryden*, ed. Earl Miner (New York: Random House, 1969), 222. Professor Miner suggests that Dryden's Shimei may be Slingsby Bethel, "a determined opponent of the throne and a London Sherrif in 1680," n. 585, 223.

37. Starkey, *The Dignity of Kingship*, 175.

38. Ibid., 175.

39. See Michael Lieb, *The Poetics of the Holy: A Reading of Paradise Lost* (Chapel Hill: University of North Carolina Press, 1981), 34.

40. Keeble, "Restoration Images," 12.

41. C. H. Firth and R. S. Rait, eds., *Acts and Ordinances of the Interregnum: 1642–1660*, 3 vols. (London: His Majesty's Stationery Office, 1911), 2:410.

42. The act, which allowed for a statute of limitations of six months, further stipulated that public preaching or publishing of blasphemous opinions was punishable by imprisonment for six months for the first offense and banishment on pain of death for the second. The act did not, however, seek to reach private conversations.

43. Anonymous, *A true Relation of The Life, Conversation, Examination, Confession, and just deserved Sentence of James Naylor the grand Quaker of England* (London, 1656), title page.

44. James Nayler, *A Discovery of the First Wisdom from beneath, and the Second Wisdom from above, Or, The difference betwixt the two Seeds, The one after the Flesh, the other after the Spirit* (London, 1653), 3–4.

45. Ibid., 4.

46. Ibid., 4.

47. Ibid., 11–12.

48. Ibid., 13.

49. Ibid., 19.

50. Ibid., 17.

51. Ibid., 21.

52. Ibid., 21.

53. Ibid., 9.

54. Ibid., 24.

55. Ibid., 24.

56. Granger, *A Familiar Exposition*, 212.

57. Ibid., 202–3. Many Royalists thought that unrighteous rulers were rare. The Elizabethan Peter Muffett earlier remarked that bad princes "pill and poll the poore people and undoe them by taxes and extreme extortion, that they may have money to supply all thir voluptuous and luxurious desires." *A Commentarie on the Booke of the Proverbes of Salomon* (London, 1592), 146.

58. Thomas Fuller, *The Marvellous Wisdom and Quaint Conceits of Dr. Thomas Fuller, D.D.* (London: Pickering and Chatto, 1893), 149.

59. Joan Bennett demonstrates the close connections between Charles I and Milton's Satan: "The fundamental similarity between Charles and Satan can be understood by analyzing their claims to divine right to power. Whereas seventeenth-century royalists argued that the English king was a representative of God's power, Milton argued that the man Charles was, like Satan, a usurper of that power." *Reviving Liberty*, 35. Robert Fallon argues that Satan is a composite portrait that incorporates some of Milton's disillusionment with Cromwell. See *Divided Enemies: Milton's Political Imagery* (University Park: Penn State University Press, 1995), especially 55–81.

60. Knoppers, *Historicizing Milton*, 86.

61. Granger, *A Familiar Exposition*, "The Epistle Dedicatory," Sig. A7r–A7v.

62. Ibid., 2–3. The image of laying a foundation conveys in part the typological relationship between law and wisdom, since "Torah" is derived from the verb for laying or casting the foundations of the universe. This sense of Torah as a foundation is central in the Book of Job, and recalls again the distinction between creator and creature established by Abdiel. See James A. Sanders, *Torah and Canon* (Philadelphia: Fortress Press, 1972), 1.

63. Richard Lanham lists the following cognates for prolepsis: Ante occupatio; Anticipatio; Praeceptio; Praeoccupatio; Praesumptio; Procatalepsis. He defines prolepsis as "Foreseeing and forestalling objections in various ways." *A Handlist of Rhetorical Terms*, 2nd ed. (Berkeley: University of California Press, 1991), 120.

64. Pemble, *Salomons Recantation*, 10.

65. Granger, *A Familiar Exposition*, 61.

66. Herle, *Wisdom's Tripos*, 200.

67. Dennis Danielson, "Through the Telescope of Typology: What Adam Should Have Done," *Milton Quarterly* 23 (1989): 121–27.

68. Reichert, *Milton's Wisdom*, 220–22.

69. Hardy, *Wisdomes Character*, 3–4.

70. Lewalski, *Paradise Lost and the Rhetoric of Literary Forms* (Princeton: Princeton University Press, 1985), 277. See also Joseph Wittreich, *Feminist Milton* (Ithaca: Cornell, 1987), 104; Cheryl H. Fresch, "Whither thou goest": *Paradise Lost* XII, 610–23 and the Book of Ruth," *Milton Studies* 32 (1995): 111–30.

Chapter 3. "Contrary Blasts"

The opening epigraph is from Spencer, *The Righteous Ruler*, 5.

1. John Price, *A Sermon Preached before the Honourable house of Commons At Saint Margarets in Westminster on Thursday the 10 of May, being a day of solemn Thanksgiving appointed by the Parliament, for the mercies God had bestowed on the Nation through the successfull conduct of the Lord Generall Monck* (London, 1660), 19.

2. Ibid., 18.

3. Starkey, *Royal and Other Innocent Bloud*, 2.

4. John Bunyan, *Grace Abounding to the Chief of Sinners* (London: Dent, 1928; reprint, 1984), 1.

5. The word translated as "riddle" occurs only nine times in Judges and a total of eighteen times in the Bible as a whole. It is translated as "dark speech" in Numbers 12:8, for example.

6. Robert Alter, *The Art of Biblical Narrative* (New York: Basic Books, 1981), 100.

7. Gerhard von Rad, *Old Testament Theology,* 2 vols. (New York: Harper and Row, 1962), 1:334.

8. Book of Enoch, *The Apocrypha and Pseudepigraphica of the Old Testament in English*, ed. R. H. Charles, 2 vols. (Oxford: Clarendon, 1913), 2:192.

9. Justin Martyr, *Second Apology Writings of Saint Justin Martyr*, trans. Thomas Falls, in *The Fathers of the Church* (Washington: Catholic University of America Press, 1948, reprint, 1965), 6:124.

10. Alter, *The Art of Biblical Narrative*, 100.

11. Spencer, *The Righteous Ruler*, 49.

12. Ibid., Sig. A2r.

13. Derek Wood, "Intertextuality, Indirection and Indeterminacy in Milton's *Samson Agonistes*," *English Studies in Canada* 18 (1992): 271.

14. Noam Flinker, "Typological Parody: Samson in Confrontation with Harapha," *Milton Quarterly* 24 (1990): 140.

15. Jesus cites the text in Matthew 21:42, establishing a typological resonance Ellis uses to compare the monarch to Christ: "Jesus saith unto them, Did ye never read in the scriptures, The stone which the builders rejected, the

same is become the head of the corner: this is the Lord's doing, and it is marvellous in our eyes?"

16. Ellis, *Happy Restauration*, 7.

17. Ibid., 31.

18. Ibid., 25.

19. Aristotle, *Poetics*: *Literary Criticism from Plato to Dryden*, ed. Alan H. Gilbert (Detroit: Wayne State University Press, 1962), 49b20, 76.

20. Alter, *The Art of Biblical Narrative*, 33.

21. In her study of the role of the Chorus, Kathleen Swaim summarizes the patterns of doubleness which are apparent in the poem. She cites the double annunciation of Samson's birth, Samson's betrayal by two women, the two entries of the Philistine officer who summons Samson to the temple, the "bi-form" nature of Dagon who is half man and half fish, and the two shouts which are audible from the pagan festival "off stage." As Swaim suggests, readers gain perspective on "the various doublenesses operating throughout *Samson Agonistes*, particularly the junctures of metaphorical and metaphysical, poetic and spiritual, verbal and transcendent, pagan and Christian, experiential and faith-full." See "The Doubling of the Chorus in *Samson Agonistes*," *Milton Studies* 20 (1984): 225–45, 225, 240.

22. Proponents of the "regenerationist" reading of the poem include Don Cameron Allen, "The Idea as Pattern: Despair and *Samson Agonistes*," *Twentieth-Century Interpretations of Samson Agonistes,* ed. Galbraith Crump (Englewood Cliffs: Prentice-Hall, 1968), 51–62; Raymond Waddington, "Melancholy Against Melancholy: *Samson Agonistes* as Renaissance Tragedy," *Calm of Mind: Tercentenary Essays on Paradise Regained and Samson Agonistes in Honor of John S. Diekhoff,* ed. Joseph Wittreich (Cleveland and London: The Press of Case Western Reserve University, 1971), 259–87; and Mary-Ann Radzinowicz, *Towards Samson Agonistes: The Growth of Milton's Mind* (Princeton: Princeton University Press, 1978). See also F. Michael Krouse's *Milton's Samson and the Christian Tradition* (Hamden, Conn.: Archon Books, 1963). Regeneration offers an answer to Samuel Johnson's charge that the poem has no "middle" because its "middle" episodes do not precipitate the catastrophe. In the regenerationist position, the middle episodes are related to the climax because each episode prepares Samson for the climax and shows his progress towards it. In *Interpreting Samson Agonistes* (Princeton: Princeton University Press, 1986), Joseph Wittreich sees Samson as a demonic parody of the true heroism of Jesus in *Paradise Regained*. Wittreich's dissent from previous regenerationist readings has brought new attention to the poem, and particularly to its complex, irreducible tensions, as is demonstrated in the work of Derek Wood and others. As I argue, Milton is not motivated to create only a demonic parody in Samson, and would certainly revalue classical *anagnorisis* in biblical terms. The psychic and political dissonances that find a rhetorical analogy in the biblical fragments that inform the poem also seek clarity in the moment of recognition, signaling a potential distinction between license and liberty, presumption and wisdom, in Milton's assessment of Samson.

23. Mary-Ann Radzinowicz, "How Milton Read the Bible: The Case of *Paradise Regained*," *The Cambridge Companion to Milton*, ed. Dennis Danielson (Cambridge: Cambridge University Press).

24. Hugh MacCallum, "*Samson Agonistes*: The Deliverer as Judge," *Milton Studies* 23 (1987): 265.

25. Hardy, *Wisdomes Character*, 11–12.

26. See Leonard Mustazza, "The Verbal Plot of *Samson Agonistes*," *Milton Studies* 23 (1987): 241–58.

27. Kermode, *Sense of an Ending*, 59.

28. Adela Yarbro Collins, *Crisis and Catharsis: The Power of the Apocalypse* (Philadephia: Westminster, 1984), 141.

29. Ibid., 141.

30. Edward Taylor, *Milton's Poetry: Its Development in Time* (Pittsburgh: Duquesne University Press, 1979), 109.

31. Ibid., 110.

32. Ibid., 110.

33. A number of critics have remarked on this comparison. See Jacqueline DiSalvo, "Make War Not Love: On *Samson Agonistes* and *The Caucasian Chalk Circle*," *Milton Studies* 24 (1988): 203–31. See also DiSalvo's "Milton and Shaw Once More: *Samson Agonistes* and *Saint Joan*," *Milton Quarterly* 22 (1988): 115–20. The figure of Deborah in Milton's work is also discussed by Stevie Davies in *The Feminine Reclaimed: The Idea of Woman in Spenser, Shakespeare and Milton* (Lexington: University Press of Kentucky, 1986). Joseph Wittreich discusses Dalila, Jael, and Deborah in *Feminist Milton*, 126–27. Stella Revard comments on the relation between Dalila and Jael, the heroine of the Song of Deborah, in "Dalila as Euripidean Heroine," *Papers on Language and Literature* 22 (1987): 291–302. Mieke Bal's comparison of Dalila and Jael is found in *Death and Dissymmetry* (Chicago: University of Chicago Press, 1988).

34. Heather Asals has noted the "anagogic" meaning of this reference: "Generated out of the tale of the lion and the honeycomb traditional to the Samson story, the 'honied words' of Dalila, in the context of Christian exegesis, identify her with the Word and the Gospel." See "In Defense of Dalila: *Samson Agonistes* and the Reformation Theology of the Word," *Journal of English and Germanic Philology* 74 (1975): 184. The metaphor of scripture as honey was commonplace since the Middle Ages. In "The H. Scriptures I" Herbert writes: Oh Book! infinite sweetness! let my heart / Suck ev'ry letter, and a honey gain." See *The Complete English Works*, 56.

35. See *Harper's Bible Dictionary*, ed. Paul J. Achtemeier et al. (San Francisco, 1985), 214.

36. Williams, *Those Who Pondered Proverbs,* 25. See also Claudia Camp, *Wisdom and the Feminine in the Book of Proverbs* (Sheffield: Almond Press, 1985), 115–20, as well as Williams, *Women Recounted*. Citations that illustrate the primacy of seductive language include Proverbs 2:16, 6:24, 7:5, 7:21, and 22:14, in addition to Proverbs 5:3.

37. Her prediction can be compared with the Song of Deborah, especially Judges 5:24–26.

38. Stanley Fish has examined the act of interpretation in the motif of marking or writing upon a blank surface. See "Spectacle and Evidence in *Samson Agonistes*," *Critical Inquiry* 15 (1989): 563.

39. Peter Muffett, *A Commentarie on the Booke of the Proverbes of Salomon* (London, 1592), 317.

40. Thomas Wilcocks, *The Works of that Late Reverend and Learned Divine Mr. Thomas Wilcocks, Minister of Gods Word, Containing an Exposition upon the Whole Booke of Davids Psalmes, Salomons Proverbs, the Canticles, and part of the 8. Chapter of St. Pauls Epistle to the Romans* (London, 1624), 150.

41. Cawdray, *Treasurie*, 828.

42. Draxe, *Bibliotheca Scholastica*, 238.

43. Henry Delaune, *Patrikon Doron or A Legacy to His Sons, Being a Miscellany of Precepts; Theological, Moral, Political, Oeconomical, Digested Into Seven Centuries of Quadrins,* 2nd ed. (London, 1657), century I; quatrain 78, 20. Barbara Lewalski remarks on the *Basilikon Doron*: "the absolute power of God the Supreme Patriarch is imaged in the absolute monarch of the state, and in the husband and father of a family. A woman's subjection, first to her father and then to her husband, supposedly imaged the subjection of all English people their monarch, and of all Christians to God." See *Writing Women in Jacobean England* (Cambridge, Mass.: Harvard University Press, 1993), 2.

44. William Riley Parker, *Milton: A Biography*, 1:411.

45. Thomas Heywood, *Exemplary Lives and Memorable Acts of Nine of the Most Worthy Women of the World* (London, 1640), 6.

46. Peter Martyr, *Most Fruitfull and Learned Comentaries of Doctor Peter Martir* (London, 1564), cap. 4: fol. 96–97.

47. Ibid., fol. 93.

48. von Rad, *Old Testament Theology,* 1:327–34.

49. Gould, *Moses Unveiled*, 158.

50. Ibid., 159.

51. Mieke Bal, *Death and Dissymmetry* (Chicago: University of Chicago Press, 1988), 18. See also Mieke Bal, *Murder and Difference: Gender, Genre and Scholarship on Sisera's Death*, trans. Matthew Gumpert (Bloomington: Indiana University Press, 1988).

52. Bal, *Death and Dissymmetry,* 7.

53. DiSalvo, "Make War Not Love," 225.

54. Bal, *Death and Dissymmetry,* 24, 27.

55. Genre must also be considered in terms of gender and hierarchy. The premise that history is a male province defined by masculine acts of war and violence is criticized by both Bal and DiSalvo. An important parallel emerges between the poem and its biblical source at this point. While Judges 5, the Song of Deborah, is poetry, Judges 4, the prose narrative which records the same events, and which precedes the Song of Deborah in the Bible, was, in fact, written at a later date. The prose version appears to offer, as Frye suggests it, "one of many possible ways of explaining what happened," *Great Code,* 215. Bal argues, however, that in the culture in which the story of Jael was recorded, lyric and epic were considered feminine and masculine forms respectively, *Murder and Difference,* 124. In the culture in which Judges is recreated as

Samson Agonistes, we may further observe what Joseph Wittreich terms the "genderfication of a genre," whereby epic and prophecy especially, but also tragedy, were considered male domains. See *Feminist Milton,* 73. The presiding criterion for the "masculinity" of these genres is overt concern with history.

56. In a similar way, in *Paradise Regained*, Jesus dismisses Satan with proverbs such as "Man lives not by Bread only" (1:349) and "Tempt not the Lord thy God" (4: 561). The literary devices of wisdom, which include the parable, are a distinctive feature of the Gospels.

57. As Achsah Guibbory puts it: " 'This day' and 'now' emphasize newness, the break with the past, and God's announcement that all 'shall bow' similarly divides future behavior from the pattern set in the past." *The Map of Time: Seventeenth-Century English Literature and Ideas of Pattern as History* (Urbana and Chicago: University of Illinois Press, 1986), 181.

58. Samuel Johnson, *The Rambler*, 16 July 1751, in *Milton: Comus and Samson Agonistes: A Casebook*, ed. Julian Lovelock (London: Macmillan, 1975), 157–63.

59. von Rad, *Old Testament Theology*, 2:107.

CHAPTER 4. "THE PROMIS'D KINGDOM"

The opening epigraph is from *To The Most High and Mighty Prince Charles the II* (London, 1660), 30.

1. Hill, *The English Bible*, 118.

2. Richard Baxter, *A Holy Commonwealth*, ed. William Lamont (Cambridge: Cambridge University Press, 1991), 83. Lamont notes the joint burning of Baxter's and Milton's writings, xxiii.

3. Arthur Barker, *Milton and the Puritan Dilemma, 1641–1660* (Toronto: University of Toronto Press, 1942; reprint, 1971), 289.

4. Erasmus, *The Education of a Christian Prince* (1515), ed. Lester Born (New York: Octagon, 1965), 200.

5. Ibid., 200.

6. Ibid., 203.

7. James I, *Workes*, 149.

8. David Loewenstein observes how Milton's *Eikonoklastes* attacks the typologies linking the Stuarts to David, Solomon, and Christ in both the *Basilikon Doron* and *Eikon Basilike*. See *Milton and the Drama of History* (Cambridge: Cambridge University Press, 1990), 55–56.

9. James I, *A Speach in Star Chamber, 20 June, 1616, Workes*, 550.

10. Ibid., 549, emphasis mine.

11. Ibid., 550–51.

12. William Prynne, "Admonitorie Preface," *Thomas Campanella, an Italian Friar and Second Machiavel, His Advice to the King of Spain for Attaining the Universal Monarchy of the World* (London, 1659), Sig. A3r–A3v.

13. Sir Walter Raleigh, *The Cabinet Council*, ed. John Milton (London, 1658), 56, 42.

14. Ibid., 46.

15. Ibid., 80.

16. Ibid., 82–83.

17. Ibid., 83.

18. Ibid., 85.

19. Ibid., 85–86.

20. Ibid., 86.

21. James I, *Workes,* 197.

22. Ibid., 203.

23. Ibid., 208.

24. Thomas Hobbes, *Leviathan*, ed. Richard Tuck (Cambridge: Cambridge University Press, 1996), 269.

25. Ibid., 83.

26. Ibid., 280.

27. Ibid., 323.

28. Ibid., 323.

29. Ibid., 256.

30. Ibid., 257.

31. Ibid., 373.

32. Richard Tuck, "Hobbes and Locke on Toleration," *Thomas Hobbes and Political Theory*, ed. Mary Dietz (Lawrence: University Press of Kansas, 1990), 162.

33. Ibid., 165.

34. Hobbes, *Leviathan*, 283.

35. Ibid., 427–28.

36. Victoria Kahn, "The Metaphorical Contract in Milton's Tenure of Kings and Magistrates," *Milton and Republicanism*, ed. David Armitage, Armand Himy, Quentin Skinner (Cambridge: Cambridge University Press, 1995), 88.

37. Hobbes, *Leviathan*, 283–84.

38. *Ibid.*, 283.

39. J. G. A. Pocock, "Time, History and Eschatology in the Thought of Thomas Hobbes," *Politics, Language, and Time: Essays on Political Thought and History* (New York: Atheneum, 1971), 158.

40. David Quint, "David's Census: Milton's Politics and *Paradise Regained*," *Remembering Milton*, ed. Mary Nyquist and Margaret Ferguson (New York and London: Methuen, 1987), 144.

41. James Harrington, "Historical Introduction," *Political Works*, 5.

42. Harrington, *Political Works*, 175.

43. Ibid., 178.

44. Harrington, "Historical Introduction," *Political Works*, 80.

45. Harrington, *Political Works*, 332.

46. Matthew Wren, *Monarchy Asserted, Or the State of Monarchicall & Popular Government* (Oxford, 1659), 64.

47. Ibid., see chapter 7, "Whether the Ten Commandments were professed by God or Moses, and voted by the People of Israel," 64–65.

48. Starkey, *The Dignity of Kingship*, 75.

49. Ibid., 76.

50. Starkey, *Britan's Triumph*, st. 59.

51. Lactantius, *Lactantius: The Divine Institutes I–VIII*, trans. Sister Mary Francis McDonald (Washington: Catholic University of America Press, 1964), book 3, chapter 2, 166.

52. Justin Martyr, *The First Apology of Saint Justin Martyr,* in *Writings of Saint Justin Martyr,* trans. Thomas Falls (Washington: Catholic University of America Press, 1948; reprint, 1965), 81.

53. Clement of Alexandria, *Stromateis: Books One to Three*, trans. John Ferguson (Washington: Catholic University of America Press, 1991), book 1, 42. See also Alister McGrath, ed., *The Christian Theology Reader*, 4–6.

54. Tertullian, *On Prescription against Heretics, The Writings of Quintus Sept. Flor. Tertullianus*, trans. Peter Holmes, 3 vols. (Edinburgh: T. T. Clark, 1884), 2:9.

55. Augustine, *On Christian Doctrine, A Select Library of the Nicene and Post-Nicene Fathers,* ed. Philip Schaff (Grand Rapids: Eerdman's, 1983), 2: ch. 40:554.

56. John Bunyan, *Miscellaneous Works of John Bunyan*, ed. Roger Sharrock et al., 13 vols. (Oxford: Clarendon Press, 1976–94), 2:16.

57. Michael Mullett, *Bunyan in Context* (Pittsburgh: Duquesne University Press, 1997), 23.

58. Hardy, *Wisdomes Character*, 5, 6.

59. Ibid., 7.

60. Herle, *Wisdom's Tripos,* title page.

61. Ibid., 10.

62. Ibid., 77–78.

63. Ibid., 191–92.

64. Ibid., 209.

65. Douglas Bush, *The Renaissance and English Humanism* (Toronto: University of Toronto Press, 1972), 125.

66. Granger, *A Familiar Exposition*, 28.

67. H. R. MacCallum argues that *Paradise Regained* recreates the "twofold audience" of the Gospels. See "Jesus as Teacher in *Paradise Regained,*" *English Studies in Canada* 14 (1988): 136. Jesus simultaneously addresses his teaching to an audience of hard-hearted Pharisees and an audience of earnestly searching common people who, as we read in Mark, "heard him gladly" (Mark 12:37).

68. MacKenzie observes that Mary "has down the ages been represented by various symbols, such as Noah's dove, the Ark of the Covenant, Star of the Sea, the Sheep that bore the Lamb of God, and the Church's Diadem." See *A Reader's Guide to Gerard Manley Hopkins* (London: Thames and Hudson, 1981), 157.

69. Martin Luther, *The Magnificat*, trans. A. T. W. Steinhauser, in *Luther's Works,* ed. Jaroslav Pelikan, 55 vols. (Saint Louis: Concordia, 1956), 21:326.

70. Haskin, *Milton's Burden*, 134.

71. Sanders, *Torah and Canon*, 1.

72. Dayton Haskin notes that Mary's "pondering" is conveyed by the Greek verb *symballousia*—to throw or cast together. See *Milton's Burden*, 133.

73. Luke uses the same verb—*bale*, from *ballein*—to throw, or cast.

74. John Shawcross demonstrates that Milton viewed the Old Testament as prophetic and typological, with the New Testament as its antitype. See "Milton and Covenant," 174–75. The Jesus of *Paradise Regained* is the subject of Old Testament prophecy, but the *Torah* is clearly the foundation of Jesus' self-awareness in the poem.

75. Northrop Frye, *Words With Power* (New York: Viking, 1990), 31.

76. Jason Rosenblatt, *Torah and Law in Paradise Lost*, (Princeton: Princeton University Press, 1994), 67.

77. Northrop Frye, *Myth and Metaphor: Selected Essays, 1974–1988*, ed. Robert Denham (Charlottesville: University Press of Virginia, 1990), 236.

78. Williams, *Those Who Pondered Proverbs*, 40.

79. John Diodati, *Pious and Learned Annotations Upon the Holy Bible* (London, 1651), Sig. Zz2v.

80. Haskin, *Milton's Burden*, 179, 180.

81. Diodati, *Pious Annotations*, Sig. Zz2v.

82. Haskin, *Milton's Burden*, 125.

83. Richard Brathwaite, *The English Gentlewoman*, in *The English Gentleman and The English Gentlewoman* (London, 1631), 48.

84. Ibid., 51.

85. Ibid., 45–46.

86. Elizabeth Jocelin, *The Mothers Legacie to her Unborne Childe* (London, 1624), 3–4.

87. Ibid., Sig. B5r.

88. Ibid., 17.

89. Ibid., 12, 13–14.

90. Radzinowicz, "How Milton Read the Bible," 71.

91. Williams, *Those Who Pondered Proverbs*, 17.

92. MacCallum, "Jesus as Teacher," 138.

93. Frye, *The Great Code*, 121.

94. While Milton's authorship of the *Christian Doctrine* has been questioned and defended in the last decade, we should consider here how the similitude of Father and Son in the poem differs from the precise articulation of an unorthodox Christology in the treatise. The *Christian Doctrine* argues that the Father imparts "as much as he wished of the divine nature" (*CPW* 6:211) to the Son but that the Father and the Son cannot be one in essence: "Two distinct things cannot be of the same essence. God is one being, not two" (*CPW* 6:212). The climax of *Paradise Regained* does not explicate the theology of the *Christian Doctrine*. Like the Joban theophany that may be its model, the climax is a visionary moment that exceeds the capacities of its interpreters. Interpretive energy must therefore be invested in symbolic community rather than in material evidence. Mary demonstrates the former, and Satan the latter.

95. A central critical question concerns the theme of identity: is Milton occupied with Satan's attempt to expose Jesus' share of the divine nature and

thereby to know it as Jesus does? Or is Milton occupied with a spectrum of ethical issues as they are interpreted by the Son of God who divests himself of divinity in order to be "fully tried / Through all temptation" (1:4–5) and thereby to grow in wisdom and understanding? Both themes are established in the poem. Edward Tayler interprets the climax as a revelation of the divine identity that Jesus has understood all along. See *Development in Time*, 171. MacCallum argues that Jesus' understanding of his identity matures through a process that combines "continuity and discovery." See "Jesus as Teacher," 136. I argue that the event of recognition or *anagnorisis* is both individual and social. Jesus' consistent identification with scripture in the face of temptation is exemplary to the scriptural society that will in turn identify itself with the word expressed through him.

96. *A Dialogue With Trypho,* qtd. in Marina Warner, *Alone Of All Her Sex: The Myth and Cult of the Virgin Mary* (London: Weidenfield and Nicolson, 1976), 59–60.

97. Joseph Hall, *Contemplations upon the remarkable passages in the life of the holy Jesus* (London, 1679), 12.

98. Ellis, *Happy Restauration*, 27.

99. Ibid., 7.

100. Luther, *The Magnificat*, 306–7.

101. Anthony Stafford lists seventeen, including flaming bush, mystic rose, ivory tower, morning star, David's bower, rod of Moses and of Jesse, a fountain sealed, Gideon's fleece, woman clothed with the sun, garden shut, living spring, throne of Solomon, tabernacle, altar breathing incense, untouched lily, and honeycomb. *The Femall Glory* (London, 1635), sig. D4v–D5v. Milton does not share Stafford's Catholic approach to Mary. Stafford's treatise is, nevertheless, a valuable source of Marian traditions and commentary.

102. The Council of Ephesus convened to resolve the dispute between Cyril of Alexandria and Nestorius, patriarch of Constantinople. The dispute concerned the nature of the Incarnate Christ. Cyril promoted the title of "Theotokos" or Mother of God for Mary in the belief that the Christ she bore was a unity of two natures: the divine and the human. Nestorius could not accept that Mary gave birth to that which existed from all eternity: he denied this in the belief that Christ's divine and human natures were separate. See Geoffrey Ashe, *The Virgin* (London: Routledge & Kegan Paul, 1976), 189. Nestorius was suppressed and Mary was proclaimed the Mother of God in the city where, according to tradition, she is supposed to have lived after Jesus' Ascension. See Warner, *Alone Of All Her Sex*, 8. Rejecting a coeternal Trinity, the *Christian Doctrine* asserts that God begets the Son "within the bounds of time" (*CPW* 6:209). For this reason, unorthodox or heretical views of the Incarnation, such as Nestorianism and Arianism, are points of comparison for, though not identical with, the subordinationist Christology of the *Christian Doctrine*.

103. Dayton Haskin, "Milton's Portrait of Mary as a Bearer of the Word," *Milton and the Idea of Woman,* ed. Julia Walker (Urbana and Chicago: University of Illinois Press, 1988), 180.

104. Williams, *Those Who Pondered Proverbs*, 40.

105. Alberto Manguel, *History of Reading* (Toronto: Alfred A. Knopf, 1996), 71.

106. Haskin, *Milton's Burden*, 133.

107. Manguel, *History of Reading*, 72.

AFTERWORD

1. Frye, *The Great Code*, 226.

Bibliography

Primary Sources

Allen, Robert. *Concordances of the Holy Proverbs of King Solomon*. London, 1612.

Anon. *A true Relation of The Life, Conversation, Examination, Confession, and just deserved Sentence of James Naylor the grand Quaker of England*. London, 1656.

———. *A Dialogue Conteyning the Number of the Effectual Proverbs in the English Tongue*. London 1566.

Aristotle. *Poetics: Literary Criticism from Plato to Dryden*. Edited by Alan H. Gilbert, 69–124. Detroit: Wayne State University Press, 1962.

Augustine. *On Christian Doctrine*. Translated by J. F. Shaw. *A Select Library of the Nicene and Post-Nicene Fathers*. 14 vols. Vol. 2. Edited by Philip Schaff. Grand Rapids: Eerdman's, 1983.

Baxter, Richard. *A Holy Commonwealth*. Edited by William Lamont. Cambridge: Cambridge University Press, 1991.

Beza, Theodore. *Ecclesiastes, or the Preacher*. Cambridge, 1589.

Blake, William. *The Complete Poetry and Prose of William Blake*. Edited by David Erdman. New York: Doubleday, 1988.

Book of Enoch. *The Apocrypha and Pseudepigraphica of the Old Testament in English*. 2 vols. Edited by R. H. Charles, 163–281. Oxford: Clarendon, 1913.

Brathwaite, Richard. *The English Gentleman and The English Gentlewoman*. London, 1631.

Brayne, John. *A Treatise Of the High Rebellion of Man against God in Blasphemy*. London, 1653.

Brinsley, John. *An Antidote Against the Poysonous Weeds of Heretical Blasphemies*. London, 1650.

Browne, Edward. *Rules for Kings, and Good Counsell for Subjects: Being a Collection of certaine places of holy Scripture, directing the one to Governe, and the other to obeye*. London, 1642.

Bunyan, John. *Grace Abounding to the Chief of Sinners.* London: Dent, 1928; reprint, 1984.

———. *Miscellaneous Works of John Bunyan.* 13 vols. Edited by Roger Sharrock et al. Oxford: Clarendon Press, 1976–94.

Cawdray, Robert. *A Treasurie or Storehouse of Similies: Both pleasaunt and delightful, and profitable, for all estates of men in generall.* London, 1600.

Clement of Alexandria. *Stromateis: Books One to Three.* Translated by John Ferguson. Washington: Catholic University of America Press, 1991.

Culpepper, Nicholas. *Catastrophe Magnatum Or, The Fall of Monarchie, A Caveat to Magistrates deduced From the Eclipse of the Sunne.* London, 1652.

Delaune, Henry. *Patrikon Doron or A Legacy to His Sons, Being a Miscellany of Precepts; Theological, Moral, Political, Oeconomical, Digested Into Seven Centuries of Quadrins.* 2nd ed. London, 1657.

Diodati, John. *Pious and Learned Annotations Upon the Holy Bible.* London, 1651.

Dod and Cleaver. *A Plaine and Familiar Exposition of the Thirteenth and Fourteenth Chapters of the Proverbs of Salomon.* London, 1608.

Draxe, Thomas. *Bibliotecha Scholastica Instructissima or Treasurie of ancient Adagies, apol sententious Proverbes.* London, 1633.

Dryden, John. *Selected Poetry and Prose of John Dryden.* Edited by Earl Miner. New York: Random House, 1969.

Ellis, Clement. *A Sermon Preached on the 29th of May 1661, The Day of his Majestie's Birth and Happy Restauration After a Long Exile, To His Crown and Kingdome.* Oxford, 1661.

Erasmus, Desiderius. *The Education of a Christian Prince.* Edited by Lester Born. New York: Octagon, 1965.

Evans, Arise. *To The Most High and Mighty Prince Charles the II.* London, 1660.

Firth, C. H., and R. S. Rait, eds. *Acts and Ordinances of the Interregnum: 1642–1660.* 3 vols. London: His Majesty's Stationery Office, 1911.

Fuller, Thomas. *The Marvellous Wisdom and Quaint Conceits of Dr. Thomas Fuller, D.D.* London: Pickering and Chatto, 1893.

Gauden, John (attributed to Charles I). *Eikon Basilike.* London, 1649.

Gould, William. *Moses Unveiled; or, those Figures Which Served unto the pattern and shadow of heavenly things, pointing out the Messiah Christ Jesus, briefly explained.* London, 1658.

Granger, Thomas. *A Familiar Exposition or Commentarie on Ecclesiastes, Wherein the worlds vanity, and the true felicity are plainely deciphered.* London, 1621.

Griffith, Matthew. *The fear of God and the King, Press'd in a Sermon, Preach'd at Mercers Chappell, on the 25th of March, 1660.* London, 1660.

Hall, Joseph. *Contemplations upon the remarkable passages in the life of the holy Jesus.* London, 1679.

————. *Salomon's Divine Arts*. London, 1609.

Hardy, Nathaniel. *Wisdomes Character and Counterfeit*. London, 1656.

Harrington, James. *The Political Works of James Harrington*. Edited by J. G. A. Pocock. London: Cambridge University Press, 1977.

————. *Aphorisms Political*. London, 1659.

Herbert, George. *George Herbert: The Complete English Works*. Edited by Ann Pasternak Slater. London: Everyman, 1995.

Herle, Charles. *Wisdom's Tripos Or Rather its Inscrition, Detur Sapienti, in Three treatises*. London, 1670.

Heywood, Thomas. *Exemplary Lives and Memorable Acts of Nine of the Most Worthy Women of the World*. London, 1640.

Hobbes, Thomas. *Leviathan*. Edited by Richard Tuck. Cambridge: Cambridge University Press, 1996.

Hooker, Richard. *The Laws of Ecclesiastical Polity*. Edited by Arthur Stephen McGrade. Cambridge: Cambridge University Press, 1989.

James I, King of England. *The Workes of the Most High and Mightie Prince, James*. London, 1616.

Jocelin, Elizabeth. *The Mothers Legacie to her Unborne Childe*. London, 1624.

Johnson, Samuel. *The Rambler*, 16 July 1751. *Milton: Comus and Samson Agonistes: A Casebook*. Edited by Julian Lovelock, 157–63. London: Macmillan, 1975.

Lactantius. *Lactantius: The Divine Institutes I–VIII*. Translated by Sister Mary Francis McDonald. Washington: Catholic University of America Press, 1964.

L'Estrange, Roger. *No Blinde Guides, In Answer to a Seditious Pamphlet of J. Milton's, Intituled Brief Notes upon a Late Sermon*. London, 1660.

Luther, Martin. *The Magnificat*. Translated by A. T. W. Steinhauser. *Luther's Works*. 55 vols. Vol. 21. Edited by Jaroslav Pelikan. Saint Louis: Concordia, 1956.

Martyr, Justin. *Writings of Saint Justin Martyr*. Translated by Thomas Falls. *The Fathers of the Church*. Vol. 6. Washington: Catholic University of America Press, 1948; reprint, 1965.

Martyr, Peter. *Most Fruitfull and Learned Comentaries of Doctor Peter Martir*. London, 1564.

Milton, John. *John Milton: The Complete Poems and Major Prose*. Edited by Merritt Y. Hughes. Indianapolis: Bobbs-Merrill, 1984.

————. *Complete Prose Works of John Milton*. 8 vols. Edited by Don Wolfe et al. New Haven: Yale University Press, 1953–82.

————. *The Works of John Milton*. 18 vols. Edited by Frank Allen Patterson. New York: Columbia University Press, 1931–38.

Morley, George. *A Sermon Preached at the Magnificent Coronation of the Most High and Mighty King Charles the II ^{d}*. London, 1661.

Muffett, Peter. *A Commentarie on the Booke of the Proverbes of Salomon*. London, 1592.

Nayler, James. *A Discovery of the First Wisdom from beneath, and the Second Wisdom from above, Or, The difference betwixt the two Seeds, The one after the Flesh, the other after the Spirit.* London, 1653.

Ogilby, John. *The Relation of His Majestie's Entertainment Passing through the City of London, To His Coronation.* London, 1661.

Patrick, Symon. *A Sermon Preached before the King and Queen at Whitehall, April 16, 1690, Being the Fast-Day.* London, 1690.

———. *A Paraphrase upon the Books of Ecclesiastes and the Song of Solomon.* London, 1685.

Pemble, William. *Salomons Recantation and Repentance: or, the Book of Ecclesiastes Briefly and Fully Explained.* London, 1627.

Phillips, Edward. *The Life of Milton. John Milton: The Complete Poems and Major Prose.* Edited by Merritt Y. Hughes, 1025–37. Indianapolis: Bobbs-Merrill, 1984.

Price, John. *A Sermon Preached before the Honourable house of Commons At Saint Margarets in Westminster on Thursday the 10 of May, being a day of solemn Thanksgiving appointed by the Parliament, for the mercies God had bestowed on the Nation through the successfull conduct of the Lord Generall Monck.* London, 1660.

Price, Laurence. *The Shepherds Prognostication Fore-Telling the Sad and Strange Eclipse of the Sun.* London, 1653.

Pynne, William. "Admonitorie Preface." *Thomas Campanella, an Italian Friar and Second Machiavel, His Advice to the King of Spain for Attaining the Universal Monarchy of the World.* Translated by Edward Chilmead. London, 1659.

Raleigh, Sir Walter. *The Cabinet Council.* Edited by John Milton. London, 1658.

Ramesay, William. *A Short Discourse of the Eclipse of the Sunne, On Monday, March 29, 1652.* London, 1652.

Reynolds, Edward. *Annotations on the Book of Ecclesiastes.* London, 1669.

Sadler, Anthonie. *Mercy in a Miracle, Shewing, The Deliverance, and the Duty, of The King, and the People. A Sermon Preached at Mitcham in Surry, June 28, 1660, In a Solemne Congratulation for the Restoration of his Majesty to his Royal Throne.* London, 1660.

Spencer, John. *The Righteous Ruler, A Sermon Preached at St. Maries in Cambridge, June 28, 1660.* Cambridge, 1660.

Stafford, Anthony. *The Femall Glory: or, the Life, and Death of our Blessed Lady, the Holy Virgin Mary, Gods Owne Immaculate Mother.* London, 1635.

Starkey, George. *The Dignity of Kingship Justified.* London, 1660.

———. *The Dignity of Kingship Justified.* G.S. Reproduced in Facsimile from the Edition of 1660 with an introduction by William R. Parker. New York: Columbia, 1942.

———. *Britan's Triumph for Her Imparallel'd Deliverance, And her Joyfull Celebrating the Proclamation of Her Most Gracious, Incomparable King Charles the Second.* London, 1660.

————. *The Royal and Other Innocent Bloud Crying Aloud to Heaven for Due Vengeance*. London, 1660.

Stillingfleet, Edward. *A Sermon Preached before the King, March 13, 1666*. London, 1667.

Tertullian. *On Prescription against Heretics, The Writings of Quintus Sept. Flor. Tertullianus*. 3 vols. Vol. 2. Translated by Peter Holmes. Edinburgh: T. T. Clark, 1884.

Wilcocks, Thomas. *The Works of that Late Reverend and Learned Divine Mr. Thomas Wilcocks, Minister of Gods Word, Containing an Exposition upon the Whole Booke of Davids Psalmes, Salomons Proverbs, the Canticles, and part of the 8. Chapter of St. Pauls Epistle to the Romans*. London, 1624.

Wren, Matthew. *Monarchy Asserted, Or the State of Monarchicall & Popular Government*. Oxford, 1659.

SECONDARY SOURCES
(including citations in footnotes)

Achinstein, Sharon. *Milton and the Revolutionary Reader*. Princeton: Princeton University Press, 1994.

Achtmeier, Paul J. and et al, eds. *Harper's Bible Dictionary*. San Francisco: Harper's, 1985.

Allen, Don Cameron. "The Idea as Pattern: Despair and *Samson Agonistes*." *Twentieth Century Interpretations of Samson Agonistes*. Edited by Galbraith Crump, 51–62. Englewood Cliffs: Prentice-Hall, 1968.

Alter, Robert. *The Art of Biblical Poetry*. New York: Basic Books, 1985.

————. *The Art of Biblical Narrative*. New York: Basic Books, 1981.

Asals, Heather. "In Defense of Dalila: *Samson Agonistes* and the Reformation Theology of the Word." *Journal of English and Germanic Philology* 74 (1975).

Ashe, Geoffrey. *The Virgin*. London: Routledge & Kegan Paul, 1976.

Ashley, Maurice, ed. *Cromwell*. Englewood Cliffs, N.J.: Prentice-Hall, 1969.

Bal, Mieke. *Murder and Difference: Gender, Genre and Scholarship on Sisera's Death*. Translated by Matthew Gumpert. Bloomington: Indiana University Press, 1988.

————. *Death and Dissymmetry*. Chicago: University of Chicago Press, 1988.

Barker, Arthur. *Milton and the Puritan Dilemma, 1641–1660*. Toronto: University of Toronto Press, 1971.

Bennett, Joan. *Reviving Liberty: Radical Christian Humanism in Milton's Great Poems*. Cambridge, Mass.: Harvard University Press, 1989.

Bush, Douglas. *The Renaissance and English Humanism*. Toronto: University of Toronto Press, 1939; reprint, 1972.

Camp, Claudia. *Wisdom and the Feminine in the Book of Proverbs*. Sheffield: Almond Press, 1985.

Collins, Adela Yarbro. *Crisis and Catharsis: The Power of the Apocalypse*. Philadephia: Westminster, 1984.

Copeland, Thomas. "Raphael, The Angelic Virtue." *Milton Quarterly* 24 (1990): 117–28.

Danielson, Dennis. "Through the Telesope of Typology: What Adam Should Have Done." *Milton Quarterly* 23 (1989): 121–27.

Davies, Stevie. *The Feminine Reclaimed: The Idea of Woman in Spenser, Shakespeare and Milton*. Lexington: University Press of Kentucky, 1986.

DiSalvo, Jacqueline. "Make War Not Love: On *Samson Agonistes* and the *Caucasian Chalk Circle*." *Milton Studies* 24 (1988): 203–31.

———. "Milton and Shaw Once More: *Samson Agonistes* and *Saint Joan*." *Milton Quarterly* 22 (1988): 115–20.

Fallon, Robert. *Divided Enemies: Milton's Political Imagery*. University Park: Penn State University Press, 1995.

Fish, Stanley. "Spectacle and Evidence in *Samson Agonistes*." *Critical Inquiry* 15 (1989).

Flinker, Noam. "Typological Parody: Samson in Confrontation with Harapha." *Milton Quarterly* 24 (1990).

Fontaine, Carole. "Proverbs: Introduction." *Harper's Bible Commentary*. Edited by James L. Mays et al., 495–99. San Francisco: Harper and Row, 1988.

———. *Traditional Sayings in the Old Testament: A Contextual Study*. Sheffield: Almond Press, 1982.

Fresch, Cheryl H. "Whither thou goest": *Paradise Lost* XII, 610–23 and the Book of Ruth." *Milton Studies* 32 (1995): 111–30.

Frye, Northrop. *The Great Code*. Toronto: Academic Press, 1982.

———. *Words With Power*. New York: Viking, 1990.

———. *Myth and Metaphor: Selected Essays, 1974–1988*. Edited by Robert Denham. Charlottesville: University Press of Virginia, 1990.

———. *The Double Vision: Language and Meaning in Religion*. Toronto: University of Toronto Press, 1991.

Guibbory, Achsah. *The Map of Time: Seventeenth-Century English Literature and Ideas of Pattern as History*. Urbana and Chicago: University of Illinois Press, 1986.

Haskin, Dayton. *Milton's Burden of Interpretation*. Philadelphia: University of Pennsylvania Press, 1994.

———. "Milton's Portrait of Mary as a Bearer of the Word." *Milton and the Idea of Woman*. Edited by Julia Walker, 169–84. Urbana and Chicago: University of Illinois Press, 1988.

Hill, Christopher. *The English Bible and the Seventeenth-Century Revolution*. London: Penguin, 1993.

Honeygosky, Stephen R. *Milton's House of God: The Invisible and Visible Church*. Columbia: University Press of Missouri, 1993.

Kahn, Victoria. "The Metaphorical Contract in Milton's *Tenure of Kings and Magistrates*." *Milton and Republicanism*. Edited by David Armitage, Armand Himy, Quentin Skinner, 82–105. Cambridge: Cambridge University Press, 1995.

Keeble, Neil. *The Literary Culture of Nonconformity in Later Seventeenth-Century England*. Athens: University of Georgia Press, 1987.

———. " 'Till one greater man / Restore us . . .': Restoration Images in Milton and Bunyan." *Bunyan Studies* 6 (1995–96): 6–33.

Kermode, Frank. *The Sense of an Ending: Studies in the Theory of Fiction*. London: Oxford University Press, 1966.

Kerrigan, William. *The Prophetic Milton*. Charlottesville: University Press of Virginia, 1974.

Knoppers, Laura Lunger. *Historicizing Milton: Spectacle, Power and Poetry in Restoration England*. Athens: University of Georgia Press, 1994.

Krouse, F. Michael. *Milton's Samson and the Christian Tradition*. Hamden, Conn.: Archon Books, 1963.

Lanham, Richard. *A Handlist of Rhetorical Terms*, 2nd ed. Berkeley: University of California Press, 1991.

Lewalski, Barbara. *Paradise Lost and the Rhetoric of Literary Forms*. Princeton: Princeton University Press, 1985.

———. *Writing Women in Jacobean England*. Cambridge, Mass.: Harvard University Press, 1993.

Lieb, Michael. *The Poetics of the Holy: A Reading of Paradise Lost*. Chapel Hill: University of North Carolina Press, 1981.

Loewenstein, David. *Milton and the Drama of History*. Cambridge: Cambridge University Press, 1990.

———. "Treason against God and State: Blasphemy in Milton's Culture and *Paradise Lost*." *Milton and Heresy*. Edited by Stephen Dobranski and John Rumrich, 176–98. Cambridge: Cambridge University Press, 1998.

Luxon, Thomas. *Literal Figures: Puritan Allegory and the Reformation Crisis in Representation*. Chicago: University of Chicago Press, 1995.

MacCallum, Hugh. "*Samson Agonistes*: The Deliverer as Judge." *Milton Studies* 23 (1987): 259–90.

———. "Jesus as Teacher in *Paradise Regained*." *English Studies in Canada* 14 (1988) 135–51.

MacKenzie, Norman. *A Reader's Guide to Gerard Manley Hopkins*. London: Thames and Hudson, 1981.

Manguel, Alberto. *A History of Reading*. Toronto: Alfred A. Knopf, 1996.

McGrath, Alister, ed. *The Christian Theology Reader*. Oxford: Blackwell, 1995.

McKane, William. *Proverbs: A New Approach*. Philadelphia: Westminster, 1970.

Melbourne, Jane. "Biblical Intertextuality in *Samson Agonistes.*" *Studies in English Literature* 36 (1996): 111–27.

Mueller, Janel. "Milton on Heresy." *Milton and Heresy.* Edited by Stephen Dobranski and John Rumrich, 21–38. Cambridge: Cambridge University Press, 1998.

Mullett, Michael. *John Bunyan in Context.* Pittsburgh: Duquesne University Press, 1997.

Mustazza, Leonard. "The Verbal Plot of *Samson Agonistes.*" *Milton Studies* 23 (1987): 241–58.

Norbrook, David. *Writing the English Republic.* Cambridge: Cambridge University Press, 1999.

Parker, William Riley. *Milton: A Biography.* 2 vols. Oxford: Clarendon Press, 1968.

Pocock, J. G. A. "Time, History and Eschatology in the Thought of Thomas Hobbes." *Politics, Language, and Time: Essays on Political Thought and History,* 148–201. New York: Atheneum, 1971.

Quint, David. "David's Census: Milton's Politics and *Paradise Regained.*" *Remembering Milton.* Edited by Mary Nyquist and Margaret Ferguson, 128–47. New York and London: Methuen, 1987.

Radzinowicz, Mary-Ann. *Towards Samson Agonistes: The Growth of Milton's Mind.* Princeton: Princeton University Press, 1978.

———. "How Milton Read the Bible." *The Cambridge Companion to Milton.* Edited by Dennis Danielson, 207–24. Cambridge: Cambridge University Press, 1989.

Reichert, Paul. *Milton's Wisdom.* Ann Arbor: University of Michigan Press, 1992.

Revard, Stella. "Dalila as Euripidean Heroine." *Papers on Language and Literature* 22 (1987): 291–302.

Rosenblatt, Jason. *Torah and Law in Paradise Lost.* Princeton: Princeton University Press, 1994.

Sanders, James A. *Torah and Canon.* Philadelphia: Fortress Press, 1972.

Shawcross, John. "Milton and Covenant: The Christian View of Old Testament Theology." *Milton and Scriptural Tradition.* Edited by Leland Ryken, 160–91. Columbia: University of Missouri Press, 1984.

Swaim, Kathleen. "The Doubling of the Chorus in *Samson Agonistes.*" *Milton Studies* 20 (1984): 225–45.

Tayler, Edward. *Milton's Poetry: Its Development in Time.* Pittsburgh: Duquesne University Press, 1979.

Tuck, Richard. "Hobbes and Locke on Toleration." *Thomas Hobbes and Political Theory.* Edited by Mary Dietz, 153–71. Lawrence: University Press of Kansas, 1990.

von Rad, Gerhard. *Old Testament Theology.* 2 vols. New York: Harper and Row, 1962.

Waddington, Raymond. "Melancholy Against Melancholy: *Samson Agonistes* as Renaissance Tragedy." *Calm of Mind: Tercentenary Essays on Paradise Regained and Samson Agonistes in Honor of John S. Diekhoff.* Edited by Joseph Wittreich, 259–87. Cleveland and London: The Press of Case Western Reserve University, 1971.

Warner, Marina. *Alone Of All her Sex: The Myth and Cult of the Virgin Mary.* London: Weidenfield and Nicolson, 1976.

Williams, James G. *Those Who Pondered Proverbs.* Sheffield: Almond Press, 1981.

———. *Women Recounted: Narrative Thinking and the God of Israel.* Sheffield: Almond Press, 1982.

Wittreich, Joseph. *Visionary Poetics: Milton's Tradition and His Legacy.* San Marino, California: Huntington Library, 1979.

———. *Interpreting Samson Agonistes.* Princeton: Princeton University Press, 1986.

———. *Feminist Milton.* Ithaca: Cornell University Press, 1987.

Wood, Derek. "Intertextuality, Indirection and Indeterminacy in Milton's *Samson Agonistes.*" *English Studies in Canada* 18 (1992): 261–72.

Index